The
Modern-Day
PIONEER

The
Modern-Day
PIONEER

SIMPLE LIVING

 IN THE

21ST CENTURY

CHARLOTTE DENHOLTZ

Avon, Massachusetts

Published by
Adams Media, a division of F+W Media, Inc.
57 Littlefield Street, Avon, MA 02322. U.S.A.
www.adamsmedia.com

ISBN 10: 1-4405-5179-0
ISBN 13: 978-1-4405-5179-6
eISBN 10: 1-4405-5180-4
eISBN 13: 978-1-4405-5180-2

Printed in the United States of America.

10   9   8   7   6   5   4   3   2   1

This publication is designed to provide accurate and authoritative information with regard to
the subject matter covered. It is sold with the understanding that the publisher is not engaged
in rendering legal, accounting, or other professional advice. If legal advice or other expert
assistance is required, the services of a competent professional person should be sought.
—From a *Declaration of Principles* jointly adopted by a Committee of the American Bar
Association and a Committee of Publishers and Associations

Many of the designations used by manufacturers and sellers to distinguish their product are
claimed as trademarks. Where those designations appear in this book and Adams Media was
aware of a trademark claim, the designations have been printed with initial capital letters.

Interior illustrations by Eric Andrews and Kathie Kelleher.
Additional spot art © Juniper Images Corporation.

This book is available at quantity discounts for bulk purchases.
For information, please call 1-800-289-0963.

For all the pioneers,
from antiquity through today,
who have blazed trails and
changed the world.

CONTENTS

SIMPLICITY
at Your Fingertips,

THE WILDERNESS
at Your Doorstep

"It is not easy to be a pioneer—but oh, it is fascinating! I would not trade one moment, even the worst moment, for all the riches in the world."

— ELIZABETH BLACKWELL —

FROM THE LATE 1700s through the nineteenth century, thousands of Americans looked across the horizon, toward the setting sun, and felt an itch for adventure.

Hungry for freedom and a different way of life, the pioneers left behind everything they'd ever known. They were urged to "Go West, young man," but women and families also migrated in droves. They traveled in covered wagons and caravans across the Great Plains and along the Oregon Trail.

Once they arrived, these daring men and women started their lives anew. They built cabins in the wilderness and lean-tos on the prairie. They braved deep snow and long droughts to grow their own food and raise their own meat.

The original pioneers were literally trailblazers—carving out paths where there were none.

But as the Wild West became tamed, and the rugged plains became suburbs and highways, we lost sight of the mindset that made the pioneers so inspiring. In modern times, life is quick and easy. You can eat tomatoes in the middle of December, get pizza delivered to your doorstep in half an hour, and buy anything you need with just the click of a mouse. But this comes at a cost. Hothouse tomatoes could never compare to vegetables plucked from your own garden. And there's no better feeling than nestling underneath a quilt you've made yourself.

It's hard to imagine living exactly like the original pioneers. You can't go backwards, and there are times when quick and easy is exactly what you need. But while most of you don't want to leave your lives behind and build a log cabin, many of you do want to be more self-sufficient. And sometimes, when you eat fast food or pull out your credit card for an overpriced bar of fancy soap, you feel the same itch that your forefathers had.

In *The Modern-Day Pioneer*, you'll discover all of the secrets of simple living that America has forgotten over the years. You'll learn how to use whatever land you have—whether that's an acre, a backyard, or a windowsill—to grow your own food. Then you'll learn to can and preserve, allowing you to enjoy that food all year round. You'll learn how to keep yourself in fresh eggs, meat, and honey by raising chickens, rabbits, and bees. Inside *The Modern-Day Pioneer* are recipes for easy and economical meals, from hearty bread that a pioneer would eat on the frontier to nutritious cuisine that can cure everything from depression to a runny nose. You'll discover the magic of fermentation first hand with an introduction to brewing your own beer.

This book will introduce you to crafts that are both practical and therapeutic. You'll take the first steps toward becoming a master quilter, soapmaker, and candlemaker. You'll learn to mend clothes and sew buttons. You don't need to know these skills to survive, the way the pioneers did. But as a Modern-Day Pioneer, you'll enjoy exploring each of these activities, discovering which ones bring out your frontier spirit.

The Modern-Day Pioneer connects you with an entire community of homesteaders. Like the original pioneers, who found camaraderie through quilting bees and barn raisings, these men and women are constantly meeting new people and striking up friendships through shared interests. More than a series of hobbies, *The Modern-Day Pioneer* is the doorway into an entire culture.

By holding this book, you have taken the first step toward leading a more rewarding life. And the next time you look out across the horizon and feel an itch, you'll know exactly how to scratch it.

"Where there is an open mind, there will always be a frontier."

— CHARLES KETTERING —

CHAPTER 1

HOW A PIONEER TENDS:
Using the Land You Have

"Earth is here so kind, that just tickle her with a hoe and she laughs with a harvest."

— Douglas William Jerrold —

13

WHEN THE ORIGINAL PIONEERS TRAVELED WEST, they found an unmitigated wilderness vastly different from the gilded cities back East. It was up to them to turn the rugged frontier landscape into terrain that could support their survival. Slowly they cultivated the prairie, turning it into gardens that could grow vegetables and herbs, orchards that provided fruit, and farmland where they could raise cattle.

Modern-Day Pioneers live all over the world, in apartment complexes, suburbs, and farms. You can use your space to grow and cultivate food—whether it's a garden, a back porch, or a windowsill. In this chapter you'll learn how to keep rabbits, chickens, and bees. You'll even learn how to make compost and recycle rainwater to keep your plants growing strong.

THE PRAIRIE IN YOUR BACKYARD

I F YOU HAVE ENOUGH LAND TO GARDEN, you must contemplate several factors when deciding what to plant.

First, look at your climate and the amount of sunlight your plot will get. If you get full sun all day, some plants will grow better than if the area only gets a few hours of sunlight. If your site is shady, choose the plants that can tolerate a bit less sun, or if it is a bit wet, make sure the plants can take a little extra moisture at certain times of the year.

Vegetables that do well with four to six hours of sunlight:

+ Carrots   + Peas
+ Lettuce   + Swiss chard
+ Kale

Vegetables that need more sunlight (at least six to eight hours):

+ Cucumber   + Peppers
+ Eggplant   + Squash
+ Tomatoes

Planting Methods

Next, take a look at the landscape of your land. If it's possible, choose a level site for your garden with good drainage and easy access. A hilly area will drain quicker than a flat one, making it more difficult to keep the plants well watered.

Row Gardening

If you are lucky enough to have flat land with good soil, row gardening is your best growing method. Row gardening is usually used on larger plots, but this method of growing can be easily utilized in small spaces, such as in flat, sunny backyards. When planning a row garden, it is important to make sure you allow space for pathways between and at the end of each row to accommodate a place for you to walk and use any larger tools, like a rototiller or wheelbarrow. Walking on the soil where you will be planting your vegetables can compact it and harm the soil structure. When designing this style of garden, make designated pathways.

Rows can be as long or as wide as you want or need them to be. Often the width is dependent on the type of equipment you will be using to till the beds. If you are going to use a rototiller, measure the width of the tines. This will give you an idea of how wide you want your bed to be. When choosing the width of your garden bed, consider how long your reach is; if you are weeding on one side, can you easily reach across the bed without straining your back?

Growing in Raised Beds

If your land is not flat, or if the soil quality is poor, raised beds may be a better option for your garden. Raised garden beds have four sides and hold soil. If you want to grow in a moist area that has poor drainage, this method will allow you to better control where your water goes. If you have a sloped or terraced garden site, raised beds will help define these areas and make it easier to grow plants in the more difficult to reach areas. Another great reason for using raised beds is that the bed can be made to any height. If you cannot bend easily, the raised bed can work very well for you. Make sure it is built to the height that is comfortable. If it is a low bed, adding a ledge on the top will allow you to sit while gardening.

Wood, stones, bricks, and cement are the most common materials used when making raised beds. Wood is easy to find and

FIGURE 1-1: Raised wooden garden bed

build with, and it is often not that expensive. When building your beds with wood, you want to choose wood that will not rot easily. If you can, choose wood such as cedar or redwood, as both these are more resistant to rot because of their natural oils. Stay away from pressure-treated wood or wood covered in creosote, as these products contain heavy metals and poisons such as arsenic, copper, and chrome. These chemicals can leach into your garden soil and ultimately into your food.

If wood is not the look you want, rocks are also often easy to find and can be very attractive. However, one disadvantage to using rock is that it does not have the same barrier from weeds and grass as solid wood sides do. You may need to use cement to fill in the crevices and cracks between the rocks for a sturdier barrier.

If you want a more defined raised bed but do not want to use wood or stone, try using cement blocks, standard masonry bricks, or larger interlocking bricks. They come in various colors and sizes and can be easily stacked to increase the height of your raised bed if that is a concern. For a more involved and a permanent option, you can also make your raised beds with cement.

This design is for a 4-foot-wide, 8-foot-long, 12-inch-high wood raised bed. The first thing you want to do is decide exactly where you want your raised bed to be, as you want to build it on that same spot.

BUILDING A RAISED BED

Here is your list of materials for one raised bed:

- Three 8-foot-long (12-inch-wide by 2-inch-thick) boards (wood made from cedar or redwood), one cut in half to make two 4-foot-long boards
- One 4-foot-long (2-inch-thick by 4-inch-wide) board, cut into four 1-foot-long (2-inch-thick by 4-inch-wide) boards (two-by-fours)
- Twenty-four 4-inch wood screws for full dimension wood or 3-inch wood screws for planed wood
- Drill
- Screwdriver to match the wood screw heads

Most building supply stores will cut the pieces of wood for a minimal charge, saving you time. You now have two (8-foot-long by 12-inch-wide by 2-inch-thick) pieces and two (4-foot-long by 12-inch-wide by 2-inch-thick) boards to make your rectangular box; you also have four pieces of 1-foot lengths of two-by-fours.

Directions for construction:

1. Lay each 8-foot length on the ground; place a piece of two-by-four at each end and using three screws on each, attach the two-by-four length to each flat end of the board. Drilling a hole not quite the length of the screw into the wood first will make screwing the pieces together easier. Attaching the two-by-four to the board will give the sides of your raised bed more support.
2. These 8-foot boards will be used as the sides of your box. The 4-foot lengths are the ends of your rectangular box. Attach each 4-foot length to the two-by-fours using three screws on each corner. You now have a four-sided raised bed.

Rotation Gardening

The pioneers understood that it wasn't enough to plant their crops in the right places at the right times; they also needed to plan their farming land for years to come. An unplanned crop could transform bountiful, rich soil into dead dirt. Vegetable rotation is a process used to ensure that certain vegetables or a family of vegetables is not planted in the same spot in successive years. Different plants require different amounts of nutrients from the soil to grow well. You should add compost (which you'll learn how to make later in this chapter) to your soil each year. However, it is also important to move your plants around each year so as not to deplete the nutrients. One year you may grow a vegetable that uses a lot of nitrogen, and the following year you may plant a crop that uses more phosphorus. By rotating your vegetable layout the soil can have time to rebuild the nitrogen in that area.

Moving your vegetables to different areas of your garden each year will also help cut down on pests and diseases. Some plants attract certain pests and diseases, which often live in the soil. If you move this vegetable to another area of the garden, the pests or diseases will die. Different plants also will repel certain pests.

The best way to keep track of your plant rotation is to categorize the plants you're interested in growing. There are four basic categories of vegetables:

+ Heat-loving vegetables such as tomatoes, peppers, eggplants, and squash.
+ Brassica crops like broccoli, cabbage, cauliflower, Brussels sprouts, and kale.
+ Root vegetables such as beets, carrots, garlic, leeks, onions, potatoes, radishes, and turnips.
+ Other vegetables like beans, lettuce, peas, and Swiss chard.

FOUR-YEAR VEGETABLE ROTATION

Divide your garden plot into sections, and plant vegetables from the same category in the same section. Then each year, rotate the kind of plants you grow in each part of your garden. A four-year plan should look like this:

	YEAR 1	YEAR 2	YEAR 3	YEAR 4
BED ONE	Cabbage family	Heat-loving vegetables	Root vegetables	Everything else
BED TWO	Heat-loving vegetables	Root vegetables	Everything else	Cabbage family
BED THREE	Root vegetables	Everything else	Cabbage family	Heat-loving vegetables
BED FOUR	Everything else	Cabbage family	Heat-loving vegetables	Root vegetables

Planting Fruit Trees

For the Modern-Day Pioneer, what could be better than biting into a perfectly ripe and juicy piece of fruit from your own garden? Common fruit trees for home gardens include apple, cherry, peach, pear, and plum trees.

The fruit trees that are most suitable for home gardens are dwarf stock, which can be grown as individual trees or as a horizontal cordon or fan espalier. Espalier is a lattice made of wood or wire on which to train fruit trees by selecting lateral branches to grow horizontally on each side of a main stem. Training fruit trees to grow on an espalier is one of the best tree forms for a small-space garden. The tree will have a single stem with no major spreading branches. It will take up little space, be easy to manage, and have a high yield for a small tree. The most popular dwarf trees are apples and pears.

Planting Your Tree

Most trees or shrubs are bought in containers and are best planted between mid-fall and early spring. Fruits do not like waterlogged soil, so make sure the area where you will be planting is well drained. You also want to make sure the soil is not frozen. When you are ready to plant, dig a hole wide enough so you can spread the plant's roots outward and deep enough so the roots will be covered by 3 or 4 inches of soil.

Place a stake deeply and firmly in the center of the hole. You want the stake to be tall enough to reach the point where the stems begins to branch. Place 4 to 6 inches of aged manure or compost into the hole and work this into the existing soil. If the tree roots are dry, soak them in water for a couple of hours. Plant the tree no deeper than it was in the container, which is indicated by the soil mark around the stem. Fill the hole with topsoil, shaking the tree a few times to settle the soil around the roots. Once the roots are covered, firm the soil around the base of the tree by gently treading on it. Tie the tree to the stake.

PIONEER TIP!

When purchasing a tree, choose one that is one or two years old. Older trees will be too hard to reestablish. In the first year, only the main stem grows; in the second season the side shoots (branches) grow from the main stem. In the third year, the side shoots grow from the first branches, and so on.

It is best not to grow grass around your tree for two or three years.

Growing Herbs

Throughout this book you'll learn about the many ways a Modern-Day Pioneer can use herbs. In almost every culture in history there are references to using herbs for preparing and preserving food, scenting the air, and treating illness and wounds. Most herbs are wild, tough plants that have not changed despite being cultivated for centuries.

When planning your herb garden, first decide where you would like to locate the plants. If you're keeping your herbs outside, consider growing them near the back or front door so that the plants will be easily accessible to the kitchen.

When harvesting herbs, be sure to pick them early in the morning. The best time is just after the dew has dried, but before the sun has hit the leaves. The reason for this timing is that the essential oils found in the herb leaves lose their quality of flavor and fragrance once the leaves are exposed to heat.

When harvesting perennial herbs such as thyme, mint, and lavender, it is important not to harvest too much of the plant in the first year of growth. If the plant is cut back too much, the root system will not be able to develop properly. A light trim will help to shape the plant and encourage bushiness. Once the plant has become established, you can harvest up to two-thirds of the plant each season.

Most annual and biennial plants can be cut several times over the season, and a good rule of thumb is to cut the top half of the plant at each cutting. Just before the first frost, either pull the plant or cut it at ground level. The same is true when harvesting biennials such as parsley. If you are growing to save herb seeds, find a way to mark the plant early in the season and do not cut it so that it will produce a large amount of seeds. If you're growing the plant in a container, write a note on the pot. If you're planting it in the ground, perhaps place it on the edge of your herb garden; anything to remind you that you're treating that plant differently from the others. Biennials will not produce seeds until the second year.

THE PRAIRIE IN THE CITY

I F YOU ARE A MODERN-DAY PIONEER in the concrete jungle, the only outdoor space you have may be a balcony or porch. Growing your vegetables in containers is a great solution.

When space is tight, it is best to concentrate on growing small quantities of several different crops and choosing smaller or dwarf varieties of larger plants. Planting in pots is probably the easiest and most common way to grow food on a balcony or patio, as there is usually no earth space available.

When planning your space, looking for how much sunlight the area gets is the first step. Most vegetables, herbs, and fruit or berry bushes need at least six hours of sun, so take the time to check this out. If you get less than six hours, there are fewer options, but you can still grow many of the vegetables listed earlier in this chapter such as lettuce or Swiss chard. You should also consider the proper-sized container in which to grow your plants. You will want to give your plants enough space so they can grow to maturity. Most herb and vegetable plants need a pot with at least a depth of one foot of soil to grow their best.

Finding Containers

Containers can be purchased at your local nursery or hardware store. The most common kinds available are traditional oak barrels, pots made from reconstituted paper, terra cotta, ceramic, wood, plastic, and resin. If you are planning to grow your vegetables in a container for several years, choose a good-quality one that will last. Containers need to be cleaned on a regular basis to keep them looking good, as well as pest- and disease-free, so choose a container that you can take care of easily.

To save money, you can recycle items that are no longer fulfilling their original purpose. You can use many different kinds of small containers for growing lettuce: tin cans, milk cartons, a bucket, or an old cooking pot are all wonderful options. When you purchase garden pots, there usually are holes in the bottom of them already; however, if you are recycling a container, make sure you make at least one good drainage hole so excess water can easily drain.

If you want to grow root crops (such as potatoes and carrots) or beans and peas, you'll need a larger container. Some good choices include Styrofoam coolers, wooden crates, plastic crates (which may need a liner such as landscape fabric in order to hold the soil), and plastic ice cream buckets (ask at your local ice cream parlor for their empties). Garbage cans, wooden barrels, metal washbasins, old wheelbarrows that have become rusty and full of holes, or plastic clothes hampers are great options for planting larger crops such as tomatoes, potatoes, and squash.

What Grows Well in a Container

The following are suitable vegetables to grow in containers:

- Beans
- Beets
- Broccoli
- Carrots
- Cucumber
- Lettuce
- Peas
- Peppers
- Radishes
- Spinach
- Tomatoes

To grow lettuce, spinach, salad greens, radishes, and green onions, you need a container approximately 8 to 10 inches wide and at least 6 inches deep. In this size container you could grow two or three of your leafy greens and up to a dozen radishes or green onions. For growing carrots, beets, peas, and beans—just remember your peas and beans will produce a better harvest if they are grown on a trellis or supported in some way—the best size container is approximately 12 to 16 inches wide and at least 10 inches deep. If you choose a rectangular container, you could make great use of the space by growing your peas and beans in the back and planting your root crops in front of them.

Larger vegetables, such as tomatoes, cucumbers, cabbage, broccoli, peppers, potatoes, or dwarf corn, need a container at least 16 inches wide and with at least 18 inches of soil to grow well. For best results, use transplants when growing these vegetables (except for potatoes and corn). Grow only one of these plants in

PIONEER TIP!

If you want to grow a lot of vegetables on your balcony or patio, emphasize your vertical space by using trellises or fences. Grow vegetables that can be trained to grow upright, such as snow peas, shelling peas, pole beans, cucumbers, and tomatoes. Choose attractive materials like bamboo, metal, or wood to make trellises or stakes for your plants.

each container. To fill up the pot and make it look more attractive, plant lettuce or herbs around the base of the larger plant.

There are also fruits that do well in containers:

+ Blueberries
+ Raspberries
+ Kumquats, lemons, and dwarf varieties of other fruit trees (must be grown in large pots on a patio in the summer and brought indoors or sheltered when the weather gets cold)

Do not use only potting soil for your fruit trees and shrubs because there is not enough organic matter in it for the plant's needs. Compost is best, or mix the compost with topsoil. For peaches, nectarines, apricots, and cherries, reduce the topsoil by one quarter and add in sand.

Once the tree is planted, mulch the top of the container with wood chips to help conserve moisture. Give potted fruit trees and shrubs a thorough watering whenever the top inch of soil feels dry. A little fertilizer, like an inch or so of compost or fish fertilizer, should be applied every spring when blossoms start to form. Most fruit trees or shrubs grown in containers will need to be brought indoors or at least protected from the colder winter weather.

Planting in a Container

Here are eight easy steps for planting your containers.

1. Select an appropriate-sized container that has drainage holes for the plants you are growing.

2. Fill the container with potting soil to within an inch of the top of the container.

3. Moisten the soil and let it absorb the water before planting (lukewarm water will be absorbed faster than cold water).

4. You can grow several plants in the same pot (except very large ones like tomatoes or squash). They can be crowded in a bit, as about ten small plants will fit into an 18-inch pot.

5. Set taller plants in the center of the pot and insert stakes prior to planting any other plants around the larger one. If you will be trellising plants, the larger ones can be placed at the back of the container so they will climb on the trellis, and others can be planted in front.

6. Water once the plants are in the soil; this will help settle the soil, and the roots will get established quickly.

7. Add more soil, if needed, after watering.

8. Keep the container moist and well fertilized.

Window Boxes

Even without a balcony or patio to put some pots on, most Modern-Day Pioneers will have a sunny windowsill that may work just as well. The best option would be to hang the box outside a window that opens; the plants will get more natural light and you can easily reach to water and fertilize the plants.

Most window boxes are approximately two to three feet in length and 6 to 8 inches deep, although there are many different sizes to choose from. If you do not have a sturdy window ledge to support the box, a lightweight option is probably best. There are some great hooks and hangers for supporting a window box over a balcony rail or on the windowsill.

A window box is not usually very large, so the options are more limited; however, you can still grow some of your own food.

Some plants that will grow well in a window box that does not get a lot of heat:

+ Lettuce
+ Swiss chard
+ Spinach

FIGURE 1-2: Window box with herb garden

If your window box gets a great deal of sun, these plants would be a better option:

+ Parsley
+ Chives
+ Basil
+ Peas
+ Beans (if they can be trellised in some way)

When planting your window box, choose plants that will work best for your location. If the area is not too hot, lettuce or spinach will grow in a shallow window box; however, if the area gets a lot of heat, some annual herbs such as basil, parsley, and chives could a better option for you.

Many herbs can be grown in pots indoors during the winter months. Place them in proper-sized containers and position them in a sunny window so you can enjoy using them all winter long. Grow perennials such as marjoram, chives, mint, and winter savory from divisions or cuttings taken in the fall. Basil, dill, and parsley are annuals and will need to be started from seed outdoors (in pots) in late summer and then transplanted into larger pots in the fall. When growing herbs indoors make sure you use a light, well-draining potting soil, and water as needed. Try not to let the plants dry out or be overwatered.

Bagged Garden

Another option is growing your herbs and vegetables in a bagged garden. You can get a shallow plastic container and place the bag of potting mix or a burlap sack into it. Make sure you poke a few drain holes in the bag, then turn it over and cut a flap into the top of the bag to expose the soil for planting. The plastic container will hold moisture as well as keep the area clean; it will act the same as a tray under a container. Just make sure there is no water sitting in the plastic container, as most plants do not like their roots to be too wet—they can start to rot.

The bagged garden is an excellent option for growing the following:

+ Tomatoes
+ Potatoes
+ Carrots
+ Beets
+ Cabbage

FIGURE 1-3: BURLAP SACK GARDEN

COMPOSTING

MAKING COMPOST CAN BE a huge benefit for your garden or potted plants. It does take some work but for a little time and effort, the rewards are great. You will learn about two methods of creating your own compost: backyard composting and worm composting. A compost pile makes use of kitchen waste that would otherwise go into the garbage, and is an excellent spot to recycle your weeds (just make sure they have not gone to seed). You can allow other garden debris to decompose in the pile rather than having it go to the landfill. The resulting compost is perfect for using in your garden beds, containers, or window boxes.

Backyard Composting

This is the perfect composting method for the Modern-Day Pioneer with outside land where he or she can leave a compost pile for three to six months. The best times to make a new compost pile are in the spring or in the fall, as the heat of the summer or the cold in winter will not slow down the decomposition process. The final result should be a rich, dark-colored material that smells earthy and crumbles easily in your hands.

To make your compost pile:

1. Lay down 4 to 6 inches of carbon material—for example, straw, shredded or dried leaves, small sticks, corn or broccoli stalks (chopped into smaller pieces or put through a chipping machine, if possible).

2. Cover that with 4 to 6 inches of green material—for example, leaves, grass, and kitchen waste.

3. Add in a handful of organic fertilizer with lime if you want, but this is optional.

4. Cover with a thin layer of soil or animal manure to keep the flies and odor down.

5. Repeat the above steps.

For best results, make the pile at least three feet high by three feet wide before leaving it to sit. Temperature is an important factor in making compost; the larger the pile, the easier it is for the material in it to get to the high temperatures needed to kill any weed seeds or diseased plant material. A temperature that is either too low or too high can slow down the decomposition process, while warm weather has a tendency to speed it up a bit. The pile usually starts out cool, and then as the materials start to decompose, the temperature inside the pile increases. Once your compost pile has reached approximately three feet by three feet, let that one sit and start a new pile. Most plastic compost bins will be approximately this size when they are full so you can move the bin, leaving the pile to work, or have two bins if you have a large amount of debris.

Never let your compost pile dry out, especially in the summer months. Keeping the pile covered will keep the sun from drying it out and prevent the rain from making it too wet.

Take a handful of compost from the middle of the pile; if it is crumbling and slightly moist to the touch, there is enough moisture. If it forms a hard ball, the pile is too wet.

Turning your pile will also allow more air circulation, and is especially important if your pile is too wet. A lot of gardeners never turn their compost and that method does work; however, taking the time to turn your pile over regularly will hasten the decomposition process.

A simple compost structure is a three-sided bin made by stacking concrete blocks, railroad ties, wooden boards, bales of straw, or pallets. Wire fencing or wire mesh can also be used to make a less solid bin as long as the holes are small enough to hold the materials you have. Bending the wire into a circular shape is often the easiest and the sturdiest shape to set up. Make sure the walls are about four feet high and the area inside is a minimum of three feet by three feet.

There are also many different types of plastic compost bins on the market; they are compact and great for a tiny space. Plastic bins are lighter to move around, can last longer than wooden bins, and are enclosed so they can protect your compost from the rain and sun. They come in round shapes, square shapes, solid-sided containers, tumblers, and ones with removable and stackable sides. Most have a capacity of twelve cubic feet, which is the size needed for your compost to heat up.

Apartment Worm Composting

If you live in an apartment or a condominium and do not have access to a backyard, composting with earthworms can be an easy way to turn your kitchen waste into nutritious compost that is great to add to your vegetable containers. An earthworm has the ability to consume its own weight in soil and organic matter each day. It leaves behind castings that are rich compost. Generally, a pound of earthworms will compost one pound of kitchen waste, making one pound of compost each day.

MAKING A WORM BIN

To make this worm bin you need the following items:

- Two (15-gallon) plastic bins
- Bucket
- Burlap sack or newspaper
- Small pail of pebbles
- Peat moss
- Potting soil (or a mixture of organic materials such as straw, soil, and aged manure, if you have it)
- Worms
- Water

Here are the steps to make your earthworm compost:

1. Drill at least six holes in the bottom of one of the containers, and then place it into the second container. The second container will hold any liquid that drains from the first bin. Lift out the top bin every few weeks and use the liquid from the second one as a tea for your garden plants.
2. Prepare the bedding by filling a bucket one-third full of peat moss, one-third full of a combination of good garden soil, dried straw or leaves, and manure (if you have some available). Finally, fill the last third of the bucket with water.
3. Soak this mixture overnight, and the next day squeeze out any excess water.
4. Cover the bottom of the plastic bin that has holes with a layer of small pebbles.
5. Lay 4 inches of the bedding mixture over the pebbles. Leave the bin to stand one day, as the mixture may heat up too much and kill the earthworms if they are put in right away.

continued on next page

6. Move some of the bedding to the side of the bin and place the earthworms from their shipping container into the center of the bin. Lightly cover the earthworms with the bedding you pulled aside.

7. Place a burlap sack or some newspapers on top of the bedding and moisten with a watering can. Keep the bedding material moist but not soggy.

8. The bin will begin to drip from the holes in the bottom, so make sure the first bin is inserted into the second one so the second can catch the drippings.

9. Start feeding the worms slowly. If you give them more than they can eat, the extra vegetable waste will attract flies and heat up the bedding, which can kill the earthworms. Start feeding them soft foods like cooked vegetables, bread scraps, and soups, leftover cereal with the milk, cornmeal, or coffee grounds. After a few weeks your earthworms will be ready to handle raw vegetables. Do not give the earthworms strong foods like onions or garlic.

10. Every few weeks add a thin layer of soil on top of the decomposing pile.

11. Every two weeks turn the compost with your hands (wear gloves) to aerate it. Reduce the amount of food you give the earthworms for a few days as the earthworms will not come to the surface for a few days after you turn the compost.

12. After one month, add another 2 inches of bedding to accommodate the increased worm population (they will have increased over the month).

13. After three months the compost will be ready to use; however, you will need to start a new bin in which to move the earthworms. When you are ready to divide the existing box, use a large table covered with a plastic sheet and dump the bedding and worms onto the table. Heap the compost into a pile in the center of the table. Pick out the rocks and put them back into the bin. Any worms exposed to the light will burrow into the center of the pile. Scrape the top of the pile of bedding into a bucket and wait ten minutes while any exposed worms burrow deeper. After several scrapings your worms will be at the bottom of the pile, making it easy to put them back into the bin you are using. If there are a lot of worms, start a second bin.

COLLECTING AND USING RAINWATER

I F YOU LIVE IN A CLIMATE that gets a fair amount of rain, install a rain barrel. A rain barrel is a closed container where water is collected from roof gutters. The water from the gutter is directed to the barrel by having the downspout enter the top of the rain barrel. It is best to have a barrel with a spigot at the bottom of the barrel; that way you can easily pour the water into your watering can to use in the garden.

There are a variety of types and sizes of rain barrels that can be purchased at your local hardware store or garden center. They can fill up fairly quickly, so find one that works for your area and your average rainfall. Collecting rainwater to water your plants, rather than using your tap water, is an easy way to conserve your overall water usage. During the summer months a lot of areas have water restrictions, so collect-

ing rainwater will allow you to have more than enough to keep your vegetable plants healthy.

FIGURE 1-4: RAIN BARREL

RAISING YOUR MEAL

THE PIONEERS grew their own fruit and vegetables, but that was only part of their diet. They also ate hearty rabbit stew, hard-boiled eggs, and honey smeared on sourdough bread (which you'll learn to make in Chapter 4, "How a Pioneer Bakes").

Not all Modern-Day Pioneers can keep chickens, rabbits, or bees. You'll need enough outside land to house the animals and enough free time to tend to them. Make sure that the chickens and rabbits have enough room to roam, and build sturdy structures that will keep predators at bay. Be sure to check your local zoning laws to make sure that you can keep animals on your land. Beekeeping, in particular, has been subject to many laws limiting the places where one can build an active hive. But if you are able to keep your own animals, you'll find that your meals will taste so much better when all of the ingredients come from your own backyard.

Chickens for Eggs

Egg layers are often divided into two groups, Bantams and Standards.

Bantams

Bantams are very small birds and come in a variety of colors and types. They require less room and less feed than standards do, but they produce smaller eggs (three bantam eggs equal two regular eggs in a recipe). Bantams are often raised as pets because they have great personalities, but don't let that fool you into thinking they aren't producers. Bantams make the best brooders (hens that sit on their eggs so they hatch), and soon you'll have a good-sized flock of bantams.

Standards

Standards range from heavy breeds to light breeds. They include many of the breeds you might be familiar with—Wyandotte, Rhode Island Red, White Plymouth Rock, and Barred Rock. Standards also include fairly unknown breeds like Turkens (naked-necked chickens that look like turkeys); crested breeds, which have tufts of feathers around their heads; and feather-footed breeds. They can produce brown eggs or white eggs and some can even produce colored eggs. No matter what color is on the outside of an egg, the inside is the same. However, if you are thinking about selling some of your excess eggs, brown eggs will bring you more money per dozen. If you are raising a self-propagating flock, look for breeds that are good brooders.

Chickens for Meat

If you are raising chickens for meat you will find the most efficient feed-to-flesh conversion ratio with the Cornish Rock broiler. These hybrid chickens grow quickly and produce broad breasts and big thighs (think white meat and dark meat). But if you are buying chickens in order to create a flock that self-propagates, these are not the chickens for you. First, because they are hybrid, the chicks will not turn out like the parents. Second, because these chickens have been bred to grow so rapidly, they have been known to have heart attacks after three or four months. There are slower growing breeds that are both egg laying and meat producing and those breeds are a wonderful choice for growing a small farm flock. The meat growth will take more time and you will have a lower feed-to-flesh conversion ratio, but you will not have the expense of buying new chicks year after year because you will be able to

hatch your own. Generally in these situations, you take the roosters (males) and grow them for meat, because you only need one rooster (and perhaps a backup rooster) for your flock.

PIONEER TIP!

When you receive your day-old chicks, dip the beak of the chicks in the water before you turn them loose. A baby bird will not instinctively go to the water and can die of dehydration standing right next to a waterer.

Raising Rabbits

Rabbits have a higher feed-to-flesh conversion ratio than any other livestock. They are quiet, gentle animals that can be raised almost anywhere. They are well known for their ability to reproduce and provide mild, lean meat that tastes a lot like poultry. Perhaps you are wondering why, if you're going to raise an animal that tastes like poultry, you wouldn't just raise chickens instead. The reason is that rabbits are more efficient and productive than chickens are. A female rabbit (doe) can produce up to one thousand times her body weight in food in a single year. You can process (skin and butcher) five rabbits in the same time it takes to process one chicken. Rabbits naturally live in dens and holes, so they can be raised in closer quarters than chickens can.

A diet of mixed grains like oat, soft wheat, and grain sorghum is a rabbit's favorite. You need to supplement that with protein from good legume hay like alfalfa or timothy. Besides grain and hay, a plentiful supply of fresh water is essential for healthy rabbits.

You can raise rabbits in hutches or cages, or create rabbit runs with an outdoor fenced-in area. Letting your rabbits "run" decreases stress, increases their fur density, and gives you better meat because of the exercise.

PIONEER TIP!

One baby rabbit is called a kit; there are six to ten "kittens" in a litter. A rabbit's gestational period is one month. When they are two months old, kittens should be weaned from their mothers. You can breed the female again once her litter has been weaned. A doe potentially can give birth to forty kittens in a year's time.

Beekeeping: A Short Introduction

The pioneers knew that bees produced more than honey—they helped the farming cycle renew each year. Bees are an essential part of agriculture, necessary for pollinating plants to ensure better fruits and bigger crops. In this section, you will learn the basics of beekeeping, but this is an intense process only for a very dedicated Modern-Day Pioneer. Before beginning this hobby, make sure you have a thorough understanding of the complexities of keeping bees.

Honeybees can be kept almost anywhere there are flowering plants that produce nectar and pollen. Choose a site for beehives that is discreet, sheltered from winds, and partially shaded. Avoid low spots in a yard where cold, damp air accumulates in winter.

The Hive Location

The best beehive location is one where your best source of pollen and nectar is within two square miles of your hive; the closer the better. Because bees actually use pollen and nectar to produce their own energy, the farther they have to travel for it, the more they have to consume themselves. In contrast, if you can place them closer to their food source, you can collect more honey.

Position your hive so the entrance faces east. This way the early morning sun will alert them to the new day. Because flower nectar will often evaporate in the morning hours during the summer, the sooner bees are out of their hive foraging, the more honey they will produce. The best position for a hive is where it will also have afternoon shade, shielding the hive from the summer sun. Shade, rather than sunlight, will give the bees more time to concentrate their effort on making honey, because they won't need to work on carrying water back and forth to cool the hive.

Basic Beekeeping Equipment

A manmade hive is built to imitate the space that bees leave between their honeycombs in nature. The dimensions are fairly standard and should be copied exactly if you decide to make you own beehives.

The following equipment is used within a hive:

+ **Bottom board:** a wooden stand that the hive rests upon. Bottom boards can be set on bricks, concrete blocks, cinder blocks, or any stable base to keep the hive off the ground.
+ **Hive body or brood super:** a large wooden box that holds eight to ten frames of comb. In this space, the bees rear their brood and store honey for their own use. Up to three brood supers can be used for a brood nest.
+ **Queen excluder:** a frame made with wire mesh placed between the brood super and the honey super.
+ **Honey supers:** shallow boxes with frames of comb hanging in it for bees to store surplus honey.
+ **Frames and foundation:** frames hang inside each super or box on a specially cut ledge, called a rabbet. Frames keep the combs organized inside your hive and allow you to easily and safely inspect your bees.
+ **Inner cover and outer cover**

+ **Smoker:** this calms bees and reduces stinging; pine straw, sawdust, chipped wood mulch, grass, and burlap make good smoker fuel.
+ **Hive tool:** used for prying apart supers and frames.
+ **Bee suit or jacket, veil, gloves, ankle protection, and gauntlet:** this is all protective personal gear worn when working with bees.
+ **Feeders:** these hold sugar syrup that is fed to bees in early spring and in fall.

Purchasing Bees

Usually the best way to start keeping bees is to buy established colonies from a local beekeeper. Often a local beekeeper might even have a colony he or she wants to give away. It's better to get two colonies at the beginning, because that allows you to interchange frames of both brood and honey if one colony becomes weaker than the other and needs a boost.

Have the beekeeper open the supers. The bees should be calm and numerous enough that they fill most of the spaces between combs.

Moving a hive is a two-person job. It's easiest to move a hive during the winter when they are lighter and populations are low. The first thing you want to do is close the hive entrance. You can accomplish this with a piece of folded window screen. Then look for any other cracks and seal them with duct tape. Make sure the supers are fastened together and the bottom board is stapled to the last super. Remember to open hive entrances after the hives are relocated.

PIONEER TIP!

If you are buying the colonies, realize that the condition of the equipment usually reflects the care the bees have received. If you find the colonies housed in rotting hives, don't purchase them.

You can also buy packaged bees and queens. Bees are commonly shipped in two- to five-pound packages of about 10,000 to 20,000 bees. Keep the packages cool and shaded when they arrive. To transfer bees to their new hive, set up a bottom board with one hive body and remove half of the frames. Spray the bees heavily with sugar syrup (one part sugar to one part water) through the screen on the package; the bees will gorge themselves with syrup and become sticky, making them easy to pour.

The next step is to move the queen, which will be in a separate cage. Pry off the package lid, remove the can of syrup provided for transit, find and remove the queen suspended in her cage, and reclose the package.

The queen cage has holes at both ends plugged with cork. Under the cork at one end you will see that it is filled with white "queen candy." Remove the cork from this end and suspend the queen cage between two center frames in your hive. Worker bees will eventually eat through the candy and release the queen.

Shake the original package lightly to move all bees into a pile on the bottom. Take the lid off the package again and pour the bees into the hive on top of the queen. As they slowly spread throughout the hive, carefully return the frames to their original positions. Replace the inner and outer covers on the hive. You must now feed the bees sugar water until natural nectar starts to appear.

Beekeeping Throughout the Year

You want your bees to be at their maximum strength before the nectar flow begins. This way, the created honey is stored for harvest rather than used to build up their strength. Feeding and medicating your bees should be done in January through February. Because the queens will resume egg laying in January, some colonies will need supplemental feedings of sugar syrup.

By mid-February, you should inspect your hives. You should be looking for population growth, the arrangement of the brood nest, and disease symptoms. If one of your colonies has less brood than average, you can strengthen it by transferring a frame of sealed brood from your other colony.

If you use two brood supers and find that most of the bees and brood are in the upper super, reverse the supers, placing the top one on the bottom. You want to do this because it relieves congestion. When a colony feels congested it swarms, looking for another place to live. If you only have one brood super, you will need to relieve congestion by providing additional honey supers above a queen excluder.

Annual requeening can be done in early spring or in the fall. Most feel that requeening is one of the best investments a beekeeper can make. Young queens not only lay eggs more prolifically, but they also secrete higher levels of pheromones, which stimulate the worker bees to forage.

In order to requeen a colony, you must find, kill, and discard the old queen. Then you need to allow the colony to remain queenless for 24 hours. After that period of time, you can introduce the new queen in her cage, allowing the workers to eat through the candy in order to release her.

By mid-April your colonies should be strong enough to collect surplus nectar. This is when you should add honey supers above the hive bodies. Add enough supers to accommodate both the incoming nectar and the large bee population. Adding supers stimulates foraging and limits late-season swarming.

During late summer and early autumn, the brood production and the honey production drops. At this point, you should crowd the bees by giving them only one or two honey supers. This forces bees to store honey in the brood nest to strengthen the hive. Colonies are usually overwintered in two hive bodies or in one hive body and at least one honey super. Make sure that if you overwinter in one hive body and a honey super, you remove the queen excluder so the queen can move up into the honey super during winter. If your colony is light on stores, feed them heavy syrup (two parts sugar to one part water). Bees should have between fifty to sixty pounds of stores going into winter. A hive with a full deep frame weighs six pounds and a full shallow frame weighs three pounds. You can pick up the frame to estimate the weight of the hive and stores. Never allow stores to drop below twelve to eighteen pounds.

Gathering Honey

It's best to harvest your honey on a sunny, windless day, since bees are calmest then. Remove the bees from the hive by blowing smoke into the hive opening. After a few minutes, pry the outer cover loose and lift it off. Blow more smoke through the hole in the inner cover. Now you can remove the inner cover. After the inner cover is removed, once again blow smoke into the hive to finally drive the bees downward and out of the way.

Remove the super and pry the frames loose with the hive tool. Be careful not to crush any bees. A crushed bee releases a scent that stimulates other bees to attack. Gently brush off any bees that are clinging to the frames. A comb that is ready to be harvested should be about 80 percent sealed over.

Uncap the combs in a bee-proof location, like a tightly screened room. Bees will want to take the honey, if they can get to it. Slice off the comb tops with a sharp knife warmed in hot water. A heavy kitchen knife is fine. It's best to use two knives, cutting with one while the other is heating. Once the honey is extracted, return the emptied combs to the hive for the bees to clean and use again. With care, combs can be recycled for twenty years or more.

If you do keep bees, remember that you can use your honeycombs to obtain wax for your candlemaking in Chapter 8, "How a Pioneer Lights the Way."

CHAPTER 2

HOW A PIONEER PREPARES:
Canning and Preserving

"In seed time learn, in harvest teach, in winter enjoy."

— WILLIAM BLAKE —

SUMMER WAS A GOOD TIME FOR THE PIONEER. The land was alive with fresh food and healthy livestock. But that only lasted a season. When autumn came to the prairie, the pioneers knew that it was time to prepare for the long winter ahead. If they didn't preserve their fruits, vegetables, and meat, they could starve to death. And so they harvested diligently, canning their vegetables and drying their meat into jerky. They made berries into jam and cucumbers into pickles. And so, when the snow was all around them, they were able to go into their root cellar, open a jar of peach preserves, and taste the summertime.

As a Modern-Day Pioneer, you've worked hard to grow your own food. In this chapter, you'll learn how to eat that yield all year round.

CANNING

CANNING is one of the most common methods of preserving and a good way to keep nearly any kind of food—as long as it is correctly harvested and prepared.

When canning, it's important to start out with fresh and unspoiled food. Remove any spots of decay. Wash foods thoroughly in clean water. Keep cold foods, especially meats, cold until you are ready to can them.

There are two methods of canning food—using a water-bath canner and using a pressure canner. Which one you use will depend on your food's pH content. The more acidic the food, the less heat and time is required to destroy bacteria. Most fruits are more acidic and can be canned using a water-bath method. Foods with less acidity need more time and more heat in order to be safe. Vegetables like corn and beans, for example, are less acidic and so must be canned using a pressure cooker. Tomatoes have always been in the middle, and using a water-bath canner is often fine, though the acidic content of tomatoes can depend on where they were grown as well as their variety and ripeness.

It is very important that you can your foods for the correct amount of time in the correct manner. Otherwise you may expose yourself to botulism toxin, one of the most deadly poisons known on earth. Botulism is caused by a certain kind of bacterium, *Clostridium botulinum,* that is practically everywhere in the soil. The bacteria themselves are not poisonous in their dormant state. However, when heated, the spores in the bacteria begin to grow and form a toxin. Luckily, the number of botulism cases is rare, but one death is too many. Don't be frightened of home canning, because hundreds of thousands of Modern-Day Pio-

PIONEER TIP!

Botulism toxin spores are resistant to heat and thrive in an airless, low-acid, and low-sugar-content atmosphere. They are killed, however, by the 240°F temperature achieved by heating under pressure.

neers successfully can their produce every year. But remember not to take shortcuts when it comes to preserving your food.

Most produce can be canned either raw (cold pack) or precooked (hot pack). In cold packing, you fill your jars with the fruit or vegetables and pour boiling water over them. In hot packing, you precook the produce before putting the food in your jars. Then you'll pour the cooking liquid or boiling water over them before canning. In this chapter, you will find directions for both methods.

When storing your canned goods, you will want to put them in a cool, dry, dark place. Dampness will erode the lids and cause leaking. Warmth can affect the quality of the vegetable, and freezing can break the jars. A basement room or pantry is a great place to store your canned vegetables.

The Equipment

There is some basic equipment you will need to have on hand to start canning your foods. Many of these supplies can be found in secondhand stores and can be reused over and over again, year after year. The only items that cannot be recycled are the snap-on lids. Once these have been sealed, they will not seal again properly so you will need to purchase new lids every year.

First, you'll need a canner. There are two kinds:

+ Water-bath canner with rack (for high-acid foods)
+ Pressure canner with rack (for low-acid foods)

Which canner you'll use will depend on the kind of food you're canning. But whatever method you use, you'll also need the following:

+ Jars
+ Screw band lids
+ Snap-on lids
+ Potholders
+ Spoons
+ Spatula
+ Soup ladle
+ The freshest and best-quality fruits and vegetables possible

Before you begin canning, look at your equipment, especially your jars. Throw away any chipped or cracked jars and any old canning lids. Rings can be used over and over again, unless they don't fit tightly. For food safety, your pressure canner gauge must be accurate and should be tested each year. It can be tested and calibrated by most university, state, or county extension services.

Water-Bath Canning

The pioneers used water-baths full of boiling water to can their produce, and this is still the perfect way to process high-acid foods like fruits.

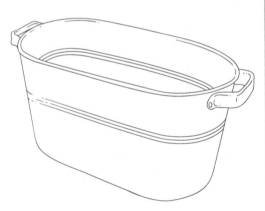

FIGURE 2-1: OLD-FASHIONED CANNER
WITHOUT LID

Place the prepared fruit in sterile, clean, hot jars, covered with either water or syrup depending on your recipe. Put the lid and ring on immediately and tighten. Lower the jar into your kettle of boiling water. You will need a rack on the bottom of your kettle for the jars to sit on. Without a rack, the jars could break. The kettle has to be tall enough and the water deep enough so the water will cover the jars by at least 1 to 2 inches at all times. If the processing will take a long time, have an auxiliary kettle filled with boiling water waiting to replace the evaporated water. Once you have filled the kettle with your jars, make sure the water is at a boil, place the lid on the kettle, and set your timer.

Once the correct amount of time has passed, remove the jars with a jar lifter and place them on top of a towel or wooden board on your table or counter. As they cool you will hear popping sounds, which indicates that the lids have sealed.

Start timing your next batch once the water has come to a boil again.

Water-Canning Your Fruits

In Chapter 1, "How a Pioneer Tends," you learned how to cultivate your own fresh fruit. Here are some tips on how to can your harvest to enjoy all year.

CANNING APPLES

Preparation: Wash, peel, core, and cut into pieces. Apples will turn brown quickly, so drop peeled fruit into a solution made of 2 tablespoons vinegar or lemon juice to 1 gallon of water to prevent this.

Hot pack: Precook apples for 5 minutes in a syrup, then pack into hot jars. Leave 1 inch of headspace, then fill the jar with hot syrup, making sure to leave a ½ inch of headspace. Seal and process in a water-bath canner.

Kind of syrup: thin

Number of minutes needed in boiling water-bath: 15 for pints; 20 for quarts

CANNING BERRIES

Preparation: Wash and remove any stems from the berries. Drain well.

Cold pack: Pack the berries into hot jars, leaving about 1 inch of headspace. Pour in hot syrup to about ½ inch from the rim of the jar. Seal and process in a water-bath canner.

Hot pack: Berries can be precooked for 3–5 minutes in a syrup. Use ½ cup of syrup for every cup of berries. Pour into jars, leaving about ¼ inch of headspace. Seal and process in a water-bath canner.

Kind of syrup: medium (a heavier syrup than what you'll find when canning apples)

Number of minutes needed in boiling water-bath: 10 for pints; 15 for quarts

CANNING PEACHES

Preparation: Wash, then blanch to loosen the skins. Dip into cold water and then remove the skins. Cut fruit into halves or slices and remove the pit. Peaches will turn brown quickly, so drop peeled fruit into a solution made of 2 tablespoons vinegar or lemon juice to 1 gallon of water to prevent this.

Cold pack: Drain well before placing peaches into hot jars, leaving 1 inch of headspace. Pour in hot syrup to about ½ inch from the rim of the jar. Seal and process in a water-bath canner.

Hot pack: Simmer the peaches in boiling syrup for 3–5 minutes. Pack into hot jars, leaving 1 inch of headspace. Pour in hot syrup to about ½ inch from the rim of the jar. Seal and process in a water-bath canner.

Kind of syrup: medium

Number of minutes needed in boiling water-bath: cold pack—25 for pints, 30 for quarts; hot pack—20 for pints, 25 for quarts

CANNING TOMATOES

Preparation: Use only firm, ripe tomatoes. Wash gently so as not to bruise the fruit. Place the tomatoes into a blanching basket and dip them into boiling water to loosen the skins. Immediately place them into cold water, gently peel off the skins, and cut off the stem ends. If you want less seeds in your canning, scrape out excess seeds.

Cold pack: Place tomatoes into hot jars. Press them down until they are covered in their own juice, leaving ½ inch of head-space. Do not add any other liquid. Add salt and ½ teaspoon lemon juice to pints and 1 tablespoon lemon juice to quarts. Seal and process in a water-bath canner.

Hot pack: Place the tomatoes into a large saucepan and bring them to a boil for five minutes, stirring occasionally to prevent sticking. Pour into hot jars, leaving ½ inch of headspace. Add salt and ½ teaspoon lemon juice to pints and 1 tablespoon lemon juice to quarts. Seal and process in a water-bath canner.

Kind of syrup: none

Number of minutes needed in boiling water-bath: cold pack—40 for pints, 50 for quarts; hot pack—35 for pints, 45 for quarts

Water-Canning Recipes

Because high-acid fruits and tomatoes can be used to make so many delicious spreads and condiments, jams and sauces are great candidates for water-bath canning.

Tomato Ketchup

This is a real homemade treat for everyone.

INGREDIENTS + MAKES 4 PINTS

13 pounds tomatoes
2 cups cider vinegar
1 cup sugar
2 tablespoons salt
2 tablespoons finely chopped onion

½ teaspoon ground red pepper
2 teaspoons whole allspice
1½ sticks cinnamon
1 teaspoon celery seed

1. Peel and seed the tomatoes. To peel and seed a tomato, make an "X" at the bottom of the tomato with a sharp knife. Place the tomato into boiling water for 15–20 seconds. Remove it and plunge it into ice water. The skin will slip right off after it has cooled for a bit. To remove the seeds, cut the tomato in half and squeeze each half in your hand.

2. Blend tomatoes to a smooth purée, and then pour through a strainer or cheesecloth.

3. Pour tomato purée into a large pot, then add vinegar, sugar, salt, onion, and red pepper.

4. Tie remaining spices into a cheesecloth bag and add it to the mixture.

5. Bring mixture to a boil and keep it there until the volume of the mixture is reduced by about half, stirring frequently to prevent any scorching on the bottom.

6. Remove the spice bag and pour mixture into hot sterilized jars. Leave ½ inch of headspace.

7. Process in a hot water-bath for 5 minutes; start timing when water is at a full boil.

Blackberry Preserves

This recipe is flexible; substitute raspberries or a blend of raspberries and blackberries if you prefer. Spread this on your homemade bread (from Chapter 4, "How a Pioneer Bakes") for a delicious breakfast.

INGREDIENTS + MAKES ABOUT 6 PINTS

3 quarts blackberries
7½ cups sugar
2 (3-ounce) pouches liquid pectin

1. Rinse fully ripe blackberries in cold water and drain.

2. Place berries into a stockpot.

3. Crush with a potato masher to extract juice. Stir in sugar, mixing well.

4. Bring to a full rolling boil over high heat, stirring constantly.

5. Add pectin and return to a full rolling boil. Boil for 1 minute. Remove from heat.

6. Skim off foam. Ladle preserves into sterilized jars. Wipe rims. Cap and seal.

7. Process in water-bath canner for 5 minutes.

Maple Apple Jam

Just for fun, leave ½ inch of space at the top of the jars and sprinkle hard-crack caramel and chopped nuts on top of the jam. The tasty result is similar to a candy apple at the fair.

INGREDIENTS + MAKES 8½ PINTS

6 pounds mixed apples, chopped
6 cups sugar
1 cup maple syrup
½ teaspoon cinnamon

½ teaspoon allspice
½ teaspoon nutmeg
½ teaspoon ginger
¼ teaspoon cloves

1. Combine all ingredients in a large, nonreactive pot. Bring to a boil over medium-low heat.

2. Continue boiling, stirring frequently, until the jam holds its shape when put on a cold platter.

3. Pour hot into hot jars, leaving ¼ inch headspace. Cap and process in a water-bath canner for 10 minutes.

Pressure Canning

Pressure canning is the best way to preserve low-acid foods, which include most vegetables, meats, poultry, and fish. Vegetables do not have natural acidity, so they need to be cooked at high enough temperatures when canning to kill any potential dangerous organisms or bacteria in the food. A pressure canner reaches a temperature (240°F) that is high enough to destroy any potentially dangerous bacteria-causing organisms.

The exception to this is when you are making pickles, relishes, or sauerkraut from vegetables. The vinegar or brine used adds the acidity needed to make them safe for eating without having to be cooked at a high temperature. (See the information on pickling later in this chapter.)

Unlike a water-bath canner, the jars do not need to be completely covered with water in a pressure canner. The directions that come with your specific brand of pressure canner tell you how many cups of water to add for it to generate the right amount of pressure.

A pressure canner is a heavy kettle-like container with a steam-tight lid that clamps securely in place. Properly maintained, it is a safe device. A gauge records the pressure inside the pot, and a safety valve opens the lid automatically whenever the pressure reaches a certain point. Air and steam can also be released manually by opening the vent (or petcock) on the lid.

Steps for Pressure Canning

No matter what food you are canning, there are certain steps to follow when using a pressure canner:

1. Make sure your pressure canner is clean before using it. Do not immerse the lid with the gauge into water; just wipe it clean. To clean the vent, draw a string or thin piece of cloth through the hole.

2. Place the specific amount of water into the canner, along with the rack.

PIONEER TIP!

A pressure canner can also be used as a water-bath canner for high-acid fruits; just make sure you leave the vent open so the steam is continually released. A rack is also used to keep the jars from touching the bottom as well as making it easier to lower them into the pot and pull them up again.

---

3. Place the canner on the burner and bring the water to a boil.

4. Place the filled jars, already fitted with lids, on the rack in the canner.

5. Place the canner lid on the canner and twist to seal it down. Initially leave the pressure weight off the vent port until the water boils and steam escapes strongly from the open vent.

6. Let the steam flow for ten minutes.

7. Place the weight on the vent.

8. Once the pressure gauge has indicated the proper pressure, or the weight has begun to rattle, you can start timing your jars according to the recipe you use. Adjust the stove temperature to maintain the desired pressure.

9. Once the time has elapsed, turn the heat off and allow the canner to cool down until the pressure is vented.

10. Once the canner has cooled, lift off the weight, open the top, and remove the jars. Carefully place the jars onto a towel or wooden board. DO NOT try to open the canner while there is still pressure inside. This can cause a serious scalding.

Pressure Canning Your Vegetables

In the last chapter you learned about the many vegetables that you could grow, no matter how much land you had. Here are instructions for canning some of the most popular homegrown vegetables.

FIGURE 2-2:
CANNED VEGETABLES

CANNING SNAP OR WAX BEANS

Preparation: Sort beans by size and color, using the nice colored and shaped ones for canning whole. The other ones can be cut into 1-inch pieces. Snip off the ends and wash thoroughly.

Cold pack: Pack raw beans into hot jars, leaving 1 inch of headspace. Add salt if desired and cover with boiling water to ½ inch from the rim of the jar. Process in a pressure canner.

Hot pack: Blanch beans for 2 minutes. Pack into hot jars, leaving 1 inch of headspace. Add salt if desired and cover with boiling liquid to ½ inch from the rim of the jar. Process in a pressure canner.

Number of minutes needed in canner: 20 for pints; 25 for quarts

CANNING BEETS

Preparation: Do not peel beets before cooking them. Cut off the leaves, leaving 1 inch of stem and the root intact so as not to lose color when cooking them. Cook beets for 10–15 minutes, then plunge into cold water. The skins will easily slip off after this. You can leave baby beets whole or cut larger ones into ½-inch pieces.

Hot pack: Pack into hot jars, leaving 1 inch of headspace. Add salt if desired and cover with boiling liquid to ½ inch from the rim of the jar. Process in a pressure canner.

Number of minutes needed in canner: 30 for pints; 35 for quarts

CANNING CARROTS

Preparation: Scrub with cold water, remove tops, scrape, and wash again. Save the smoothest and similar-sized carrots whole for canning. Cut the rest into ½-inch pieces.

Cold pack: Pack raw carrots into hot jars, leaving 1 inch of headspace in pints and 1½ inches in quarts. Add salt if desired and cover with boiling water to ½ inch from the rim of the jar. Process in a pressure canner.

Hot pack: Place carrots into a pot of boiling water and then let it boil again. Pack into hot jars, leaving 1 inch of headspace. Add salt if desired and cover with boiling liquid to ½ inch from the rim of the jar. Process in a pressure canner.

Number of minutes needed in canner: 25 for pints; 30 for quarts

CANNING EGGPLANT

Preparation: Wash thoroughly, then peel and slice into cubes. Sprinkle eggplant with salt and cover with cold water. Let stand for 45 minutes and drain well.

Hot pack: Boil eggplant in a small amount of water for five minutes. Drain. Place into hot jars, leaving 1½ inches of headspace. Cover with boiling water to ½ inch from the rim of the jar. Process in a pressure canner.

Number of minutes needed in canner: 30 for pints; 40 for quarts

CANNING FRESH GREEN PEAS

Preparation: Shell and wash peas.

Cold pack: Pack raw peas into hot jars, leaving 1 inch of headspace. Add salt if desired and cover with boiling water to ½ inch from the rim of the jar. Process in a pressure canner.

Hot pack: Cover peas with boiling water and bring to a boil again. Pack peas loosely into hot jars, leaving 1½ inches of headspace. Add salt if desired and cover with boiling liquid to 1 inch from the rim of the jar. Process in a pressure canner.

Number of minutes needed in canner: 40 for both pints and quarts

CANNING PEPPERS

Preparation: Use medium-size sweet bell peppers that are crisp and firm. Wash thoroughly under cold water. Cut out stem, remove seeds, and quarter or slice.

Hot pack: Boil peppers for three minutes. Place into hot jars, leaving 1½ inches of headspace. Add salt it desired. Also add vinegar—½ teaspoon for a pint and 1 teaspoon for a quart. Cover with boiling water to 1 inch from the rim of the jar. Process in a pressure canner.

Number of minutes needed in canner: 35 for pints; 45 for quarts

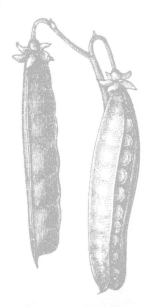

Canning Problems

When canning foods, be sure to watch for signs of spoilage. Air bubbles, murky liquid, strange color or odor, mushiness, sliminess, mold, leaky jars, bulging caps, or foam are all signs something has gone wrong. The food should not be eaten if any of these signs present themselves. Make sure it is destroyed so no person or animal will eat it.

A properly sealed jar is necessary for your canning and preserves to keep. If a jar that had been properly sealed opens in your cupboard, the jar may be cracked or the food may be spoiled. Examine jars of canned food carefully before opening them, looking for signs that the seal may be broken or the food may be discolored. After opening the jar, check to see if there is any odor. If in doubt, do not eat the food as it may contain mold or bacteria.

PROBLEMS WITH CANNED FRUITS

PROBLEM	THE CAUSE	PREVENTION
Fruit dark after removing from jar.	Fruit was underprocessed.	Make sure you follow the correct time for processing fruits. Start counting time once the water is boiling.
Floating fruit.	The syrup weighs more than the fruit.	Use ripe, firm fruits. Use a light to medium syrup and pack tight without crushing the fruit.
Pink in canned pears, peaches, and other fruits.	Some fruits naturally change color when processed.	Add 1 tablespoon of lemon juice to each quart of fruit before processing it.

PROBLEMS WITH CANNED VEGETABLES

PROBLEM	THE CAUSE	PREVENTION
Brown vegetables.	Overcooking or vegetables are too ripe.	Precook and process foods for the times given in the recipe. Choose vegetables that are firm and not overripe.
Color fades.	High temperatures will break down the green color of vegetables. Some foods fade naturally to a black or brownish color. This happens when the acids in foods contact minerals and metals in water and utensils.	Use stainless steel pots and utensils when canning.
Foods are dark at the top of the jar.	Food was not properly covered or was underprocessed.	Make sure foods are covered completely with a liquid, follow proper canning methods, and use the correct processing times when canning.
Liquid lost during processing.	Food packed cold. Food packed too tight. Not enough water to cover jars in the canner. Liquid was absorbed by starchy veggies.	Next time, precook the food. Leave more space in the jar. Keep 2 inches of water above the jars during processing. Allow extra room for starchy vegetables to expand.
Liquid is murky.	Food is spoiled, do not eat it. Table salt fillers.	Follow proper processing methods and cooking times. Use pure canning salt rather than table salt.

PICKLING

PICKLING IS ONE of the oldest methods of preserving food and is a process that can be applied to vegetables, meats, eggs, and fruit. Pickling is the preserving of food in an acid, such as vinegar, and it is this acidic environment that prevents growth of undesirable bacteria.

The varieties of pickled and fermented foods are classified by ingredients and method of preparation. Most dill pickles and sauerkraut are fermented and cured for about three weeks. Refrigerator dills are fermented for about one week. Fresh-pack or quick-process pickles are not fermented; some are brined several hours or overnight, then drained and covered with vinegar and seasonings. Fruit pickles usually are prepared by heating fruit in seasoned syrup acidified with either lemon juice or vinegar. Relishes are made from chopped fruits and vegetables that are cooked with seasonings and vinegar.

Most pickled foods are salted or soaked in brine first to draw out moisture that would dilute the acid used to safely preserve the food.

As mentioned before, the safety of canning relies on the acidity of the contents of the jar. Make sure you are using vinegar with a 4 to 6 percent acid to be safe, although many food-safety professionals are now advising 5 percent. Do not alter vinegar, food, or water proportions in a recipe and do not use vinegar with unknown acidity. Use only recipes with tested proportions of ingredients. Select fresh, unspoiled, and unblemished fruits or vegetables. Use canning or pickling salt. White vinegar is usually preferred when a light color is desirable, as is the case with fruits and cauliflower.

Bread and Butter Pickles

These pickles will keep in your fridge for several months.

INGREDIENTS + MAKES 6–7 PINTS

7 cups thinly sliced cucumbers
1 cup thinly sliced onion
1 cup thinly sliced green pepper
1 tablespoon pickling salt
1 tablespoon celery seed
2 cups sugar
1 cup vinegar

1. Place the cucumbers, onion, and green pepper into a large bowl.

2. Mix together the pickling salt, celery seed, sugar, and vinegar.

3. Pour over the vegetables. Stir well. Pack into jars, seal, and refrigerate.

Easy Dill Pickles

You can easily make one jar of pickles at time with this recipe.

INGREDIENTS + MAKES 1 JAR

1 pound small cucumbers
1 clove garlic
1 tablespoon pickling salt
½ cup vinegar
Pinch of dill

1. Wash cucumbers. Peel garlic and chop in half.

2. Sterilize a quart jar in boiling water for 10 minutes; boil jar lids and rings for 2–3 minutes.

3. In each jar, put the salt, vinegar, garlic, and dill. Pack in cucumbers, leaving ½ inch of room at the top of the jar.

4. Fill to almost overflowing with boiling water. Seal and tighten ring. Ingredients will mix by themselves.

Caramelized Red Onion Relish

Although this is a vegetable, the added acid of the vinegar means that you can use a water-bath to can.

INGREDIENTS + MAKES 6 PINTS

6 large red onions, peeled and very thinly sliced
¾ cup firmly packed brown sugar
1 tablespoon extra-virgin olive oil

3 cups dry red wine
½ cup aged balsamic vinegar
½ teaspoon fine sea salt
½ teaspoon freshly ground pepper

1. In a heavy nonstick skillet, combine onions and brown sugar with olive oil; heat over medium-high heat.

2. Cook uncovered for 25 minutes, or until onions turn golden and start to caramelize, stirring frequently.

3. Stir in wine, vinegar, salt, and pepper; bring to a boil over high heat. Reduce heat to low and cook for 15 minutes, or until most of the liquid has evaporated, stirring frequently.

4. Ladle into sterilized jars, leaving ½ inch of headspace. Remove air bubbles. Wipe rims. Cap and seal, then process in a water-bath canner for ten minutes.

PIONEER TIP!

The fastest way to peel an onion is to cut off both ends, slice the onion in half crosswise, and peel each half.

Sauerkraut

This recipe is based on a traditional method of making kraut in a brine crock. You'll need a large 3-gallon crock.

INGREDIENTS + MAKES 4 QUARTS

12 pounds cabbage
¼ pound salt

1. Wash the cabbage head; remove any leaves that have dark spots.

2. Cut cabbage into quarters; remove core and shred into ¼-inch pieces.

3. Mix cabbage with salt in a mixing bowl and let it sit for 5 minutes. The salt will pull liquid from the cabbage, which is called brine.

4. Fill crock by firmly packing in the cabbage and liquid, leaving 5 inches of headspace. If the brine has not covered the cabbage, boil some water, cool it, and then add it to the crock until the cabbage is completely covered.

5. Cover the cabbage with a clean white muslin cloth, then use a small bowl, plate, or other weight at the top to push the cabbage down. The weight should force the juice to come to the bottom of the cover but not over it. The cloth should be moist but not covered with the juice. Cover crock with an air-tight lid.

6. Check the sauerkraut often. If the juice level is too high, remove some of the water, or if not enough, increase the amount of water. Room temperature is recommended for fermenting cabbage (75°F is the best temperature). The sauerkraut will be ready in 2–3 weeks. Fermentation is indicated by the formation of bubbles.

7. Scum will form on the surface of the brine. It is important to skim it off every few days. Wash the cloth and weight and replace on the sauerkraut each time.

8. Pack into hot sterilized jars, leaving ½ inch of headspace. For quart jars, process for 20 minutes in hot water-bath.

FREEZING

FREEZING FOOD is an excellent method of food preservation. It allows many foods to be stored for weeks or even months longer than they can be in the refrigerator and to be defrosted as needed, with no or very little loss of quality and nutrients.

You will need a good-quality freezer if you plan to freeze large quantities of food. Look for a size that fits your family and budget. You generally need two to five cubic feet per person, depending on how much frozen food you use. If you buy bulk meat or plan to freeze a large quantity of fresh vegetables, you will want to get the largest freezer you can afford and have space for.

Chest freezers are usually less expensive than uprights. They are also cheaper to run, as they do not lose as much cold air when the freezer is opened and can be more tightly filled. They also require less maintenance, saving you additional money. They do, however, have some disadvantages. It is difficult for a small person to reach the bottom, and lifting out heavy packages can be tricky for any sized person. You will need to have a plan when packing your frozen food so it can be easily found again, as you will be stacking items on top of each other. Also, a large chest freezer can take up a lot of space. If you decide to consider a chest freezer, be sure to look for extras like baskets, an interior light, rollers, a drain hole, a lock, and a key.

An upright freezer is more expensive to purchase and run. The advantages over a chest freezer are that an upright freezer may be easier to find a space for in your home, and the foods placed in it are more accessible. When purchasing an upright freezer, look for extras like a heavy-duty magnetic door seal and a drainage outlet that will make cleaning your freezer easier.

If you do not have the space or the need for a chest or upright freezer, most refrigerators have a freezer on the top or bottom that can be used for freezing smaller amounts of food. If you plan to use your refrigerator freezer, stacking freezer containers will help you make the most use of a limited amount of space.

The temperature of a home freezer should be 0°F or 18°C. A freezer thermometer can be used to check the temperature. The temperature should be lower than this for fast freezing, and the fast freeze switch will allow the temperature to drop to between -13° to -18°F.

Freeze food as quickly as possible after you've harvested. Never freeze food that has even the smallest degree of spoilage. When freezing nonliquid foods, such as vegetables or loose berries, fill your freezer containers as full as possible, because air dries out food. For example, when freezing blueberries you should clean the berries and air-dry them. Then pack them tightly into containers, being sure not to crush them, but filling the container to capacity.

Blanching, also known as scalding, is done to destroy enzymes in your vegetables. Enzymes will affect the color and flavor of your vegetables if they are kept frozen for any length of time. If you are planning to eat your frozen veggies such as string beans, peas, or small carrots within a month, you do not necessarily have to blanch these items. However, if you plan on defrosting throughout the winter, take the time to scald your vegetables as they will look and taste better when you get around to eating them.

To blanch your harvested vegetables, fill a pot with water and bring it to a fast boil. You can add a few teaspoons of lemon juice or salt to your boiling water to help with discoloration. Use a wire rack to hold the vegetables and lower them into the boiling water. Start timing immediately and closely watch the time, as just one minute over will give you mushy vegetables. Most vegetables will take one to four minutes. You then need to plunge the vegetables into ice-cold water for the same amount of time as you blanched them to stop the cooking process. Continue the above process with each batch of vegetables, making sure the water is at a fast boil and adding more ice to the water for cooling. Drain the vegetables and then place them on a tray or cookie sheet and put them in the freezer for an hour or so. After that time you can portion them into bags or containers and return them to the freezer. This method prevents any water crystals from forming in your bags or containers.

If you're freezing liquids, remember to leave expansion space in the containers. To keep items from freezing into one big block of produce, spread them out on cookie sheets and initially freeze them this way. Once frozen, transfer to a container.

Freezing doesn't entirely halt the action of enzymes that break down food, so anything stored longer than twelve months should be thrown away.

DRYING

RYING IS PERHAPS the most natural way to preserve your food. In its simplest form you need nothing more than a few days of hot, sunny weather. Drying is the process of removing water from food to prevent the growth of microorganisms and decay.

Drying foods is not as precise as canning and freezing because it involves so many factors, including the type of food, water content, climate, and humidity. However, there are some basic guidelines that should be followed. Start with fresh, unblemished, unspoiled food. Cut food into small, thin slices. Place food so it does not overlap. Turn food frequently to ensure a consistent dehydration. Store dried foods in a closed container at room temperature and use within one year.

You can dry many different kinds of fruits, vegetables, herbs, and meats. You are primarily looking for denser material that does not hold a lot of liquid. For example, watermelon is not a good fruit to dry. It's a good idea to start off with a small batch of whatever food you want to dry to see if you are satisfied with the taste, texture, and color of the finished product.

You might want to see which foods are commercially dried, like cherries, apples, herbs, and beef, to give you an idea of some of the things you might want to dry at first. Then feel free to use your knowledge and experiment with other foods, following the appropriate safety standards.

Sun Drying

If you live in an area that gets consecutive days of temperatures in the 90s, as well as low humidity and low air pollution, sun drying is probably a great choice for you. Sun drying has a lot of advantages, the first being its low cost. All you will need to invest in is a few drying trays, protective netting, and the food you want to dry. The sun's rays have a sterilizing effect, which slows the growth of any microorganisms in the food. Sun-dried fruits retain their color as well.

Not all food can be dried successfully in the sun; the foods need to have a fairly

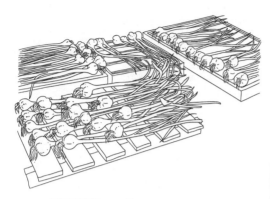

FIGURE 2-3: Sun drying garlic

high sugar and acid content so they do not spoil during the long sun-drying process. Because of this, fruits are your best choice when using this process. If you are sun drying your produce, keep a sharp eye on the sky. You are dependent on the weather when you rely on the sun to dry your food; all your time, effort, and money could be lost if it rains during the drying process. Another disadvantage is that sun-dried foods tend to have a lower quality and nutritional value than foods dried under controlled conditions.

Room Drying

Room drying is another simple method that would have been familiar to the original pioneers. And as a Modern-Day Pioneer, you may have access to thermostatically controlled cooling and heating systems that will make room drying even easier. This technique doesn't cost a lot because there is little investment needed—just a few drying trays, blocks to set them on, and a fan to keep the air circulating.

The main concern with room drying is having sufficient heat and air circulation to prevent food from attracting mold before it is completely dry. You can try drying a few items in your home if you have the proper conditions, but there are limits to what can be dried this way. For food safety reasons, stick to drying herbs, nuts in the shell, or partially dried high-acid and high-sugar fruits such as apple rings. Both citric acid and sugar are used to preserve foods, so foods that naturally have high acid or sugar contents are less likely to have bacteria or become moldy while being dried. Since these foods are less likely to quickly spoil, a slow drying process such as room drying is an option.

Begin by choosing a room that has relatively low humidity and is exposed to sunlight at least part of the day. Set the room temperature at 80°F or higher. A sunny kitchen window, a dust-free attic, or a basement are all good places for room drying. Place the foods on trays, allowing 5 to 6 inches between them for good air circulation. Use a fan to keep the air moving, and rotate the food regularly so it will dry evenly and thoroughly. This method can be used for herbs or partially dried hot peppers that have been drying in the sun and need to be brought indoors. They can be hung, allowing the foods to dry completely.

Oven Drying

This method of drying is a great choice if you only have a small amount of food you want to dry at one time. Other advantages are the wide range of possible foods that can be dried in an oven, and that you are not dependent on the weather or room temperature. You will still need to rotate the foods so they dry evenly.

Foods with a high moisture content, such as tomatoes or prunes, do not dry well in an oven, but most other foods will do well using this method. Be sure to dry strong-smelling foods like onions and garlic separately from other foods.

Start by arranging the food on drying trays, limiting to a maximum of 4 to 6 pounds of food at one time. Preheat your oven to 160°F, place the loaded trays into the oven, and prop the oven door open 2 to 6 inches. Never dry food with a closed oven door. The temperature in the oven will drop once you place the trays of food into it. Use a thermometer and try to keep the temperature around 140°F. As the food dries, less heat is needed, so adjust your oven setting accordingly.

Rotate the trays from top to bottom and front to back every fifteen minutes as you check for foods that are dried. Be sure to look at the top trays and any food on the edges of the trays since these items will dry first. To avoid scorching, remove food as it dries. Careful attention is required when drying food using this method, but you will end up with good-tasting food that is high in nutritional value.

Drying Fruits

Most fruits are covered with skin, which keeps the fruit fresh and holds the seeds and juicy flesh. For fruits to dry quickly enough not to spoil, they need to be perforated in some way so moisture can be released before you begin the drying process. Fruits such as peaches, pears, and apricots are usually cut in half with the stone removed; the skin on each of the two sides is left on to prevent all the juice from running out.

Place all sliced fruit on drying trays, making sure the fruit pieces are not touching each other. To speed up the drying process and keep timing consistent for all pieces, larger fruits should be peeled and sliced to ¼ to ½ inch thick before placing them on the trays. The shorter drying time that results will produce better quality, better tasting, and more nutritious dried fruit.

Start watching the fruits carefully when the drying process is nearly complete. Test frequently to avoid overdrying. Let a piece of dried fruit cool at room temperature and then taste it. It should be pliable, leathery in texture, and have no pockets of moisture.

Even after the drying process is complete, some pieces of fruit may still be drier than others. You will need to condition the fruit to help distribute any residual moisture as evenly as possible. This reduces the risk of spoilage, especially from mold. After the dried fruit has cooled (if you're using an oven), pack it into glass or plastic containers about two-thirds full and cover the container. Let the fruit sit for four to ten days, during which time the excess moisture in some pieces will be absorbed by the drier pieces. Shake the container daily to separate the fruits. If there is condensation inside the jar, take the fruit out of the jar and place it back into your oven.

Once your dried fruit has been conditioned, store it in plastic zip-top bags and remove any excess air. Place these smaller bags inside a larger plastic bag. Package fruits in amounts that will be used in a few days, as every time dried fruit is exposed to the air some deterioration will occur.

Fundamental Fruit Leather

This basic process will work for nearly any fruit that you'd like to make into roll-up leather. Fruit leather has a great shelf life and makes a wonderful, healthy snack.

INGREDIENTS + MAKES 1 BAKING SHEET OF LEATHER

4 cups fruit purée—apples, pears, berries, peaches, or a mixture of your favorite fruits
Honey or sugar to taste

1. Wash and peel fruit, making sure to remove any overripe parts.

2. Purée fruit in a food processor or blender.

3. Taste; sweeten to preference.

4. Heat entire mixture in a saucepan adding as little water as possible to have the fruit purée come to a low rolling boil; cool.

5. Coat fruit leather tray with spray-on oil.

6. Cover the oiled surface with purée no more than ⅛ inch thick.

7. Dry at 135°F in a conventional oven for about 12 hours.

8. Wrap in plastic for storing.

Drying Vegetables

Drying vegetables takes some extra effort. Some vegetables, such as broccoli, asparagus, and cauliflower, do not rehydrate very well, so it is better to freeze these vegetables rather than dry them. Other vegetables, like potatoes and carrots, can be easily stored or purchased at a reasonable price all year round. It is really not worth the time and effort to dry these types of vegetables, unless you are doing it for convenience or for backpacking supplies. Vegetables have less sugar content than fruits, so they are best dried under controlled conditions. Sun or room drying may be less effective than using an oven. The drying time and temperature is crucial to getting a good-quality item in the end.

Start by cutting your vegetables into uniform pieces. The drying time is proportional to the thickness of the cut vegetables. A ¼-inch dice dries in two hours; a ½-inch dice will take eight hours. Preheat the oven. Arrange the vegetables on drying trays, placing similar sized pieces on the same tray and leaving a bit of space between each piece for air circulation. Place the trays into the oven, and maintain a controlled temperature throughout the drying process so that the internal temperature of the vegetables does not exceed 140°F.

DRYING BEANS

+ Harvest after pods have faded to a tan color.
+ Wash pods, remove beans from pods, and wash beans again.
+ Water blanch for 3–5 minutes.
+ Dry for one hour at 150°F.

DRYING GARLIC

+ Remove the shell.
+ Slice to ⅛ inch thickness or leave whole.
+ Dry at 160°F for 1–2 hours.
+ Reduce to 130°F until dry.

DRYING ONIONS

+ Trim the bulb end and remove the peel.
+ Slice ⅛–¼ inch thick.
+ Dry at 160°F for 1–2 hours.
+ Reduce to 130°F until dry.

DRYING PEPPERS

+ Wash and cut into 1-inch dice, in halves, or leave whole.
+ Dry at 140°F for 2 hours.
+ Reduce to 130°F until dry.

Remember that dried vegetables will not keep as long as dried fruits. It is best to use them within six months; any longer and they will become less tasty and have less nutritional value.

Drying Herbs

Drying is a particularly good way of preserving the herbs you've grown. Bunches of herbs can be hung, or screens of herbs can be placed in a dry attic, around a hot water heater, or on top of a refrigerator. You can also place screens of herbs covered with paper towels in your car and park it in a shady spot; the warmth in the car will quickly dry them. If the weather is not cooperating or you do not have time to let the herbs dry naturally, you can place them in a warm oven to speed up the drying process. Set the temperature to 80°F to 100°F. Make sure you monitor the process until the leaves are crispy dry. It will usually take three to six hours for them to dry completely.

For drying in bunches it is best to use long-stemmed herbs. Tie the stems into one-inch bunches; then tie the string to a clothes hanger and hang it in a dark, dry, cool place. If dust is a problem, place the bunch into a brown paper bag to protect the herbs from collecting any dust. The hanging methods for drying can take up to two weeks for the herbs to become dry enough to store.

CURING MEATS

CURING MEATS IS DEFINED AS DRY-ING, smoking, adding seasonings or salt, or any combination of these methods. Adding some natural preservatives such as sugar, vinegar, or curing salts may also be involved in the curing process. Curing meat and fish will maintain the quality of the product while allowing it to be stored for a period of time.

Often the curing process involves brine, which is simply a solution of salt and water. The purpose of brine is to draw the natural sugars and moisture from foods and to form the lactic acids that protect the food against spoilage bacteria. Alone, meat is a low-acid food, so be careful to follow the preparation instructions to avoid bacterial growth.

The curing process lengthens the storage life of meats while adding a distinctive flavor. Ham and bacon are the most common cuts of meat cured; however, pork chops, ribs, lamb, chicken, and turkey are all tasty when cured.

PIONEER TIP!

Dry meat until it is tough and chewy. This can take up to 12 hours; check by tasting a small piece after 4–6 hours and then every hour after that until it is the consistency that you like.

Teriyaki Jerky

This recipe is fantastic for any type of meat that you enjoy with a rich teriyaki flavor.

INGREDIENTS ✦ MAKES 3½ POUNDS

5 pounds meat
2½ cups soy sauce
2½ cups teriyaki sauce
3 tablespoons dark brown sugar
3 tablespoons garlic powder

3 tablespoons onion powder
2 tablespoons powdered ginger
1 (5-ounce bottle) Liquid Smoke
½ cup honey
5 teaspoons curing salt

1. Slice the meat as thinly as possible (a mandoline or meat slicer helps with this). About ³⁄₁₆ inch is recommended.

2. Mix all the remaining ingredients together and put into a marinating dish with the meat.

3. Cover and refrigerate for at least 24 hours and at most 48 hours, stirring regularly. Drain meat completely.

4. Put the meat on a cookie tray and set your oven to 150°F. Turn regularly over the next six hours.

5. Cool and store in an airtight container or food-storage bag.

Corned Beef

The "corn" in this recipe's title refers to the coarse salt used when curing the beef. You can add saltpeter (potassium nitrate) to the brine to help retain the beef's pink color.

INGREDIENTS + SERVES 12–16

6 pounds beef brisket (flank or neck may be used)
8 cups water
1 cup Morton Tender Quick Salt
3 tablespoons sugar
1 teaspoon ground pepper
2 teaspoons mixed pickling spice
2 bay leaves
2 cloves garlic, minced

1. Cover meat with water in a large kettle. Bring to boil, then let water cool for a few minutes. Add remaining ingredients.

2. When liquid is lukewarm, cover with a clean triple-folded piece of cheese-cloth. Weigh down meat to keep submerged in brine.

3. Leave to cool for 36 hours or more.

Homemade Salami

You may substitute onion salt or garlic salt for the powder in this recipe if you prefer your salami on the salty side. For the recipe to succeed, you must use either curing salt or quick cure.

INGREDIENTS ✦ MAKES 6–8 SMALL ROLLS

5 pounds ground beef

6 teaspoons salt

5 hot peppercorns, crushed

2 teaspoons garlic powder

1½ teaspoons mustard seed

2½ teaspoons hickory seasoning

1½ teaspoons smoked salt

2 teaspoons onion powder

5 teaspoons Morton Tender Quick Salt

2 teaspoons ground caraway seed

1. Combine all ingredients in a large bowl; knead for 5 minutes. Cover tightly with plastic wrap and refrigerate for 24 hours.

2. Knead mixture for 5 minutes. Cover tightly with plastic wrap; refrigerate another 24 hours.

3. Knead for 5 minutes, then form meat into 6–8 small rolls. Place on a broiler pan and bake for 8 hours at 150°F, turning every hour. Turn oven off; let salami cool on broiler rack while still in the oven until it reaches room temperature.

4. Wrap tightly in plastic wrap. Refrigerate and slice. Serve on crackers or bread.

Smoked Rainbow Trout

This fish can be eaten as is once it has been smoked. You will not need to cook the trout after carrying out this recipe.

INGREDIENTS + MAKES 2 POUNDS

1 cup brown sugar
1 cup canning salt
2 pounds freshly caught trout

1. Mix sugar and salt together.

2. Clean the trout well, then sprinkle a tablespoon of the salt and sugar mixture on the inside and outside of the fish. Place the fish into plastic bags, then into a pan or bucket, packing close together. Do not add water. Let stand for 12 hours. Rinse well and hang tail end up overnight.

3. Make a fire in your smokehouse and bring the temperature to 170°F using a candy thermometer to check the temperature. Hang fish in the smokehouse without touching each other.

4. Keep the temperature at 170°F for 2–3 hours; then it can cool to 140°F for 2 hours.

PIONEER TIP!

There are many types and styles of smokehouses, so the type you build depends upon the type of smoking you want. All smokehouses require a vent at the top to get rid of moisture. When smoking fish, always be selective about the wood you use. Never use evergreen and keep in mind that alder and willow work well.

CHAPTER 3

HOW A PIONEER EATS:
Simple Meals Using the Fruit (or Vegetables) of Your Labor

"A man seldom thinks with more earnestness of anything than he does of his dinner."

— SAMUEL JOHNSON—

THE ORIGINAL PIONEERS WERE UP AT SUNRISE, tending to their household, their animals, and their fields. They did not stop working until well after nightfall, when they'd finally blow out their candles and put away their needlework.

There was no room for idleness in the wilderness. The pioneers needed to be at their strongest and best all day, all year. And they knew that eating filling, healthy meals was an important part of staying robust. Hungry, weak farmers could not harvest all of their crops before the winter came. Hungry, preoccupied homesteaders might become forgetful and drop stitches while quilting, or miss steps while making soap.

The pioneers knew what was in season and what they had in their kitchen. They prepared hearty meals with their preserved foods in the winter, and nourishing summer dishes with fresh fruit and vegetables. In this chapter, you will learn to put together mouthwatering, pioneer-inspired menus for any occasion.

THE PIONEER'S KITCHEN

T̲HE MOST IMPORTANT ITEMS a tradesperson has are his or her tools. You wouldn't want to be a carpenter, plumber, or electrician without the proper specialized equipment. The same could be said about the tools around a kitchen, especially a kitchen that is going to be an essential part of your daily life.

Cookware

Look for quality kitchen hand tools that will last and won't melt when exposed to hot surfaces. Have at least one good set of measuring cups and spoons and several larger Pyrex multi-cup measuring cups. Make sure you have enough good-quality mixing bowls and bakeware. You will likely be making multiple dishes at a time, and there's nothing worse than realizing you're one pan short just as everything is going into the oven.

Cooking Equipment

While the only tools a Modern-Day Pioneer needs to make most of the dishes in this chapter are a sharp, solid knife and a good cutting board, the following items

---

PIONEER TIP!

Think twice before buying a highly specialized appliance like a bread machine. Often you will be baking more bread than the machine can handle, and you will be wasting both money and space for a machine that can only do one thing. In Chapter 4, "How a Pioneer Bakes," you'll learn to make bread as the original pioneers did, without a machine.

---

will make certain jobs much easier and more professional looking.

+ **Wire Whisk:** A "balloon whisk" has fine wires that incorporate air into foods, lightening their texture. This tool is also essential for making dressings and sauces where insoluble ingredients like oil and vinegar are combined.
+ **Standing Electric Mixer:** A strong hand with a good utensil will do the job, but an electric mixer ensures

a uniform job and makes tasks like kneading dough, whipping cream, and softening butter move along much more quickly.

+ **Food Processor and Blender:** With a good strong knife and some elbow grease, you can chop anything into a purée, but using a processor or a blender will save time and effort, especially for dressings. Use a blender for smoother mixtures, and a processor for rougher jobs with dry ingredients.

Cast Iron in Your Kitchen

The pioneers needed cookware that could withstand the demands of a rustic kitchen, and cast iron was the perfect material for their hearth. For the Modern-Day Pioneer, there are several benefits to using cast iron in your kitchen.

Cast iron can withstand a level of heat that nonstick and other lightweight pans cannot take. You can even place your pan directly over the hot coals on a grill or over a campfire.

Every time you use the skillet you'll start to bond the oils and fats from the cooking into the surface. This is called seasoning, and as a result, cast-iron pans get better with age and use.

When you first get your skillet or cast-iron cookware, you have to season it a few times before you can cook something without worrying about it sticking. The first time you use a new cast-iron pan, preheat the oven to 350°F and place a layer of aluminum foil or a baking sheet on the bottom rack of the oven. Cut off a tablespoon-sized chunk of shortening and rub it over the entire surface of the skillet, inside and out. Place the pan upside down in the oven. Any excess will drip off the pan as it bakes. Set your timer for one hour. You'll likely notice a slight burning smell and see some smoke. This is normal and should not be a cause for concern. The oil you applied is smoking and the pan is soaking up the oil and the carbonization that it creates. Once the hour is up, turn off the heat and leave the pan in the oven to cool overnight. The surface should be darker, though it will still not be fully seasoned. It will take several uses and proper cleaning to get the desired effect.

Once you have a healthy seasoning base on the skillet, you'll find yourself cooking with less oil than you would in other pans. When you have a skillet with at least several months of seasoning, you can cut the oil called for in the recipe by a third to a half. The surface of a seasoned cast-iron pan encourages food to brown and crisp better than even the most expensive nonstick skillet on the market.

The main rule of cleaning a cast-iron skillet is never to use soap with it. Using soap won't ruin it, but will remove some of the seasoning that you've worked to build up. Most messes can be cleaned with hot water, a stiff-bristled brush, some salt, and occasionally a potato. A hot pan is easier to clean than a cold skillet because the metal is expanded and more likely to release what is stuck to it. Place a hot pan under running water and scrub it with the brush to remove the stuck-on bits.

If that doesn't work, pour ½ tablespoon of water and a tablespoon of kosher salt into the hot pan. Wad up a paper towel, hold it with tongs, and rub it over the surface of the pan to loosen anything stuck to it. The salt will help grind it away. When the salt looks dirty, dump it out, wipe the surface clean, and your pan is sealed and ready for storage.

If you have a particularly stubborn mess or if your paper towel starts to fall apart, don't break out the heavy artillery until you've tried cleaning it with oil. Pour two tablespoons of salt (kosher or pickling salt works best) in the skillet and cut a potato in half. Hold the potato like a scrub brush and rub it firmly over the surface of the skillet. The salt should act like scouring powder to help you rub off the stuck-on food. Neither the potato nor the salt will damage the surface of the pan and the potato will protect your fingertips from abrasions.

Here are the cast-iron implements that make the perfect additions to a Modern-Day Pioneer's kitchen:

+ **Stovetop Grill Pan:** Easier, healthier and more eco-friendly than charcoal or gas grills, a cast-iron pan with ridged surfaces for indoor grilling is incredibly useful.
+ **Dutch Oven:** Not an oven as we would consider it, but a deep pan with a tight-fitting lid.
+ **Skillet:** A flat-bottomed frying pan.

PIONEER TIP!

The iron from cast-iron implements will leach into your food. If you are iron-deficient, cooking with cast iron can provide supplementary nutrients. But if you have too much iron in your bloodstream, talk to a doctor before switching to cast-iron cookware.

THE PIONEER'S PANTRY

As a MODERN-DAY PIONEER, you can make the food that you might have previously purchased at the local supermarket or ordered from a nearby restaurant.

To ensure that your cooking efforts aren't frustrated by missing ingredients, make sure you have a pantry that is stocked with the essentials you need.

Here are the supplies you should keep on hand:

+ Spices and extracts
+ Baking powder, baking soda, and yeast
+ Salt: iodized, pickling, kosher, and sea salt
+ Dry milk
+ Dry buttermilk
+ Dutch cocoa
+ Cornstarch
+ Cream of tartar
+ Shortening
+ Sugar: brown sugar, confectioners' sugar, honey, molasses
+ Worcestershire sauce
+ Vinegar
+ Extra-virgin olive oil
+ Parchment paper, aluminum foil, plastic wrap, and plastic storage bags
+ Bouillon cubes (beef and chicken)

These are only initial suggestions. As you continue cooking for yourself, you may find your essentials change as you discover your favorite recipes and cooking styles.

CELEBRATING THE SUMMER BOUNTY

I N THE SUMMERTIME, make use of the crisp greens and ripe fruits for these bright, flavorful dishes. If you have a garden, serve dinner outdoors and show off your Modern-Day Pioneer lifestyle.

MENU

Appetizer:
Salad Greens with Mixed Herb Dressing

Main Course:
Rabbit Stew with Spinach Dumplings

Side Dishes:
Swiss Chard Ravioli with Fresh Pesto Sauce

Fried Green Tomatoes

Dessert:
Blackberry Stew with Sweet Biscuits

Mixed Herb Dressing

Dressings adhere to dry lettuce leaves, and run off wet ones. Be sure to thoroughly pat down your greens after washing them.

INGREDIENTS + MAKES 2 CUPS

1 cup dried parsley
½ cup dried basil
½ cup dried thyme
½ cup dried savory
½ cup dried marjoram
¾ cup olive oil
¼ cup vinegar

1. Mix together the dry ingredients and store in an airtight container.

2. To make your salad dressing, mix 1 tablespoon of the herb mixture with the ¾ cup oil and ¼ cup vinegar.

Rabbit Stew with Spinach Dumplings

If you've decided to keep rabbits (as detailed in Chapter 1, "How a Pioneer Tends"), then this is a great way to use your meat. These dumplings are delicious, but if spinach is not in season, you can always serve the stew with mashed potatoes. If you don't have access to rabbit meat, you can always substitute chicken.

INGREDIENTS ✦ SERVES 4–6

For stew:

3 pounds rabbit, cut into serving pieces
Salt and pepper to taste
⅓ cup flour
⅓ pound pancetta, diced
1 onion, diced
1 pound white mushrooms, sliced
1 (14-ounce) can diced tomatoes with roasted garlic
1 teaspoon mixed dried Italian herbs
1 cup dry red wine
2 cups chicken broth
1 tablespoon cornstarch
2 tablespoons cold water

For dumplings:

1 pound spinach
1 clove garlic, minced
1 tablespoon butter
1 pound ricotta cheese
2 cups flour
¼ teaspoon salt
3 eggs
¼ cup minced fresh parsley (for garnish)

1. To make stew, rinse rabbit pieces; pat dry. Sprinkle with salt and pepper; coat with flour. In Dutch oven, cook pancetta over medium-high heat until meat browns and fat is released. Brown rabbit in pancetta fat; remove to platter.

2. Add onion and mushrooms to Dutch oven; sauté 3–5 minutes, until vegetables soften.

3. Add tomatoes, herbs, and wine. Bring mixture to a boil; reduce heat to medium. Return rabbit to pot; add broth. Cover; simmer 1½ hours, adding water occasionally to maintain liquid level.

4. Uncover pot; cook fifteen minutes longer. Dissolve cornstarch in cold water.

5. Carefully remove rabbit pieces to platter. Turn heat to high; bring sauce to a boil.

6. Stir in cornstarch; cook, stirring, until sauce is smooth and no longer cloudy.

7. Remove from heat; return rabbit pieces to pot. Keep warm.

8. To make dumplings, cook spinach and garlic in butter; let cool. Press as much liquid as possible from spinach and garlic; finely chop. Mix spinach with ricotta, ⅔ of flour, salt, and eggs; work together until well blended. Add additional flour to make a soft dough, reserving small amount of flour. Shape into 16 small ovals. Bring large pot of water to gentle boil; add dumplings. Reduce heat to a simmer; cook 15 minutes. Drain.

9. Place rabbit pieces and dumplings in deep serving dish or casserole. Ladle sauce over all; sprinkle with parsley. Serve immediately.

Swiss Chard Ravioli

If you're growing Swiss chard in your garden, this is a great way to incorporate that vegetable into a dish.

INGREDIENTS + SERVES 8

2 tablespoons olive oil
1 medium onion, finely chopped
1 tablespoon chopped garlic (2–3 cloves)
Pinch of crushed red pepper flakes (optional)
1 large bunch (about 1½ pounds) red or green Swiss chard, stems removed
12 ounces (1½ cups) ricotta cheese
½ cup grated Parmigiano-Reggiano or Asiago cheese (use top quality here)
1 tablespoon bread crumbs
2 beaten eggs, divided
Salt and freshly ground black pepper
1 recipe Ravioli Pasta Dough (see following recipe), rolled into four sheets

1. Heat the oil in a large skillet over medium-high heat. Add the onion, garlic, and red pepper if using; cook 5 minutes until onions are translucent. Add the chard; cook until just wilted.

2. Transfer to a colander to cool and drain.

3. Once the chard has cooled, squeeze out excess moisture with your hands. Transfer to a cutting board and give it a rough chopping.

4. In a large mixing bowl, combine the chopped chard, ricotta, Parmigiano-Reggiano, bread crumbs, and half the eggs.

5. Season to taste with salt and black pepper (season it highly, as you'll only use a little in each ravioli).

6. Place 12 evenly spaced, tablespoon-sized dabs of filling onto each of 2 pasta sheets. Using a pastry brush, paint in between the filling portions with the remaining egg.

7. Loosely cover these pasta sheets with the remaining 2 sheets.

8. Press down with your hands to squeeze out any air pockets, and press firmly to seal the filling in.

9. Using a knife, or fluted pastry cutter, cut between the ravioli, separating them, and pinch the edges extra tight between your fingers. Allow them to dry for 15–30 minutes before cooking in rapidly boiling salted water.

Ravioli Pasta Dough

You can also use this dough to make any other kind of pasta: fettuccine, tagliatelle, lasagna, etc.

INGREDIENTS + YIELDS JUST UNDER 2 POUNDS

3½ cups unbleached all-purpose flour
2 large eggs (egg substitute or ½ cup hot water will also work as a vegan alternative)
½ cup plus 2 teaspoons cold water
1 teaspoon salt
1 teaspoon olive oil

1. Pulse in a food processor or vigorously hand mix the flour, eggs, water, salt, and oil until blended, being careful not to overheat the dough.

2. Knead it for ten minutes on a clean work surface, until the dough is smooth and highly elastic. The dough will be very stiff, and kneading will take a little "elbow grease."

3. Cut the dough into four pieces. It's best to let the dough rest thirty minutes before rolling it out.

4. Flatten one of the dough pieces, place on a floured work surface, and roll from the center out, turning the circle a quarter turn every few moments.

5. When the dough reaches a thickness of ⅛ inch, wrap ⅓ around the rolling pin, and draw it away from yourself, stretching it thin. Repeat this rolling and stretching process until the dough is thin enough to see your hand through. Repeat with remaining dough.

Fresh Pesto Sauce

Use fresh basil from your window box to make this pasta sauce. Add in other fresh herbs to make an unusual pesto with a kick.

INGREDIENTS + MAKES 2 CUPS

3 cups fresh basil
2 cloves garlic, puréed
¾ cup pine nuts, ground
1 teaspoon black pepper
½ cup grated Parmesan cheese
1 cup extra-virgin olive oil

1. Blend all ingredients together in a blender or food processor, or thoroughly chop and mix by hand.

2. Pour extra sauce into small containers and store in the refrigerator or freezer.

Fried Green Tomatoes

This is a perfect recipe for those pesky tomatoes that just won't ripen before the harvest. But these are so good, the Modern-Day Pioneer might want to use early tomatoes throughout the growing season.

INGREDIENTS + SERVES 6–8

1½ cups all-purpose flour
½ cup cornmeal
½ teaspoon salt, plus 1 pinch
¼ teaspoon ground black pepper

¼–½ cup milk
3–4 large green tomatoes
¼ cup vegetable oil
¾ cup ranch dressing

1. Mix together the flour, cornmeal, ½ teaspoon salt, and pepper in a large bowl.

2. Pour ¼ cup of milk into the bowl and stir to combine. If mixture looks dry, add more milk until you get a thick batter.

3. Slice the tomatoes into ¼" slices. Pat dry with paper towels.

4. Place a skillet over medium heat and add the oil.

5. Dip each tomato slice into the batter and let the excess drip off. Slide them into the skillet so they're not touching.

6. Cook each side for 1½–2 minutes.

7. Remove them and place on a rack over paper towels to keep them from getting soggy.

8. While they're still hot, sprinkle with a pinch of salt.

9. Serve with the dressing.

PIONEER TIP!

In the winter, try dredging some slices of your homemade pickles in the batter and frying them. They'll cook in about 1½ minutes and are just as tasty as fried green tomatoes.

HOW A PIONEER EATS: Simple Meals Using the Fruit (or Vegetables) of Your Labor

Blackberry Stew with Sweet Biscuits

Use the blackberries (or any small fruits) from your garden to make this lovely, easy-to-assemble cross between shortcake and cobbler.

INGREDIENTS + SERVES 6

1 cup sugar
½ cup water
6 cups blackberries
1 teaspoon lemon juice
2 cups flour

½ teaspoon salt
1 tablespoon baking powder
1 cup confectioners' sugar
½ cup very cold unsalted butter
¾ cup light cream

1. In a large saucepan, combine sugar and water. Bring to a boil over medium-high heat, stirring constantly.

2. Remove from heat; carefully add blackberries and lemon juice.

3. Return to medium-high heat; bring mixture to a boil. Immediately reduce heat to medium low; simmer fifteen minutes.

4. In a large bowl, combine flour, salt, baking powder, and confectioners' sugar; stir with whisk to blend. Add butter; cut in with a pastry blender or two knives. Work until mixture resembles coarse meal. Stir in cream to make a soft dough.

5. Coat hands and a work surface with additional flour. Knead dough briefly; roll out to 1-inch thickness.

6. Using a biscuit or cookie cutter, cut into eight biscuits. Place on a baking sheet covered with nonstick foil, at least 1 inch apart.

7. Bake at 400°F for 10–12 minutes, or until biscuits are light brown on top.

8. Ladle blackberry stew into shallow bowls; top each bowl with a hot biscuit.

A ROBUST HARVEST MEAL

s the leaves turn colors, add cool-weather produce like apples and cabbage to your diet. Using herbs and cured meats, this menu will fill the brisk autumn air with warmth and good smells.

MENU

Appetizer:
Dinner Rolls with Simple Herb Butter

Main Course:
Corned Beef and Cabbage Pie

Dessert:
Old-Fashioned Baked Apples

Simple Herb Butter

This easy spread goes perfectly with the warm dinner bread you'll learn to make in Chapter 4, "How a Pioneer Bakes." Try it with dried rosemary or thyme.

INGREDIENTS ✦ MAKES 1 CUP

1 cup unsalted butter
2 tablespoons minced fresh herbs, washed and dried well, or
 1½ teaspoons dried herbs, or ½ teaspoon herb seeds

1. Let butter soften to room temperature, and then beat in the herbs by hand or with an electric mixer.

2. For best flavor, chill for at least three hours before serving.

3. The butter can be pressed into molds, formed into balls with a melon baller, or shaved into curls.

4. Store wrapped tightly in plastic for up to a month in the refrigerator or up to three months in the freezer.

PIONEER TIP!

Put the fresh herbs into a large measuring cup and use kitchen scissors to snip them. The measuring cup will tell you how much you have. Also, use a fork to strip herb leaves off of the twigs.

Corned Beef and Cabbage Pie

Use corned beef you've cured yourself to make this rustic dish.

INGREDIENTS + SERVES 4–6

1 head leafy cabbage
1 tablespoon butter
1 medium onion, minced
2 cups heavy cream
1 tablespoon coarse mustard

2 cups shredded corned beef
2 cups finely diced boiled potatoes
Salt and pepper, to taste
2 plum tomatoes, sliced

1. Preheat oven to 350°F. Boil whole cabbage in large soup pot for about fifteen minutes, or just until leaves are tender and pliable. Set aside to cool.

2. In a large, heavy saucepan over medium-high heat, combine butter and onion; sauté five minutes.

3. Stir in cream and mustard. Bring to a boil, then reduce heat to medium. Add corned beef and potatoes, stirring gently to blend into sauce. Simmer three minutes. Remove from heat; add salt and pepper.

4. Drain cabbage; carefully remove leaves from core. In a well-buttered ceramic or glass casserole, place a layer of several cabbage leaves. Top with half of corned beef mixture, followed by another layer of cabbage. Spoon remaining corned beef mixture into casserole and top with cabbage. Cover with foil and bake for thirty minutes.

5. Remove foil and layer tomatoes over top layer of cabbage. Bake uncovered for ten minutes to roast tomatoes. Let stand ten minutes before serving.

HOW A PIONEER EATS: Simple Meals Using the Fruit (or Vegetables) of Your Labor

Old-Fashioned Baked Apples

Use the apples you've grown to make this cozy dessert on an autumn evening.

INGREDIENTS + SERVES 4

4 baking apples (Romes or Cortlands are good)
8 whole cloves
4 tablespoons butter (½ stick), softened
⅓ cup light brown sugar
½ teaspoon ground cinnamon or confectioners' sugar, plus extra for sprinkling

1. Preheat oven to 350°F. Wash and dry apples thoroughly. Using a small knife, cut a divot from the top of the apples, leaving the stem intact. This "cover" will be replaced when baking. Scoop out the seeds and core with a melon baller or small spoon. Drop 2 cloves into each apple.

2. Knead together the butter and brown sugar, along with the ½ teaspoon cinnamon, until it is a paste. Divide equally over the scooped apples, leaving enough space to replace the tops.

3. Place apples in a baking dish, with ½ cup of water on the bottom. Bake for 1 hour. Sprinkle with cinnamon or powdered sugar before serving.

A PLENTIFUL WINTER SUPPER

In the middle of a snowstorm, rely upon your preserved and canned foods, as well as root vegetables, which can last through the cold season. Serve big meals that will stick to your ribs and keep you warm until the thaw.

MENU

Appetizer:
Root Vegetables in Beef Broth

Main Course:
Sauerkraut-Stuffed Flank Steak

Side Dish:
Baked Beans

Dessert:
Sour Cream Butter Cake
with Buttercream Frosting

Root Vegetables in Beef Broth

Not only will this soup warm up the coldest day in January, but it's also a nice way of using the robust root vegetables that will last through the winter.

INGREDIENTS + SERVES 8

2 tablespoons butter
1 medium onion, diced
1 rib celery, diced
1 carrot, diced
1 turnip, diced
1 russet potato, peeled and diced
1 parsnip, diced

1 small sweet potato, peeled and diced
8 cups beef broth
2 bay leaves
½ teaspoon dried thyme leaves
1 teaspoon grated orange zest
Salt and pepper, to taste

1. In a large soup pot over medium-high heat, melt butter. Add onion and sauté for 3 minutes.

2. Add celery and carrot and sauté for 3 minutes more.

3. Add turnip, potato, parsnip, and sweet potato, then broth and bay leaves; bring to a boil. Reduce heat to medium and simmer for 25 minutes.

4. Stir in thyme, orange zest, salt, and pepper; cover. Let stand 10 minutes; remove bay leaves before serving.

Sauerkraut-Stuffed Flank Steak

Use your homemade sauerkraut from Chapter 2, "How a Pioneer Prepares," for this delicious main course. Flank steak is the boneless cut of beef that comes from the animal's lower hindquarters. It is sometimes fibrous and stringy and needs to be tenderized.

INGREDIENTS ✦ SERVES 4–6 PEOPLE

2–3 pounds flank steak
1 teaspoon salt
3 cups sauerkraut
1½ cups sliced apples
¾ cup dry bread crumbs

1 tablespoon caraway seeds
2 tablespoons flour
3 tablespoons shortening
1 onion, chopped
2 cups water

1. Spread meat open, score it, and rub the salt into the meat.

2. Mix sauerkraut, apples, bread crumbs, and caraway seeds; spread evenly over steak.

3. Roll meat firmly, tie it with heavy string. Flour the roll and sauté in the shortening until browned. Add onion and water, cover tightly.

4. Cook over low heat for 2 hours, or until the meat is tender. More water may need to be added.

Baked Beans

If you've grown and dried your own beans, you can use them to make this Colonial cold-weather classic.

INGREDIENTS ✦ SERVES 6–8

1 pound small white or pink beans

Water, as needed, plus 9 cups

4 ounces salt pork, rind removed and cut into ½" cubes

3 slices bacon, cut into matchsticks

1 medium onion, finely chopped

½ cup molasses

2 tablespoons stone-ground or brown mustard

1 tablespoon apple cider vinegar

Pinch of salt

Pinch of pepper

1. Rinse the beans and remove any bad beans or debris. Cover the beans with three inches of water and soak overnight. Place the salt pork in water in the refrigerator.

2. Preheat oven to 300°F. Place the salt pork and bacon in a Dutch oven over medium-high heat. Cook for 7–9 minutes until the bacon is crispy. Drain off almost all pork fat. Add the onion and cook for 7–8 minutes.

3. Stir in the molasses, mustard, drained beans, and 9 cups water. Turn the heat to high and bring to a boil. Stir, cover, transfer to the middle of the oven, and bake for 3 hours.

4. Remove the lid and stir. Cook for another 1–1½ hours. The liquid should thicken to a syrup consistency. Stir in the vinegar, salt, and pepper. Serve hot or warm.

Sour Cream Butter Cake

If you've been keeping chickens, use their eggs to make this rich, moist cake and the frosting that accompanies it.

INGREDIENTS + SERVES 12

4 egg yolks
⅔ cup sour cream, divided
1½ teaspoons vanilla extract
2 cups sifted cake flour
1 cup sugar

½ teaspoon baking powder
½ teaspoon baking soda
½ teaspoon salt
¾ cup (1½ sticks) unsalted butter, softened
    to room temperature

1. Preheat oven to 350°F. Grease a 9-inch cake pan, dust it with flour, and line the bottom with waxed paper. In a bowl, whisk together the yolks, ¼ of the sour cream, and the vanilla. In a large, separate bowl, mix the flour, sugar, baking powder, baking soda, and salt; whisk vigorously to combine.

2. Add the butter and remaining sour cream to the flour mixture, and mix well until flour is completely moistened. Add the egg mixture to the flour mixture in three separate additions, mixing between each addition. Pour into prepared cake pan.

3. Bake in the middle of the oven until a toothpick inserted into the center comes out clean, usually about 35–40 minutes. Start checking at 25 minutes, since oven temperatures and ingredient characteristics vary, and it might be done quicker. Cool 10 minutes, then take out of pan and cool completely on a wire rack.

4. To frost, cut laterally in half and frost both sections, then stack, smooth the sides, and refrigerate to set.

HOW A PIONEER EATS: Simple Meals Using the Fruit (or Vegetables) of Your Labor

Buttercream Frosting

INGREDIENTS ✦ YIELDS ENOUGH TO FROST 1 (9-INCH) CAKE

1½ cups sugar
½ cup water
2 large eggs plus 4 egg yolks
1 pound unsalted butter, softened to room temperature
2 teaspoons vanilla extract

1. Boil the sugar and water together without stirring until slightly thick and between 234°F and 240°F on a candy thermometer (this is called the "soft ball" stage—a thin ribbon should fall with the last drops off a spoon).

2. Whisk together eggs and yolks in a double boiler or stainless steel bowl atop a pot of simmering water. Gradually whisk in the hot sugar syrup; heat, whisking constantly, until the mixture is hot to the touch, thick, and ribbony.

3. Remove bowl from heat, and continue whisking until cool, about 5 minutes more.

4. In a mixer or bowl, beat the butter until it is fluffy and light.

5. Gradually beat the whipped butter into the egg mixture, adding it in tablespoonfuls. Add the vanilla, and whisk to incorporate.

6. If desired, flavor by adding melted chocolate, fruit liqueur, or espresso.

7. Cool over an ice-water bath until it reaches a comfortable consistency for spreading. Keeps in the refrigerator for up to one week.

CHAPTER 4

HOW A PIONEER BAKES:
Making Bread Without a Breadmaker

"All sorrows are less with bread."

— MIGUEL DE CERVANTES —

O N THE FRONTIER, if you didn't know how to make bread, you went hungry. Bread was a staple of the pioneer diet. It soaked up the gravy from their stews at supper; it filled them up at breakfast before a long day of work. Pioneers shared sourdough starters with their neighbors and taught their children to knead with gentle, firm hands. For these adventurous people who journeyed out into wild, unexplored territory, bread was a taste of home.

In this chapter, you will learn about the ingredients and techniques of breadmaking as well as basic recipes that would fill up the hungriest pioneer. You will learn how to make yeast starters that you can share with friends and family, or even pass down to your own children, creating a line of Modern-Day Pioneers for years to come.

THE MAIN INGREDIENTS

THERE ARE NOT many ingredients in bread, but everything included has a vital importance. Understanding what works, and why, will help your creative juices flow and assist in troubleshooting if problems arise.

Flour

Flour is the most important ingredient in breadmaking. It provides the structure (or "crumb") of the bread, and most of the bread's nutritional value. The grain most commonly used is wheat. Although other grains are used, wheat alone contains enough essential gluten proteins to make bread production possible.

Bread Flour

The most common flour for breadmaking is bread flour, also called high-gluten flour. The hard winter wheat in this flour is bred to have higher levels of gluten protein.

All-Purpose Flour

All-purpose is most commonly found in American kitchens. It works for bread, but is not ideal. The protein content is

---

PIONEER TIP!

All-purpose flour works fine for bread, but it isn't perfect. You can approximate the gluten protein of bread flour by adding gluten flour or vital wheat gluten, in the ratio of 1 teaspoon per cup of all-purpose flour.

---

lower than that of bread flour, balanced by an equal amount of starch. All-purpose is sometimes used in the beginning of bread recipes that require longer fermentation, taking advantage of its higher starch content as food for yeast.

Whole Wheat Flour

Another member of the wheat flour family is whole wheat. White flour production removes and discards the fibrous bran and nutrient-rich germ, leaving only the inner endosperm, which consists of starch and gluten proteins. Whole wheat flour retains the bran and germ and essential nutrients we need for good health. Most large flour production facilities make white flour first, then mix the bran and germ back in to create whole wheat. Stone-ground flours grind the whole grain and keep the flour parts together through the entire process. Wheat bran and wheat germ are also available separately to add into breads, enhancing flavor and nutrition. Graham is a similar whole grain wheat flour, with a slightly nuttier flavor. White whole wheat flour is made from a light-colored variety of wheat.

Yeast

Yeast is the one ingredient that makes bread taste like bread. That characteristic yeastiness is the fragrance we smell as we pull our loaves out of the oven. But more importantly, without yeast, our loaves would be less like bread and more like hockey pucks.

Yeast is a living organism that occurs naturally in the air all around us, and comes in different varieties. Yeast feeds on carbohydrates, and it prefers an environment that is warm and moist. When all the conditions are right, the yeast will feed and produce two byproducts, carbon dioxide and alcohol. In Chapter 5, "How a Pioneer Drinks," you'll learn how to use yeast to produce beer. But in this chapter, you'll focus on the way yeast produces carbon in the baking process.

Bubbling foam on the surface of the mixture shows that the yeast is working. As the carbon dioxide accumulates, the gluten proteins in the dough stretch, and the dough rises. The better the conditions, the more carbon dioxide is created, and the more the dough will rise. Easily absorbed carbohydrates, like sugar or honey, get to work quickly. Starches need more time to convert into sugar, so the process is slower.

Yeast Maintenance

Because yeast is alive, it can be killed. This happens eventually in the oven, but it can happen prematurely if care is not taken.

The first danger yeast encounters is water temperature. Warm water is recommended to get the yeast started, but anything over 110°F will kill it. Some bakers use a thermometer for precision, but a normal sense of touch works, too. You should be able to easily hold your finger in the warm water. That will make it slightly above body temperature (98.6°F). If you can't handle it, the yeast can't either.

Choosing Yeast

The recipes in this chapter call for active dry yeast, which is the most readily available yeast in markets today. There are other options, however. Quick-rise yeast is fed large amounts of phosphorus and ammonia, which speeds up its activity by 50 percent. Instant yeast is coated with ascorbic acid and sugar for immediate activation.

Compressed yeast, also known as fresh cake yeast, is the yeast preferred by professionals. It is perishable, and if refrigerated will hold for about a week. It may also be frozen for several months, although the consistency will change once defrosted.

Similar in consistency to a block of cheese, fresh yeast is more easily measured by weight, which is preferred by production bakers. But more importantly, fresh yeast has a superior flavor. It can be used instead of active dry (.06 ounce is equivalent to .25 ounce active dry) in the recipes in this book. Small cakes of yeast are available refrigerated in some markets, although they are often cut with cornstarch. The cornstarch accelerates fermentation, but results in a product with less flavor. If you are interested in baking with fresh yeast, try buying a 1-pound block from a local artisan baker. To store, cut it into sixteen cubes and freeze loose in a zip-top bag. Pull out ounce-sized blocks as needed.

Water

In order for the yeast to absorb nutrients, water must be present. Water can be straight from the tap, bottled, filtered, or purified. Milk, juice, tea, coffee, and eggs are commonly added in place of all or a portion of the water needed.

Many bakers insist on a certain type of water, based on taste and desired outcome. If your tap water tastes good, it is perfectly fine to use. If you are concerned about the mineral content, use a filter.

Many recipes call for water to be at a certain temperature, the optimal temperature that promotes fermentation. However, fermentation takes place even when water is cold. Cool temperatures retard fermentation, but they do not halt it until a dough is frozen. For this reason, the Modern-Day Pioneer can slow down production by making a dough in the evening, letting it rise slowly overnight in the fridge, and forming and baking it the following day. If time allows, a long rise is preferable, because more fermentation produces more flavorful bread.

Salt

While the number one reason that salt is added to any type of recipe is flavor, salt also plays a chemical role in baking yeast bread. Salt slows, and can even stop, the process of yeast fermentation. Most dough can withstand salt up to about 2 percent of its weight before the effect becomes detrimental.

Salt also helps toughen gluten by helping bond protein molecules. Salt inhibits enzymes that soften protein, essentially protecting the gluten protein from destruction. Dough made without salt will be noticeably slack or mushy, and its fermentation will be rapid and unstable. Bread made without salt will have less structure and a bland flavor.

Too much salt will prevent the yeast from feeding, causing little, if any, rise. The dough's texture will be tight and it will be too salty to eat. The right amount of salt for optimal outcome is also the precise amount needed to make bread taste good.

Sugar

Sugar makes five major contributions to bread dough. It provides food for the yeast, provides flavor for us, promotes tenderness, preserves crumb, and gives the bread a nice color.

Sugar, like salt, attracts water. This effect is evident in the moistness of a sweet bread, as well as its shelf life. The ability to hold water keeps the bread moist days longer than a sugar-free bread. The effect of holding water also means that excessive amounts of sugar will inhibit fermentation by keeping the water away from where it needs to be. In bread recipes with large amounts of sugar, it must be added in stages to prevent disruption in fermentation.

When sugar is cooked, it caramelizes. This effect also occurs inside dough, evidenced in the color of a crust. If two bread recipes are made identically, but one is made with sugar and one without, the crust of the sugar-free dough will be noticeably pale. It takes a surprisingly small amount of sugar to brown a crust, which is why most recipes contain at least a teaspoon or two. But sweet dough, with double or triple that amount, will be noticeably darker.

Fat

Fat moistens the bread, tenderizes the crumb, and prolongs the shelf life. A lean dough (fat-free dough), such as French bread, will begin to stale as soon as it cools and will last less than a day before its drying texture becomes noticeable. Rich dough (dough with fat) remains soft and moist for twice as long.

Fat slows fermentation. Oily dough is heavier, which limits the stretch of the gluten and prevents large pockets of carbon dioxide from forming during fermentation. The absence of large bubbles of gas results in the absence of large holes in the finished bread crumb. Bread with a tight crumb is preferred for recipes such as sandwiches and canapés because it holds in the fillings.

Fat is added into bread dough in several forms, including butter, milk, cream, sour cream, cheese, nut butters, and eggs. Recipes will specify how a fat is to be added, which is usually after the yeast is proofed, but before the main quantity of flour is added. It is not necessary to liquefy a solid fat before adding it. Mixing and kneading will add enough friction to warm the fats to a liquid state, making them easily absorbed by the flour.

PIONEER TIP!

Fat and oil are interchangeable; both produce the same effect on the crumb of the dough. The flavors, though, vary greatly. Neutral oils, like vegetable, salad, and canola, are good substitutes for butter. Olive oil has a strong, fruity flavor that is not always appropriate.

TECHNIQUES FOR SUCCESS

THE INGREDIENTS ARE IMPORTANT, but if you don't know what to do with them, your chances of success are limited. One cannot simply throw everything listed together in a bowl. The proper order of mixing and kneading is key for the Modern-Day Pioneer.

Mixing

Mixing should be done in a large bowl to prevent overflows. The initial mixing can be done with your tool of preference, but for ease of cleanup, a simple dinner fork is the best tool. Spoons do not incorporate ingredients enough, and a whisk only works well until flour is added, at which time the dough clumps into the center of the whisk. As soon as the dough holds together, the mass should be turned out onto a lightly floured work surface for kneading.

Kneading

Kneading is the most important step in breadmaking. This is the stage when the gluten is created, and the dough becomes capable of holding the carbon dioxide that is built up during fermentation. There are many ways to knead. The key is to keep the dough moving around the table. It must be well agitated. Some bakers fold and press, others lift and slap, others roll and drop. As long as it is kept moving for 8–10 minutes, any method will work. As the dough is kneaded, it may be necessary to add more flour.

The Right Consistency

When dough is kneaded, it transforms from a slack, lumpy dough to a tight, smooth one. This transformation is key to the outcome of your bread. After 10 minutes the dough should be tight and elastic and spring back into shape when poked or stretched. If it does not, rest the dough for five minutes and check it again. It is possible to over-knead (although it is difficult to do by hand). The over-kneaded dough looks much like the under-kneaded dough, lumpy and rough. The difference is that the over-kneaded dough will feel tight, not slack.

Kneading and Flour

Bread baking is an inexact science, and the amount of flour a particular recipe will require depends on several variables, including human error. Air temperature, ingredient temperature, humidity, measurement accuracy, and the type of flour and its manufacturer contribute to the amount of flour a recipe will take on any given day. There is only one sure way to know how much is enough, and that is by looking and feeling. The dough should be smooth and soft, but not sticky, and not so tough that it's hard to knead.

To make a loaf of bread successfully, it is necessary to reserve the last cup of flour called for, and to add it slowly, a little at a time, as the dough is kneaded. Let each addition work in completely before determining if more is necessary. The dough should be moist and soft, but not sticky. Adding a little flour at a time prevents the over-addition of flour, which makes dough tough and hard to knead, and results in a dry finished product. Sometimes a recipe will require more than what is called for, sometimes less.

Fermentation

Once the dough is kneaded, it must be put up to rise, or double. This step is called fermentation, and it is when the yeast begins feeding and consequently releases carbon dioxide. If you've kneaded properly, that gas will be trapped within the dough, and the bread will rise.

Certain things control fermentation. Yeast likes warmth, so the more warmth you provide (up to about 100°F), the faster the yeast will create gas. Conversely, if you want to slow down the fermentation, you can remove warmth. Therefore, the placement of the rising dough has everything to do with controlling the speed of fermentation. Set it in a sunny window or near a warm oven, and the dough will double in about an hour. Stored in the refrigerator,

---

PIONEER TIP!

What's the difference between proofing and fermenting?

They are the same thing. The dough is set aside to develop carbon dioxide gas through yeast feeding on carbohydrates. The terms are used interchangeably, but most professional bakers consider fermentation the main rise, when the bread doubles in volume. The proof is the final short rise just before baking.

---

the dough will rise slowly, over a period of 8–10 hours. The slower, chilled method is ideal for busy cooks who may not have time to make a dough from start to finish in any one day. Fermentation stops completely below 32°F, which makes the freezer a great place to store dough for extended periods. Defrost frozen dough in the fridge for even results.

Forming

Before a loaf can be baked, it must first be formed. Each recipe in this book includes a suggestion for form, but most doughs can easily be made in a variety of shapes.

There are two key points to remember when forming a loaf. First, the dough should be tight, smooth, and free of air pockets. This is achieved by rolling, flattening, and folding as the dough is formed. The more a dough is worked, the tighter and more elastic the gluten will become. Second, the forming should be done fairly quickly, because as long as the dough is unbaked and unfrozen, fermentation will continue. As the dough sits, gases build, gluten relaxes, and the loaf will lose its shape.

If the form is not to your liking, the process can easily be repeated, but the dough must rest for about five minutes first. Resting relaxes the gluten, allowing for more gas to build up, thus softening the dough and making it easy to form once again.

THE BAKING PROCESSES

Y ou don't need to know what happens in the oven to make delicious fresh bread, but having an idea of what steps your dough goes through will help you troubleshoot bad loaves. In the heat of the oven, several events take place. They do not happen simultaneously, but slowly, each peaking at certain temperatures.

Gas Expands

The first noticeable change is the expansion of gases. A loaf will puff up quickly, within a few minutes. This effect is known as "oven spring." In yeast breads, carbon dioxide expands through the fermentation process. In quick breads, carbon dioxide expands too, but it is created by chemical leaveners (baking soda or baking powder). In soufflés and sponge cakes, air expands during the whipping of eggs. This expansion pushes the dough up and raises the bread until the proteins solidify and form a crust.

Proteins Solidify

When proteins solidify they react just like an egg in a hot frying pan, changing from something soft to something firm.

This change creates the structure of bread as we know it. Heat causes the chains of amino acids to tighten, altering the overall structure of the protein. The most common proteins present in bread include gluten, egg, and dairy proteins.

Sugars Caramelize

Heat melts sugar and turns it brown in a process called caramelization. The higher the heat, the faster the caramelization takes place. This is not always a good thing, because the crust shouldn't brown before the interior is cooked. Therefore, oven temperature should be adjusted in accordance with the size of the loaf that is being baked. Rolls can be baked at high temperatures because heat will penetrate quickly, usually before the crust caramelizes. In a large loaf, more time is required for the heat to penetrate to the center and cook. Unless the temperature is lowered, the crust will be well browned long before the loaf is ready.

Fats Melt

Fats melt and liquefy in the oven, which allows them to be absorbed. If butter is not fully incorporated, either by accident or on purpose, it will melt away, leaving an air pocket.

Care should be taken when fermenting rich doughs. Fats start melting with very little heat, and if the dough gets too warm, the fat will run out of it, resulting in a greasy dough that is much harder to form into a loaf. Loss of fat also makes the bread less delicious.

Water Evaporates

Water evaporation in a loaf of bread is most easily observed by the weight of the finished product. A properly cooked loaf will be noticeably lighter in weight after baking because the water has evaporated. The hollow sound we listen for when determining whether a loaf is done is the echo from the hollow spaces that were once filled with water.

Water evaporation is also apparent in the making of biscuits and other recipes that use the cut-in method. Butter contains a large percentage of water. Because the butter in a cut-in dough is left in small chunks, the evaporation of its water creates steam that pushes up the dough, creating little pockets of air and a flaky texture. The same effect occurs in flaky pie dough and in puff pastry.

Starches Gelatinize

Oven heat causes starch to gelatinize. Just as cornstarch can thicken a sauce, natural starch in flour will thicken when moistened and heated. The starch is the part of flour that is not gluten protein, which means that there is abundant gelatinization in everything baked with grain. This thickening plays a major role in creating the texture of the finished crumb. Starch gives structure while remaining flexible and soft. Without starch, bread would be hard and tough.

Doneness

Recipes provide a cooking time, but the actual time it takes to completely bake a loaf can vary tremendously. The size of the oven, the size of the loaves, the thickness and material of the pans, recipe accuracy, ingredient variation, and the number of items in the oven at one time all affect the time required. The only sure way to judge doneness is by sight and feel.

A finished loaf should be golden brown in color. It should also feel lighter coming out than it was going in, and make a hollow sound when thumped. The internal temperature of a bread can be taken to determine doneness as well. Insert an instant-read thermometer into the thickest part of the loaf. The internal temperature should be in the range of 200°F–210°F when cooked.

ESSENTIAL TOOLS OF THE TRADE

THE ORIGINAL PIONEERS were able to bake bread with only the essential equipment: a bowl, a fork, a pan, and an oven. You can do the same. Here's what you need to know about basic breadmaking equipment.

Pans

Most breads can be baked on a simple baking sheet. In the professional kitchen these pans are called sheet pans. They are made of heavy aluminum, and have a ½-inch lip. These pans are indispensable to a baker and are used for just about everything.

Some breads require a loaf pan, and the market is flooded with a plethora of pans from which to choose. Heaviest is best, made from glass, ceramic, thick aluminum, or cast iron. These materials hold and spread heat evenly and reduce the chance of a burned crust. Thin baking pans will cause bread to burn, especially when used for breads that require long baking times. The same criterion applies to muffin pans.

PIONEER TIP!

Regardless of the type of pan chosen, the dough should always be placed into it seam-side down. This means that when the loaf is formed, the smooth, tight, seamless side of the dough should face up, and any rough, folded, or pleated skin should face down into the pan. The weight of the dough on these seams keeps them from opening up in an unattractive way.

Ovens

Any standard oven is suitable for baking bread. The convection oven is a common appliance in many homes but can be a little tricky for the new baker. Convection ovens were created to promote even browning of foods. They were not as successful at even browning as they were at increasing the speed of baking.

Convection ovens contain fans that move the air throughout the oven cavity, which results in an increased temperature.

This is very convenient for small items, like cookies and muffins. But larger loaves of bread need more time for the heat to penetrate the dough, and convection baking usually results in a burnt crust and doughy center.

Some convection ovens have a switch that turns the fan on and off. For large items, the fan should be turned off, and the oven used in the conventional manner. If the oven does not have the on-off capability, consider baking smaller breads, such as rolls, or bake them in a high-sided pan that can be covered in foil to prevent the moving air from reaching the loaf.

While the pioneers would bake bread on their hearth, few of you will have access to anything besides the modern oven. But if you're craving that frontier look, the traditional brick-oven appearance can be easily recreated. Use cornmeal on your baking sheet to make it look like you've fashioned a peel—a wooden paddle upon which pioneers formed and proofed their dough (after coating the surface with cornmeal themselves).

ADDITIONAL TOOLS

WHILE NOT AVAILABLE in the wilderness, this equipment may be very helpful to the Modern-Day Pioneer.

Baskets

Europeans have long used cane baskets, called banneton or brotformen, to ferment bread. They promote an even, uniform bowl shape, which is higher and rounder than a loaf proofed flat on a baking sheet. Dusted with flour, the cane leaves a decorative impression on the proofing breads. Some of these baskets are lined with linen, which needs less flour to prevent sticking. Breads are turned out of the baskets onto a baking sheet or peel before going into the oven.

A proofing linen cloth, called a cloche, is sometimes used for baguettes for the same purpose. The cloth is a simple rectangle, pleated in between each loaf to shape the dough as it is proofed.

Parchment Paper

Parchment serves many purposes, including preventing baked goods from sticking to pans. Used as a pan liner, parchment not only eases removal of the finished product, but also promotes even browning and uniform texture of the crust. In addition, parchment extends the lifetime of bakeware. Lined with paper, the pans do not come into contact with ingredients. If they did, these ingredients would burn in the oven, leaving the pan with a coating of oil and carbon. These deposits weaken the pan, as does the excessive scrubbing needed to remove them. In addition, pans left with food deposits will warp, bend, and buckle in the oven where heat flow is interrupted.

Parchment is also useful for wrapping and storage. It is frequently used by professionals to hold ingredients, and can be formed into a cone for decorating.

Racks

Cooling racks are an important last step in the production of bread. If bread is allowed to cool without a rack, condensation (also known as bread sweat) will form underneath, which results in a soggy bottom crust. A rack allows air to circulate underneath, releasing steam and evaporating any condensation for a dry, crisp crust. A rack should leave at least ¼" of space between the bread and the counter.

Buttermilk Potato Bread

Consider making this bread with your next surplus of potatoes.

INGREDIENTS + YIELDS 1 LOAF

1 medium russet (baking) potato (about ⅓ pound)

Cold water, as needed, plus 1 tablespoon

1 tablespoon sugar

1¾ teaspoons active dry yeast (1 package)

¾ cup buttermilk

1½ teaspoons plus 1 pinch kosher salt

1 tablespoon unsalted butter, at room temperature

3–5 cups bread flour

1 egg

1. Peel and quarter potato, place in a small saucepan, cover with cold water, and bring to a boil. Cook until tender, drain, and reserve liquid. Mash with a fork and set aside.

2. In a large bowl, combine ½ cup potato water, sugar, and yeast. Stir to dissolve and let stand until foamy, about 10 minutes.

3. Add potato, buttermilk, 1½ teaspoons salt, butter, and 1 cup flour. Stir to combine. Add enough remaining flour to create a firm dough. Turn out onto a floured surface and knead 8–10 minutes. Return to bowl, dust the top lightly with flour, and cover with a damp cloth or plastic wrap. Rise at room temperature until doubled in volume, about 1 hour.

4. Coat a 9" × 5" loaf pan with pan spray, and line the bottom and short sides with a strip of parchment. Turn risen dough onto a floured surface and shape into an oblong loaf. Place into prepared pan, seam-side down. Set aside to proof for 30 minutes. Preheat oven to 350°F.

5. Whisk egg with a tablespoon of water and pinch of salt, and brush lightly over the risen loaf. Bake until golden brown and hollow sounding, about 30–40 minutes. Cool 10 minutes, remove from pan, and cool completely on a rack.

WHOLE WHEAT AND GRAIN BREAD

THESE NUTRITIOUS BREADS have a heft, crunch, and lovely warm color that make them perfect for a fall or winter meal.

Cracked Wheat and Honey Bread

The hearty flavor of cracked wheat and the tang of sweet natural honey are a perfect pair. Try forming this dough into dinner rolls as well as standard loaves. If you're keeping bees, use that honey to make this bread.

INGREDIENTS + YIELDS 2 LOAVES

1½ cups boiling water
½ cup cracked wheat
1⅓ cups warm milk
¼ cup honey
1¾ teaspoons active dry yeast (1 package)

¼ cup (½ stick) unsalted butter
1 cup whole wheat flour
¾ teaspoon kosher salt
3–4 cups bread flour

1. In a medium bowl, combine boiling water and cracked wheat. Set aside for 10 minutes, stirring occasionally, until the cracked wheat has absorbed the water and has softened.

2. In a large bowl, combine milk, 1 tablespoon honey, and yeast. Stir to dissolve and let stand until foamy, about 10 minutes.

3. Add remaining honey, butter, and whole wheat flour; stir to combine. Add softened cracked wheat (drain off excess liquid if necessary), salt, and enough bread flour to create a firm dough. Add flour only to reduce stickiness. Turn out onto a floured surface and knead 8–10 minutes. Return to bowl, dust the top with flour, and cover with a damp cloth or plastic wrap. Rise at room temperature until doubled in volume, about 2 hours.

4. Coat two 9" × 5" loaf pans with pan spray, and line the bottom and short sides of each pan with a strip of parchment. Turn risen dough onto a floured surface, divide into 2 equal portions, and shape each into an oblong loaf. Place into prepared pans seam-side down, cover loosely with plastic wrap, and set aside to proof for 30 minutes, or until dough rises above the pan. Preheat oven to 375°F.

5. Dust risen loaves with whole wheat flour, and bake until golden brown and hollow sounding, about 30–40 minutes. Cool 10 minutes, remove from pans, and cool completely on a rack.

PIONEER TIP!

Cracked wheat is crushed wheat kernels with the bran intact. It is similar to bulgur, which is also crushed wheat kernels, but par-cooked, or steamed. The result is a grain that cooks a bit faster. In a pinch, cracked wheat can be replaced with bulgur in this recipe.

Oatmeal Raisin Hearth Bread

Brown sugar and oats are a sweet and comforting pair. Their combination here makes a fantastic breakfast bread, especially when smeared generously with home-made jam.

INGREDIENTS + YIELDS 2 LOAVES

2½ cups boiling water

1¾ cups steel-cut oats

1 cup raisins

1 tablespoon plus 1 pinch kosher salt

3 tablespoons butter

½ cup warm milk

3 tablespoons brown sugar

1¾ teaspoons active dry yeast (1 package)

1 cup whole wheat flour

4–6 cups bread flour

¼ cup cornmeal

1 large egg

1 cup rolled oats (not quick cooking)

1. In a large bowl, combine water, steel-cut oats, raisins, 1 tablespoon salt, and butter. Stir together, then let stand 30–45 minutes, until oats have softened. Set aside.

2. In another large bowl, combine milk, brown sugar, and yeast. Stir to dissolve and let stand until foamy, about 10 minutes.

3. Add whole wheat flour and oat mixture; stir to combine. Add enough bread flour to create a firm dough. Add flour only to reduce stickiness. Turn out onto a floured surface and knead 8–10 minutes. Return to bowl, dust the top with flour, and cover with a damp cloth or plastic wrap. Rise at room temperature until doubled in volume, about 1 hour.

4. Line a baking sheet with parchment, and sprinkle with cornmeal. Turn risen dough onto a floured surface, divide into 2 equal portions, and shape into oblong loaves. Place onto prepared pan, seam-side down. Dust with flour, cover loosely with plastic wrap, and set aside to proof for 30 minutes. Preheat oven to 375°F.

HOW A PIONEER BAKES: Making Bread Without a Breadmaker

5. Whisk egg with a pinch of salt and brush across the surface of risen loaves. Sprinkle liberally with rolled oats, and using a serrated knife, cut decorative slash marks into the surface of the dough, about ½" deep. Place a pan of cold water at the bottom of the oven to create steam, and bake until golden brown and hollow sounding, about 30–40 minutes. Cool completely on a rack before serving.

PIONEER TIP!

Scoring patterns allow bread to expand decoratively in the oven where the baker wants it to, but they are also a baker's signature. Since most bakeries produce similar breads, one way they differentiate their products from others is by the decorative slash marks in the surface of the dough. Why not create your own decorative, signature slashes?

3-Grain Brown Loaf

This dough makes a satisfying dark loaf perfect for sandwiches. It makes great rolls as well.

INGREDIENTS + YIELDS 2 LOAVES

1¾ cups warm milk
¼ cup plus 1 tablespoon molasses
1¾ teaspoons active dry yeast (1 package)
2 tablespoons canola oil
1 tablespoon cocoa powder
1 cup whole wheat flour

1 cup rye flour
1 cup rolled oats (not quick cooking)
1½ teaspoons kosher salt
3–4 cups bread flour
1 tablespoon hot water

1. In a large bowl, combine milk, ¼ cup molasses, and yeast. Stir to dissolve and let stand until foamy, about 10 minutes.

2. Add oil, cocoa, whole wheat flour, rye flour, and oats; stir to combine. Add salt and enough bread flour to create a firm dough. Add flour only to reduce stickiness. Turn out onto a floured surface and knead 8–10 minutes. Return to bowl, dust the top with flour, and cover with a damp cloth or plastic wrap. Rise at room temperature until doubled in volume, about 2 hours.

3. Coat two 9" × 5" loaf pans with pan spray, and line the bottom and short sides with a strip of parchment. Turn risen dough onto a floured surface, divide into 2 equal portions, and shape into oblong loaves. Place into prepared pans seam-side down, cover loosely with plastic wrap, and set aside to proof for 30 minutes, or until dough rises above the pans. Preheat oven to 375°F.

4. Combine remaining 1 tablespoon molasses with 1 tablespoon hot water, and brush gently onto the risen dough. Bake until golden brown and hollow sounding, about 30–40 minutes. Cool 10 minutes, remove loaves from pans, and cool completely on a rack.

BREADMAKING WITH STARTERS

BEFORE YEAST WAS READILY AVAILABLE, the creation of a starter was the only way bread could be made. Starters are often shared with friends, hence the name of this first sweet bread.

Friendship Bread Starter

This starter takes about 2 weeks to create, but will then last a lifetime!

INGREDIENTS + YIELDS 9 CUPS STARTER

3 cups milk
3 cups sugar
3 cups all-purpose flour

1. DAY 1: Combine 1 cup milk, 1 cup sugar, and 1 cup flour in a ceramic or glass bowl. Stir to combine, cover loosely with a damp cheesecloth or towel, and set aside at room temperature. Stir once a day for the next 4 days.

2. DAY 5: Add 1 cup milk, 1 cup sugar, and 1 cup flour. Stir well, cover again, and set aside at room temperature for another 5 days, stirring once a day, as before.

3. DAY 10: Again, add 1 cup milk, 1 cup sugar, and 1 cup flour. Mix thoroughly. Starter is now ready to use. To keep your starter alive, replace the quantity used for breadmaking with an equal amount of milk, flour, and sugar. Stir it every day, and feed it every 5 days by removing some starter and replacing it with an equal amount of milk, sugar, and flour (for every 1 cup used, replace with ⅓ cup milk, ⅓ cup sugar, and ⅓ cup flour). If you do not wish to feed it, but want to keep it, refrigerate it indefinitely, taking it out and repeating the process for 10 days before using it again.

Friendship Bread

This bread is the perfect gift to welcome new neighbors or cheer up a sick companion. It freezes well, which makes it easy to keep one or two on hand, just in case you need to brighten someone's day.

INGREDIENTS + YIELDS 2 LOAVES

1 cup Friendship Bread Starter (see previous recipe)

3 tablespoons canola oil, plus more as needed

1 egg

⅓ cup sugar, plus more as needed

½ teaspoon kosher salt

½ teaspoon baking soda

½ teaspoon cinnamon

3–4 cups bread flour

1. In a large bowl, combine the starter, 3 tablespoons oil, egg, and ⅓ cup sugar. Stir to combine. Add salt, baking soda, cinnamon, and enough flour to create a firm dough.

2. Turn out onto a floured surface and knead 8–10 minutes. Add flour only to reduce stickiness. Return to bowl, oil the top, and cover with a damp cloth or plastic wrap. Rise at room temperature until doubled in volume, about 1 hour.

3. Coat two 9" × 5" loaf pans with pan spray, and line the bottom and short sides of each pan with a strip of parchment. Turn risen dough onto a floured surface, divide into 2 equal portions, and shape each into an oblong loaf. Place into the prepared pans seam-side down. Dust with flour, cover loosely with plastic wrap, and set aside to proof for 30 minutes. Preheat oven to 350°F.

4. Dust the risen loaves with sugar and bake until golden brown and hollow sounding, about 35–50 minutes. Cool 10 minutes, remove from pans, and cool completely on a rack.

Sourdough Starter

The longer you keep it going, the better your bread will be. There are stories about sourdough starters that have survived for over a hundred years, passed down from generation to generation.

INGREDIENTS ✦ YIELDS 9 CUPS STARTER

3 cups water
⅛ teaspoon active dry yeast
3 cups all-purpose flour

1. DAY 1: Combine 1 cup water, yeast, and 1 cup flour in a ceramic or glass bowl. Stir to combine, cover loosely with damp cheesecloth or towel, and set aside at room temperature. Stir this mixture once a day for the next 3 days.

2. DAY 4: Add to the starter 1 cup water and 1 cup flour. Stir well, cover again, and set aside at room temperature for another 4 days, stirring once a day, as before.

3. DAY 8: Again, add 1 cup water and 1 cup flour. Mix thoroughly. Let stand at room temperature loosely covered for 6 hours, or until the starter foams and doubles in volume. The starter is now ready to use. To keep your starter alive, replace the quantity that has been used with an equal amount of water and flour (for every 1 cup used, replace with ½ cup water and ½ cup flour). Keep covered, stir it every day, and feed it every 5 days by removing some starter and again replacing it with an equal amount of water and flour. If you do not wish to feed it, but want to keep it, cover, airtight, and refrigerate indefinitely, taking it out and repeating the process (removing and replacing 1 cup as before) for 10 days before using it again.

Sourdough Boule

Boule literally means "ball," and indeed these loaves are golden spheres of delectable goodness.

INGREDIENTS ✦ YIELDS 2 LOAVES

1 cup Sourdough Starter (see previous recipe)

1 cup water

1¾ teaspoons active dry yeast (1 package)

1 cup all-purpose flour

1 teaspoon kosher salt

3–4 cups bread flour

2 tablespoons cornmeal

1. To make the sponge, combine starter, ½ cup water, and yeast. Stir to dissolve and let stand 5 minutes. Add all-purpose flour and beat 1 minute. Cover and let stand at room temperature 8–12 hours.

2. Add to the sponge remaining ½ cup water, salt, and enough bread flour to make a soft dough. Turn out onto a floured work surface and knead 8–10 minutes. Add flour only to reduce stickiness. Return to bowl, dust with flour, cover with plastic, and rise at room temperature until doubled in volume, about 1½ hours.

3. Line a baking sheet with parchment, and sprinkle with cornmeal. Turn risen dough onto a floured surface and divide into 2 equal portions. Roll into balls and place on prepared pan, seam-side down. Dust generously with flour, cover again with plastic, and rise until doubled, about 30 minutes. Preheat oven to 475°F.

4. Using a serrated knife, slice decorative slash marks into the surface of the dough, about ½" deep. Place a pan of cold water at the bottom of the oven to create steam. Bake until golden brown and hollow sounding, about 30–40 minutes. Cool completely on a rack.

Sourdough Rye Loaf

The starch content of rye flour makes it exceptional food for sourdough starter. But more important, the sweet, succulent flavor of caraway is the perfect complement to that sour flavor.

INGREDIENTS + YIELDS 2 LOAVES

1 cup Sourdough Starter (see recipe)

1 cup water

1¾ teaspoons active dry yeast (1 package)

1 cup light rye flour

1 teaspoon kosher salt

1 cup whole wheat flour

2–3 cups bread flour

2 tablespoons cornmeal

1. To make the sponge, combine starter, ½ cup water, and yeast. Stir to dissolve and let stand 5 minutes. Add rye flour and beat for 1 minute. Cover and let stand at room temperature 8–12 hours.

2. Add to the sponge remaining ½ cup water, salt, whole wheat flour, and enough bread flour to make a soft dough. Turn out onto a floured work surface and knead 8–10 minutes. Add flour only to reduce stickiness. Return to bowl, dust with flour, cover with plastic, and rise at room temperature until doubled in volume, about 1½ hours.

3. Line a baking sheet with parchment, and sprinkle with cornmeal. Turn risen dough onto a floured surface. Divide into 2 equal portions. Roll into balls and place on prepared pan, seam-side down. Dust generously with flour, cover again with plastic, and rise until doubled, about 30 minutes. Preheat oven to 475°F.

4. Using a serrated knife, slice a pinwheel or star pattern into the top of the dough, about ½" deep. Place a pan of cold water at the bottom of the oven to create steam. Bake until golden brown and hollow sounding, about 30–40 minutes. Cool completely on a rack.

CHAPTER 5

HOW A PIONEER DRINKS:
An Introduction to Homebrewing

"Shoulder the sky, my lad, and drink your ale."

— A. E. HOUSMAN —

BEER HAS A LONG AND STORIED HISTORY dating back to early Mesopotamia, where the Sumerians fermented bread with honey, dates, and spices. But the pioneers took this historic beverage and truly made it an American classic.

Ale had a prominent place among the founding fathers of the United States. Both George Washington and Thomas Jefferson ran small estate breweries.

When the original pioneers began their migration across the country, they brought with them the tradition of brewing and a fondness for ale. Brewing flourished in the Midwest and across the Great Plains. Many of America's largest breweries were founded in the Midwest and the Great Plains during the 1800s: Coors in Colorado; Anheuser-Busch in Missouri; and Miller, Schlitz, and Pabst in Wisconsin.

It's no surprise that homebrewing was so appealing out on the prairie. In a time before filtration systems and reservoirs, beer was the safe drink, free of cholera and disease. It was rich in vitamin B and iron. A good ale could quench a pioneer's thirst and complement his dinner's rich meats and crusty breads.

In this chapter, you'll find a guide to the brewing process, a close look at the ingredients and techniques you'll employ, and, finally, a step-by-step guide to making a beer that a pioneer would be proud to drink.

YOUR INGREDIENTS

THE FIRST STEP IN BREWING your ale is collecting the proper ingredients. It's possible to fulfill all your brewing needs online. But you may find it more helpful to locate and visit a local homebrew shop. A good brewshop can be an important aspect of the first-time brewer's learning experience. The clerks should act not only as suppliers but also as mentors, answering any questions you may have. When you're done brewing your first batch, bring one or two finished bottles back to the brewshop, so that the experts can taste the finished product and give you honest feedback.

There are four main components in any beer you may make. Understanding each of these ingredients, and how they affect your beer's taste, will make you a stronger brewer.

Hops

Hops are the flowering cone of a vine (*Humulus lupulus*). In their fresh form, they are bright green with sticky flecks of yellow and resemble a soft baby pinecone. They are the main source of flavoring for most beers, giving it the bitter taste and fresh smell we associate with an ale.

In addition to the bitterness, hop oils contribute to your beer's aroma. Depending on what kind of hops you use, your brew can smell piney, woody, grassy, spicy, citrusy, and a thousand other variations. If you are buying your hops from a brewshop, rather than online, take some time to smell the different variations. As a rule, hops that are added early in the brew provide the taste of your beer, and hops added toward the end of your boil affect the scent.

For the basic recipes you'll learn in this chapter you should buy your hops in pellet form.

In a good store, the hops will be kept in a cold, refrigerated area without a lot of light. Small amounts vacuum-packed in barrier bags are ideal. Bulk hops should be stored in oxygen-barrier canisters.

Your Yeast

In Chapter 4, "How a Pioneer Bakes," you learned about the yeast used for making bread. Yeast is a member of the fungus kingdom. Look at a yeast cell under a microscope and you'll see a simple, single-celled creature. For this ale, you'll be using the *Saccharomyces cerevasiae* yeast organism.

While you put together the wort (the brewing term for unfermented beer), it's the yeast that kickstarts the fermentation process and turns your creation into beer. When yeast saturates the wort, it consumes available sugar. As it is metabolized, yeast creates ethyl alcohol (ethanol) and carbon dioxide. Yeast also secretes a host of flavorful compounds. Every yeast culture produces unique concentrations of flavors. Brewers exploit these fermentation characteristics to transform barley malt and hops into a universe of beer.

There are two forms of yeast you can use for brewing, liquid or dried. Liquid yeast's strengths are freshness, variety, and a sanitary nature. Wyeast Laboratories and White Labs both offer practical and convenient liquid yeast. For a few dollars, you can purchase strains appropriate to virtually any beer style. Once you've brewed your first batch of beer, start experimenting with different yeast cultures and observe how different strains create different brews.

Most brewstores carry their yeast next to their hops. A number of styles are possible only with liquid strains. Liquid cultures should never be exposed to freezing temperatures or hot summer sun. Either extreme will kill the cells. Check the expiration dates to avoid old, dead yeast.

Dried yeast is cheaper than liquid yeast and has a longer lifespan, but you'll have less variety to choose from, and it has a reputation for being less pure.

For your first ale, you'll be purchasing the Wyeast 1007 German Ale liquid yeast slap pack, which you'll activate the day before (see the brewing directions later in this chapter for more detail). Purchase fresh yeast only; check the labels on your packet for the best-by date.

Your Extract Malt

Malted barley provides beer's soul and strength, backbone, and color. Each variety uniquely impacts beer's flavor and body. New brewers use a malt extract—a sticky, thick syrup made of concentrated wort.

Like yeast, malt extract comes in two forms—liquid and dry. Liquid malt extract retains more malt character, so that is what you will use for your first batch of beer. However, stale liquid extract can ruin a beer with metallic twangy flavors that won't disappear. So if you're in doubt about the freshness of the liquid malt your supplier carries, choose shelf-stable dried malt extract for your later brews.

When choosing extract, find a packaging or best-by date to avoid bad extract. Buy bulk liquid malt extract from drums only if the shop flushes the drums with nitrogen or speeds through a drum in a few days. Avoid extracts with sugar added.

Common Types of Extract

Maltsters use several terms to describe their extracts. Most reflect the color; some indicate the composition of the extract. Here are the malt extract types, in order of color:

+ **Light/Pale/Xtra Pale**—Pale malt-based extracts that will serve as the primary workhorse in your extract brewery. Great base for a beer and for converting a recipe to all-grain and back.
+ **Pilsner**—Pale extract based on pilsner malt, instead of pale ale malt.
+ **Wheat/Weizen**—Replicates the wheat/barley ratio of wheat beers, which consist of 40 to 60 percent malted wheat combined with pale malt. Golden color with a bready sweetness.
+ **Amber**—Extract with added crystal or toasted malts. Useful for building a stronger finishing sweetness with a bit of toastiness.
+ **Munich**—Based on a mixture of pale and Munich malts. Produces reddish tinged beers with an intense, yet not sweet, malt character.
+ **Dark**—Adding a dose of roasted malts to an amber extract yields a dark extract suitable for use in a porter or stout.

Hopped Versus Unhopped Extract

Another choice facing a brewer is the use of hopped or unhopped extract kits. Extract manufacturers add hop bittering extract to their syrups for bite. Some cans use pellets for a fresher hop character. Hopped kits are perfect for the casual brewer living far from homebrew resources.

Read the labels closely to ensure a good shelf grab. Cans labeled with a style (e.g., "IPA" or "Stout"), are more often prehopped kits. Most hopped extracts originate from Britain and Australia, so pay extra attention when looking at those.

Choose unhopped extracts when you can. Formulating recipes around hopped extracts can lead to frustration when a manufacturer switches hops based on availability or adjusts the bittering.

Your Water

Water comprises more than 95 percent of a beer, making it a very important—though often ignored—brewing ingredient. Early brewers may not have known the chemistry of water in their brewing process, but they would have understood the basics—bad water produces bad beer. As a Modern-Day Pioneer, you have the resources to understand how water reacts with the other ingredients to influence a drinker's palate. You can use water to bring your homebrew to a new level.

Using Tap Water

Can you use your municipal water for brewing? In almost all cases the answer is yes, but it might take adjustments to perfect. As long as the water is drinkable, chances are that you can use it.

If you have good water on hand, your main concern is chlorine or chloramine. Even if you can't taste or smell it, nearly all municipal water is disinfected and you must eliminate the disinfectant before introduc-

ing the malt. Malt contains aromatic compounds called phenols. Normally, they form pleasant aromas associated with beer, but combined with chlorine, they become potent, medicinal-smelling chlorophenols.

Luckily, chlorine is easy to remove from water. To dechlorinate your water, either let it sit overnight or boil and cool.

However, many municipalities now use chloramines in their water, and this is trickier to remove. Since it's naturally liquid, it won't outgas and it survives boiling. But you have a few options. Activated carbon water filters are a common solution. Sodium or potassium metabisulfite, wine sanitizers, also effectively tackle chloramine. Shops carry either powdered meta or the tablet form, campden. To drive off the chloramine, use ¼ teaspoon of powder or one crushed tablet to clear 20 gallons of water. Stir and dissolve the powder into your water and wait five to ten minutes for the chloramine to react.

During the brewing process, you'll be adding about 3 or 4 gallons of water to the fermenter after brewing. Even if your tap water does not contain chlorine or chloramines, it's always a good idea to sanitize that water by boiling it. Just make sure that you've cooled that water down before adding it to your wort. Otherwise the heat might hurt your yeast.

EQUIPMENT

I N A BREWSHOP, OR ONLINE, you can buy a basic starter kit. For around $100, you get the most basic gear for your first beer. The precise contents of the kit vary, but standard items include a fermenter (a bucket), a glass carboy, siphoning gear, a bottling bucket, a bottle capper, caps, and chemicals for cleaning and sanitizing.

However, the brew kit does not contain everything you need to brew your first batch. And if you already have some of the equipment, you may want to buy each piece of your brewery piecemeal, rather than getting the whole kit at once. Here are the basics that you should have on hand while brewing.

PIONEER TIP!

Always have backups. As your brewery grows, little parts—gaskets, clamps, and so on—creep into vital roles. Do yourself a huge favor and keep extras dedicated to the brewery. A little extra outlay up front can save you.

Brewing Gear

Thermometer

You have a few choices: the slow-reacting, fragile, cheap red alcohol floaters; the finicky and bimetal dials; and digital sticks or digital probe thermometers. Remember to calibrate your thermometer before brewing with it. You can compare it against a thermometer you know is reliable, or you can use it to take the temperature of boiling water.

Pots and Kettles

For basic brewing, you'll need two 20-plus quart pots or kettles. One is for steeping/boiling and another is for heating quarts of rinse water. Either a large soup or lobster pot or an enamel canning pot would be perfect.

Brewers debate between stainless steel and aluminum pots. Stainless steel's toughness and resistance to cleaning chemicals makes it a natural choice, but it is expensive. Large aluminum kettles cost much less, but they react to strong chemicals and some worry about health safety. If you do work with aluminum pots or kettles, make sure you clean them gently.

A Big Spoon

Never underestimate the power of a big spoon. You need something strong to thoroughly stir thick, sticky, heavy mashes and make boiling beer whirlpools. Make sure the spoon you choose has a very long handle. When you rest it in your kettle, the end of the handle should be several inches above the lip of the pot. The hope is to keep your fingers as far from the wort as possible. This lessens the chances of contamination, and keeps your hands away from the heat of the boiling worst. The modern brewer can choose steel, but avoid plastic paddles. They're flimsy and bend while stirring thick mashes.

Fermenters

Without a fermenter, beer would just be a funny-tasting drink. Fermentation is what will make your ale alcoholic.

As a novice brewer, you have two basic choices for a fermenter:

1. **Buckets**—The old reliable, buckets are cheap and unbreakable. But they scratch easily, leading to high risk of contamination that could cause off-flavors in your beer. Clean carefully with a soft sponge. Additionally, they are oxygen permeable, unsuitable for long storage. Some buckets come with spigots to eliminate siphoning. Thoroughly clean and sanitize these spigots.

2. **Glass carboys**—Glass water bottles, impervious to cleaners and oxygen, they make great fermenters. Use a brush to clean thoroughly. They are fragile to thermal shock and seriously dangerous if dropped. For that reason, care should always be taken when moving a carboy.

Airlocks

The airlock is a vitally important piece of brewing equipment. They protect your beer from contamination and allow carbon dioxide (CO_2) evolved during fermentation to escape. Best of all, their bubbling tells you that your yeast is hard at work. Airlocks attach to the mouth of your fermenter.

Aluminum Foil

Aluminum foil is the catchall for the Modern-Day Pioneer's brewing sessions; it is endlessly useful in the brewery and cheap insurance against infection. You can sanitize foil and use it to cover a starter, carboy, or bottling bucket.

The Brew Notebook

Unless you have an eidetic memory, a brewer's notebook serves as record keeper and troubleshooting guide. Batch details become muddled over time: "Did I toss in extra hops on this brew, or is this the one that I forgot the sugar?" Start a notebook on your first brew and use it faithfully to record details that might otherwise get lost in the haze.

Hydrometer

A hydrometer is a tool that allows you to calculate your beer's alcohol content. This is measured by finding the drink's Alcohol by Volume (ABV). Accurate measuring of your sugar content clues you in to the efficiency of your brewing processes.

To use a hydrometer, fill the test jar with the liquid you're measuring. Then give the hydrometer a spin and let it settle before reading the "gravity" number at the surface.

Before using a new hydrometer for a batch of beer, verify its calibration against distilled water to make sure that it's accurate.

During the brewing process, first use the hydrometer to measure the wort before you pitch the yeast. Read your sample close to calibration temperature (around 60°F). The number you get is your Original Gravity (OG), the measurement of the amount of sugar dissolved in unfermented wort. Homebrewers talk about this in units of "specific gravity."

PIONEER TIP!

After measuring the specific gravity with your hydrometer, throw out the sample you've tested. Don't pour it back into the wort, and don't drink it.

Measure the specific gravity again after the fermentation process is complete, before bottling the beer. This is called the Final Gravity (FG), a measurement of the remaining sugars and solids in a fermented beer.

The difference between the FG and the OG is "apparent attenuation." Using that difference, you can calculate an approximate ABV for your final beer by using the following equation:

$$ABV = (OG - FG) / 7.5$$

Most brew recipes will include an expected ABV, and you can use that to figure out whether or not your fermentation is complete before bottling.

Racking Gear

Moving the beer around requires a deft hand with a siphon. To siphon liquid, make sure your source vessel is above your target container.

Racking Cane

A long, straight tube with a crook. Made of either inexpensive plastic or impervious metal, a racking cane can be confusing to use at first. Fill the cane and the attached hose with sanitizer and hold both ends up. Pinch the tubing and drop the cane into the source vessel. Drop the hose into a pitcher to catch the sanitizer. Switch to the target container and let the beer flow.

Auto-siphon

A racking cane in a manual pump. A few pumps starts the siphon, but the complicated parts make the plastic gizmo prone to breakage.

Bottling Gear

Bottles need washing, sanitizing, drying, and filling, and the brewing world has gear for all those tasks.

Bottles

If you don't want the hassle of cleaning out a bunch of bottles, consider spending a little cash for new bottles from the local supply store. Start clean and keep them clean.

Bottling Bucket

A great bottling bucket has a spigot to dispense primed beer and a lid to cover the vulnerable beer. Be sure to thoroughly disassemble and clean the spigot before using.

Bottling Wand

A simple, hard plastic tube with a spring-loaded tip that you push into the bottle to pour beer.

Capper

To seal the bottle, you'll need a bottle capper. The basic "wing" model is great for light bottling tasks, but if you deal with a large number of bottles or odd bottles, an old-fashioned bench capper is a great upgrade.

CLEANING

HERE IS THE BASIC RULE for brew cleaning: Any equipment used before the boil doesn't need a scrupulous cleaning; anything following the boil needs your complete attention.

Remember the boil kills off any bacteria or wild yeasts looking to hitch a ride in your wort. Post-boil the beer begins to cool, entering the danger zone. From now until the beer splashes your glass, everything that comes in contact with the wort must be scrubbed and sanitized to prevent spoilage. This includes the boil kettle, valves, chillers, fermenters, sampling thieves, racking canes, hoses, bottles, and kegs.

You can clean gear with a brush and water alone, but better cleaning is possible through chemistry. Don't reach for the squeeze bottle of dish soap. Regular soaps leave a sticky, rinse-resistant residue.

With all chemical solutions, follow basic safety by adding chemicals to water, not the other way around. Adding water to chemicals can superheat the mixture to explode or cause splashes of ultra-concentrated solution.

Regular unscented bleach is a brewing mainstay. It's cheap, widely available, and effective. Throw a couple of tablespoons in a full bucket or carboy and let it sit for hours. To avoid corrosion, don't let metal sit in prolonged contact with bleach water. Completely rinse and air-dry before use.

Remember to rinse equipment and surfaces with hot water, which speeds the cleaning reaction. Careful rinsing ensures a clean surface. Let the gear soak just as long as needed; otherwise, etching may occur.

Cleaning Supplies

+ **Brushes**—The one piece of brewing equipment you absolutely need. The commonly employed brushes are the L-shaped carboy brush and the straight bottle brush. Bend the carboy brush to better reach the carboy shoulders where the krausen (the foamy head at the top of your fermentation vessel) piles on. Suppliers have brushes designed for many tasks, but your best investment is a new toothbrush.

+ **Plastic scrub pads**—The ease of buckets comes at a cost. You must be supremely careful not to scratch them. The tiniest scratches can harbor a spoiling army. To keep things clean and scratch free, use soft scrub pads. Gently wipe, don't dig!

+ **Wallpaper trays**—Long hoses and racking canes are challenging to clean and sanitize. It's hard to beat stacked wallpaper paste trays for soaking. Fill about halfway with a gallon of solution and drop in your long items. Draw liquid through the hoses for complete contact.

+ **Spray bottles**—Plastic spray bottles can be filled with the cleaner or sanitizer of your choice to effectively cover surfaces.

SANITATION

ANITATION IS THE ACT of killing enough "bad" critters from the wort to allow yeast to establish a foothold. As yeast cells multiply, they exhaust nutrients, lower the pH, and produce ethanol that prevents recolonization by the microscopic foes of good beer.

Bacteria and wild yeast hide in the tiniest places. Hence, the initial emphasis on good cleaning practices.

Unlike cleaning where elbow grease can win, successful sanitation requires the judicious application of chemicals or heat. Sanitation chemicals are safe when used at recommended concentrations. Use too little and proper sanitation won't happen. Use too much and you can hurt your equipment and beer.

Bleach

The cheap and available option that virtually every brewer uses at the start. A tablespoon per gallon of water sanitizes surfaces after a 20-minute soak. Rinse with freshly boiled water and dry. The chlorine needs a thorough rinsing and drying to avoid creating chlorophenols. This is a common side effect.

Oven Heat

You can sterilize beer bottles in your oven. Take clean, dry bottles and cap them with foil. Stack them in a cold oven and set the thermostat to 340°F. Bake the bottles for an hour. Shut off the oven and cool the bottles overnight. As long as the foil stays firmly in place, you have a sterile bottle.

PIONEER TIP!

The natural antimicrobial effects of boiling, alcohol, low pH, and hops make beer remarkably safe. Dangerous bacteria will have a great deal of trouble living in beer. No matter how bad your beer may taste, you won't get sick from any wee visitors. But they will produce off-flavors and aromas and so should be avoided.

Iodophor

Iodophor combines iodine with coating aids. Used at proper dilution levels, it acts as a "no-rinse" sanitizer after only two minutes of surface contact. Higher concentration levels don't sanitize better and you risk staining any plastic gear and adding an iodine flavor to your beer!

Star-San/Sani-Clean

A suspension of phosphoric acid and other chemicals, this no-rinse sanitizer works in a minute. Star-San foams with little agitation, penetrating cracks to reduce bacterial hiding spots. The foam is perfectly safe in your beer. Many brewers worry about this upon their first use, but don't fear the foam! Sani-Clean has no foaming agent. It requires more contact time. Keep a small spray bottle of fresh Star-San for quick touchups.

Isopropyl Alcohol/Ethanol

In professional brewing, spray bottles of isopropyl alcohol are used for sanitizing valves before opening and closing. At home, use a concentrated 70-percent solution of alcohol for extra insurance. Before pitching, spray alcohol on starter vessel and carboy mouths.

CLEANING AND SANITIZING GEAR RUNDOWN

WITH EQUIPMENT AND CLEANING chemicals in hand, it's time to apply them. Each piece of equipment requires a bit of special care.

Plastic Buckets

The main downside of the ubiquitous plastic bucket is sensitivity to scratches. Breathe too hard and you create a bacteria-harboring furrow. Handle your cleaning tasks with a soft sponge or a plastic scrubbing pad.

Carboys

Glass carboys are virtually bulletproof as long as you don't press too hard with any metal-tipped brushes. Carboys handle any chemical that you throw at them. For routine cleaning, spray them out to remove major debris. Mix up your favorite hot cleaner and soak overnight. A quick swipe of a carboy brush takes care of anything else.

Save sanitizer solution by filling the carboy halfway. Plug it with a solid stopper and lay it on the side. Roll it to the other side after five minutes for complete sanitation.

Bottles

If you practice good rinsing, your used bottles need a quick spritz. For a cache of dirty bottles, fill a big tub with cleaner and soak the bottles. Bleach or ammonia soaking (not together!) takes off stubborn bottle labels.

Rinsed and dried bottles can be sanitized via the oven (see previous section) or by soaking them in sanitizer. Air-dry them on your bottle tree or dishwasher rack (a bottle on each post). When dry, cover with sanitized foil.

Kettles

Kettles are the low-maintenance pieces of the brewhouse. Most sessions they just need a scrubbing. Brush out spigots to avoid mold. When the kettle interiors look brown and grimy, tackle the beerstone. Follow the directions above to restore your kettle's shine.

PIONEER TIP!

Stainless steel's corrosion resistance stands up to the strongest chemicals with nary a blemish. Aluminum kettles are cheap and reliable, but strong acids and caustics damage them easily.

Hoses and Racking Canes

For quick rinsing, get a barb adapter for your sink. Stick a hose on and let the water pressure rip. Pulse the water on and off to dislodge anything stubborn. Soak the canes and hoses in a wallpaper tray and rinse. Twirl and hang to dry hoses.

THE BREWING PROCESS

BEFORE YOU BEGIN BREWING your beer, you must understand how the hot water and sticky malt that you begin with will eventually become the alcoholic ale you can enjoy on a hot day.

The Boil

Why boil beer? Wort must be boiled to eliminate natural spoilage creatures such as lactobacillus and deadly pathogens. Hops need boiling to isomerize and dissolve the alpha acids. Boiling concentrates sugars, generating flavorful caramel and melanoidins. A vigorous boil causes proteins to clump together as "hot break" and drop out of solution. This helps clarify the beer and improves long-term stability. The boil also helps reduce the water's mineral load.

While temperature is important, the mechanical roiling plays just as big a part. The turbulence mixes the wort, hops, and nutrients, and causes the proteins to clump.

The Chill

For your first batch, a mess of cold water, a scoop of ice, and a sink of cold water are all you needed to chill the wort.

The drop from a boil is important for two reasons: sanitation and cold break. Boiling hot wort kills harmful bacteria, but as the wort loses temperature and drops below 140°F, your sanitary safe haven becomes a bacterial playground. A quick drop to a safe temperature gives yeast a headstart over bacteria. For clarity and stability purposes, a rapid chill causes additional proteins to solidify into "cold break."

The Pitch

The yeast pitch is always the same. The goal: Deliver a mass of healthy yeast into the fermenter where the wort is waiting.

You should clean and sanitize the mouth of the yeast packet and fermentation vessel. Then pour the yeast and seal up the fermenter. You will whirl the fermenter and walk away. However, while you're gone, the yeast will be hard at work transforming your wort.

The Ferment

Your fermentation efforts center on providing a safe and temperate environment for the yeast to work its magic. Lots of yeast, a little oxygen, and careful control over your temperatures will keep the beer on track.

Extract brewers need to carefully balance residual gravity-boosting measures (e.g., cara-pils, crystal malts, maltodextrin powder) with extract ferments' habits of stalling at higher than desired finishing gravities. If you find your beer's hanging higher than expected, even with copious yeast supplies, modify the recipe and reduce the presence of those malts.

Phases of Fermentation

Upon hitting the wort, the yeast begins a five-stage fermentation life cycle. It goes to work immediately, adjusting to its new environment. During this lag phase, yeast takes in the dissolved oxygen and nutrients, gearing up to convert sugar to ethanol and CO_2. Within a few hours, it enters the accelerating growth phase, a period of reproduction and energy storage.

A few hours after pitching, growth becomes exponential and fermentation apparent. During this time the yeast cells divide to saturate the wort. This exponential phase is when many yeast flavors and aromas are generated. Yeast cells treated to subpar conditions, lack of nutrients, underpitching, or too much heat release stressor chemicals, altering the beer's flavor.

Ten hours later, the fermentation hits the decelerating growth phase. The rocky krausen goes mad and alcohol production ramps up. When the airlock blurps crazily, you're here. By this point, you should have your beer at or below fermentation temperature. Fermentation generates enough heat that you can't cool the wort down.

In several days, the messy krausen falls away and the yeast enters the final stage, the stationary phase. By this point no nutrition remains and almost all of the sugar is converted. The yeast and krausen drop and the beer clears. The yeast consumes fermentation byproducts, like buttery diacetyl.

Once the yeast hits the stationary phase, the bulk of fermentation is done. Little activity occurs beyond cleanup work. Less flocculant yeast cells lag behind, consuming additional sugars before giving up the ghost.

Bottling

Bottling involves capturing carbon dioxide and dissolving it into the beer. The end result is a beer with a wonderful crisp CO_2 fizz. The first bottling step is making sure the bottles are cleaned and sanitized using the methods listed earlier in this chapter. The brewer must also remember to take apart any bottle wands and bucket spigots and clean and sanitize them completely. Remember that this is the last point of contact with the beer before drinking.

During fermentation, you could see your airlock bubbling from the production of CO_2. The goal for bottling it is to provide the leftover yeast with a little extra food and trap those bubbles in your bottle.

For your first batch, you'll learn how to make a syrup of priming sugar and boiling water for the yeast to feed on. The syrup is added to the sanitized bottling bucket. The beer is then siphoned from the fermenter into the bucket as well. It is important that the syrup be thoroughly mixed with the beer, so that the same amount of priming sugar is in each bottle.

Once both the beer and the syrup are mixed in the bottling bucket, you can open the valve or start the siphon and begin filling each bottle. While bottling your beer, you must transfer it with a minimum of aeration. Aeration at this point is detrimental because dormant yeast won't consume the oxygen. That leaves a powerful agent loose in your brew to damage the aroma and flavor.

BREWING YOUR FIRST BATCH

EVERY BREWER NEEDS A RECIPE to start. Your first beer will be a classic ale, the kind a pioneer would have gladly swigged after a long day working on the land.

Plain Pub Ale

This simple but tasty brew is perfect for the first-timer. The only thing you need to worry about is staying calm and focused. Take your time, relax, and learn each step.

INGREDIENTS

Extract

5.0 pounds Pale Liquid Malt Extract (Pilsner preferred)

Hops

0.25 ounce Hallertauer Tradition Pellet for 60 minutes

0.25 ounce Czech Saaz Pellet for 5 minutes

Yeast

Wyeast 1007 German Ale (Liquid Yeast)

Style: Blonde Ale

For 5 gallons at 1.037 OG, 3.7% ABV

60-minute boil

The Day Before Brewing

Clean All Supplies

New equipment usually only requires a good rinse, but examine them closely. Fermenters need to be clean of all dirt before you try to sanitize them. Cleaning ahead of time saves you brew-day hassles and keeps you focused. Clean everything: hoses, airlocks, test tubes, funnels, and anything else you'll use for brewing.

PIONEER TIP!

Remember that cleaning is not sanitizing! As you'll see, sanitation must be done the day of brewing.

Activate Yeast

When using a Wyeast pack, smack it the day before brewing and let it sit at a temperature of 70–75°F. The pack should start to swell, a sign that your yeast is healthy.

Brew Day

On your brew day, lay out all of your ingredients and equipment. Make sure there's nothing missing—once you start the brewing process it will be difficult to leave to buy anything you've forgotten.

1. Fill your sink with cold water and ice and plug your sink's drain, creating a chilled water bath.

2. Prepare for the day by gathering 6 to 7 gallons of water. If using tap water that contains chlorine or chloramine, make the adjustments discussed earlier in the chapter.

3. Boil 3 to 4 gallons of the water to sanitize, then set it aside to chill.

4. Fill a 20-plus quart pot with the remaining, unchilled water (it should be 3 gallons). Start boiling it on high heat.

5. While the water begins to boil, remove the yeast from the fridge to warm up.

6. Put the can of Malt Extract in warm or moderately hot water. This heat will loosen the syrup and make it easier to pour.

7. Remove the pot from the heat and stir in the Malt Extract. Mix thoroughly. Extract resting on the bottom scorches, ruining the beer.

8. Return the kettle to a boil. When the boil is roiling, add the Hallertauer Tradition hops and start a timer for 55 minutes.

9. As the wort boils, mix enough sanitizing solution to fill the fermenter. Your store has some fantastic chemicals for this, but the cheapest is a tablespoon of unscented regular-strength bleach per gallon of water. Let this soak for 20 minutes with your airlock and any other equipment (a funnel, tin foil, etc.) that might come into contact with the wort after the boil. This includes anything that might touch the yeast. Sanitize the outside of the Wyeast packet. Then rinse thoroughly and air-dry completely, upside down.

10. After 55 minutes, add and thoroughly mix in the Czech Saaz hops for 5 minutes. This brings you to the completion of the 60-minute boil.

11. After the hour's boil, turn off the heat and stir the pot rapidly to generate a whirlpool. Then tightly cover the pot.

12. Settle the pot into the sink full of cold, just running water or ice water until the contents cool to around 90°F. Make sure that none of this cold, unsanitized water gets into your wort.

13. When ready, add 2 gallons of chilled water to the fermenter. Then add the lukewarm wort.

14. Close the fermenter and place the air-lock in place.

15. Rock the fermenter back and forth for 10 minutes to thoroughly mix.

16. Take a sanitized wine thief or turkey baster (unused for poultry) and draw enough wort to float a hydrometer in your jar. Record the original gravity for your records.

17. Open the yeast pack and pour ("pitch") the yeast into the waiting wort. If you need to use a pair of scissors to open the packet, make sure they've been sanitized with the bleach solution.

18. Close up the fermenter and fill the airlock with vodka or sanitizer solution.

19. Put the vessel somewhere cool (between 60°F and 65°F preferably) and wait. Within twenty-four hours the airlock should bubble, slowly at first and then like a machine gun.

Once the airlock begins to bubble, you know that you have finished your day of brewing.

Bottling (About a Week After Brew Day)

As your beer bubbles away, it may be difficult to sit by and do nothing. But, like the original pioneers, you must practice patience and allow the natural fermentation process to transpire.

How long wort needs to ferment can vary greatly depending upon the beer you are brewing. Some projects can take years to complete. Fortunately, this ale only requires approximately a week before it's ready to bottle.

Wait until the beer ceases bubbling before proceeding to bottle; this indicates that the yeast has run its course. If you bottle the beer before fermentation has finished, the pressure that builds up inside your bottles will go far beyond normal carbonation. Unchecked, that pressure may cause the bottles to explode.

What you'll need:

+ ¾ cup corn sugar for priming
+ Bleach (for sanitization, see the directions for sanitizing your fermenter)

1. Sanitize the bottling bucket, bottling wand, hoses, and spigots.

Once the beer ceases fermenting, clean and sanitize the bottling bucket and siphoning gear. Pay close attention to any bottling wands or spouts. Failure to clean these can ruin all the hard work you've done. Wash out 50 bottles. Drop the bottles into the bucket full of sanitizer. After the appropriate soak, drain the bottles and cover with foil.

2. Create your primer.

Boil approximately ¾ cup (4.4 ounces by weight) of priming sugar in a cup of water for 10 to 15 minutes. Then add the solution to the sanitized bottling bucket and keep the bucket covered.

3. Sample a portion of the beer using your hydrometer. Once you've found the final gravity, you can approximate your beer's ABV.

4. Rack beer (via siphon) to the bottling bucket, allowing it to swirl and mix with the sugar. Carefully siphon the beer out of the fermenter into the bucket. Siphon from above the trub (the leftover protein and yeast sludge found in a fermenter) to keep the beer fairly clear. Let the beer swirl through the sugar syrup. Thorough mixing is the key to consistent carbonation from bottle to bottle.

5. Fill each bottle and cap.

Attach a hose and bottling wand to your bucket's spigot (or a siphon-ready racking cane). Press the wand to the bottom of each bottle. When the beer reaches the top of the bottle, pull the wand out. The remaining space should be perfect. Pay close attention to the beer level in each bottle as you siphon—make sure that they don't overflow. Cover the bottle with a cap and move on. Once the bottles are filled, break out the capper and crimp the caps firmly to the bottle. Press multiple times, rotating the bottle each time, to ensure a solid seal. If you have a brew partner, they can cap while you fill.

6. Set aside in a warm space for 2 weeks, then move to the refrigerator.

Set the bottles in a warmer spot (70°F) for two weeks, then place a bottle in the fridge to chill.

7. Test a bottle. If carbonated, you're ready! Otherwise, wait another week and repeat.

When you the pop the cap you should hear a reassuring hiss of escaping CO_2. Decant the beer in one smooth pour to avoid adding the accumulated yeast in your glass. If you don't hear a "pfft," check the remaining bottle temperatures. Wait another week and check again.

Enjoying Your Beer

Time to exercise patience and restraint. You'll be dying to open that first bottle, but give it a full two weeks to carbonate at 70°F. Take one bottle and chill to check carbonation. Even after two weeks, the beer may still be flat. Check a bottle every week. If the bubbles still aren't there after a month, you may have to open the bottles up and add a little dry yeast.

Store capped bottles upright for the long-term. This keeps the caps from rusting and the yeast sediment resting on the bottom. Keep the bottles cool and out of the light. Stronger beers and meads, bottled properly, can keep for years.

To avoid an exploding bottle, observe these rules: Bottle your beer only when fully fermented; carefully measure your priming sugar; and mix the priming sugar thoroughly to ensure even carbonation.

Dead Simple Hefeweizen

Here's another simple recipe that would make a perfect second batch. Use the brewing method you've just learned, but with these new ingredients and brew times.

Extract
6.60 pounds Wheat (Weizen) Liquid Malt Extract (LME)
Hops
0.5 ounce Tettnanger Pellet for 60 minutes
0.5 ounce Czech Saaz Pellet for 5 minutes
Yeast
White Labs WLP830 Hefeweizen IV, Wyeast 3650 Bavarian Wheat
Style: German Wheat Beer (Hefeweizen)
Brew Type: Extract
For 5 gallons at 1.048 OG, 4.7% ABV
60-minute boil

Beer Bread

Use your own ale to make this quick and easy bread, a great accompaniment to your beer.

INGREDIENTS + YIELDS 1 LOAF

3 cups self-rising flour
3 tablespoons granulated sugar
1 (12-ounce) can or bottle of beer

1. Preheat oven to 350°F. Coat a 9" × 5" loaf pan with pan spray, and line the bottom and short sides with a strip of parchment.

2. In a large bowl, mix together flour, sugar, and beer until just blended. Transfer batter to prepared pan; smooth the top.

3. Bake 30 minutes, until risen. Reduce oven temperature to 325°F and bake 15 minutes longer. Tent with foil if loaf browns too quickly.

4. Remove from oven and cool 10 minutes before removing from pan. Continue cooling on a rack.

PIONEER TIP!

Because it already contains leaveners, self-rising flour is perfect for quick bread baking. You can also make your own self-rising flour by combining 3 cups flour with 4½ teaspoons baking powder and 1½ teaspoons kosher salt. Blend this mixture well before measuring. Self-rising flour is not a substitute for yeast.

Beer Cheese Soup

Along with a slice of your beer bread, this soup is the perfect dinner to celebrate your burgeoning brewing talents.

INGREDIENTS + SERVES 6

2 tablespoons vegetable oil or butter
1 large onion, diced
2 ribs celery, diced
2 carrots, diced
3 cloves garlic, minced
1 teaspoon Worcestershire sauce
1 teaspoon Tabasco
2 cups water or chicken broth

2 cups beer
¼ cup flour
¼ cup butter
2 cups half-and-half
4 cups shredded Cheddar cheese
1 teaspoon Dijon mustard
Salt and pepper to taste
2 cups popped popcorn or croutons

1. In a soup pot over medium-high heat, combine oil, onion, celery, carrots, and garlic; sauté 5 minutes.

2. Add Worcestershire, Tabasco, water or broth, and beer; bring to a boil, then reduce heat to medium. Simmer 15 minutes.

3. In a saucepan over medium-high heat, combine flour and butter; cook, stirring constantly, until roux is smooth and bubbly. Reduce heat to medium; slowly whisk in half-and-half. Keep stirring until mixture thickens and half-and-half is hot. Remove from heat; add cheese, stirring until melted.

4. Whisk cheese mixture into beer broth mixture; add mustard, salt, and pepper. Simmer without boiling 10 minutes, stirring often.

5. Ladle into soup mugs; garnish with popcorn or croutons.

CHAPTER 6

HOW A PIONEER STAYS STRONG:
Prairie Remedies for Injury and Illness

"The wish for healing has always been half of health."

— LUCIUS ANNAEUS SENECA —

L IFE ON THE FRONTIER WAS OFTEN BRUTAL. When a pioneer woman went out to farm or forage, she encountered danger at every turn. There were wild animals that could bite and insects that could sting. Even in her own house, she wasn't safe. A practiced and experienced pioneer could still poke herself with a needle or sprain her ankle by tripping over a loose floorboard.

On top of the threats that might arrive from the wilderness, pioneers also had to contend with the everyday ailments and illnesses that we still deal with today. Like us, they suffered from colds and pneumonia, headaches and insomnia. They had nothing like the modern over-the-counter medicines that we use (and over-use). Yet many lived to a ripe old age on the untamed frontier. This is because the original pioneers were able to use the resources around them. They knew how to make ointments to heal burns and syrups to cure coughs. They knew which ingredients would starve off a cold and what meals would keep them calm. In this chapter you will learn how to keep yourself as strong as a pioneer.

METHODS AND TOOLS FOR HERBAL HEALING

ERBAL MEDICINE is the practice of using one or more parts of a plant—its seeds, berries, roots, leaves, bark, or flowers—to relieve physical and psychological problems, prevent disease, or just improve overall health and vitality. Herbs have a long history of use and, when the Modern-Day Pioneer uses them properly, are safe and powerful medicines.

Dosages

When using store-bought herbs, you should always follow the manufacturer's guidelines. When you don't have any—the package doesn't have dosage information or you've made the remedy yourself—you can use these. For chronic conditions, adults should take the following doses:

+ **Tea:** 3 to 4 cups a day
+ **Tincture or syrup:** ½ to 1 teaspoon, three times a day

For acute problems, adults should take the following, until symptoms subside:

+ **Tea:** ¼ to ½ cup every hour or two, up to 3 cups a day
+ **Tincture or syrup:** ¼ to ½ teaspoon every 30 to 60 minutes

The dosages given here are for non-concentrated products. Because commercial herbal extracts vary widely in their concentration, the best advice for taking a concentrated extract is to check the product's concentration level and divide that by the dosages recommended here. Generally speaking, seniors should take a quarter of an adult dose.

Here are two formulas for determining the best dosage for a child:

+ Take your child's age and add 12, then divide that number by the child's age. Then multiply the adult dosage by that number.
+ Divide the child's age at his next birthday by 24.

Using these formulas, a six-year-old would get 30 percent of an adult dose, and a twelve-year-old would be given half. If you're treating a baby younger than six months (and you're breastfeeding), you can take the appropriate herb yourself—and pass it to your baby via your breastmilk.

Here is some advice on using herbs effectively:

+ Start slowly. Take the smallest dose that's sensible, then see how you feel. Nothing? Take a bit more. Remember that herbs are almost always gentler and less potent than their pharmaceutical counterparts, so you don't want a dramatic reaction. If you're using an herb that can produce side effects you should exercise more restraint in increasing your dose than if you're using a more innocuous herb. You also should be more careful about upping the dose if you're treating a senior or a child.

+ Know what you're doing. Research the condition that you're treating, including the various treatment options—herbal and conventional—and the benefits of each.

+ Don't overdo it. Adverse reactions from the herbal remedies used most often today are extremely rare, but they can happen—most often when an herb is overused. If you take too much for too long, you can have problems.

+ Be a patient patient. Because herbs work subtly, they have what's known as a long onset of action. Unlike a pharmaceutical painkiller, for example, a dose of willow (*Salix alba*) won't get rid of your headache in a half-hour.

+ Take the long view. The general rule of thumb is to give an herbal remedy a few weeks before deciding if it's working or not.

+ Don't use short-term remedies for long-term problems. If you find yourself constantly reaching for the same type of acute remedy it's time to change tactics. Contact a professional, who can help you address the underlying problem.

Keeping and Preparing the Pioneer's Medicine Box

With only a few common tools and a few simple ingredients, which are available at most any herb shop or natural foods store, you can make your own herbal remedies. By making your own, you can control more aspects of the product you're using, and you'll gain a greater understanding of the power of plants.

Here are a few things to keep in mind when making your own remedies:

+ Herbs and herbal preparations do best when they're stored in airtight glass jars, out of direct light, in a cool area. Light, oxygen, and heat can degrade them.

+ Never use aluminum pots or containers—aluminum can react with the herbs. Stick to glass, ceramic, stainless steel, or cast iron.
+ Store all remedies and ingredients—especially essential oils and alcohol-based tinctures—out of children's reach. Many essential oils are extremely toxic, even in very small doses.

Therapeutic Teas

A tea is, without question, the simplest of herbal remedies to prepare—and use. Even the most inept of homemakers can boil water, and that's really all it takes to make a cup of tea.

To make a tea with loose herbs, put the plant material into a strainer and into a cup, then fill the cup with boiling water. Cover the cup: The medicinal value of many herbs, including peppermint (*Mentha x piperita*), is contained in the essential oils, so you'll want to keep the steam from escaping. You can also make an infusion using a French coffee press; just don't use the same one you use to make coffee.

When making tea, use about 1 teaspoon of dried herbs per cup of water. Steep for 15 minutes or longer. The more herb you use and the longer you let it steep, the stronger your tea will be.

Sweet-Tasting Syrups

Syrups are a great way to treat children with herbs. They're sweet and they go down much easier than other liquid remedies. If properly stored, syrups will last for several weeks.

To make an herbal syrup, first make a quart of an infusion and then simmer it down and mix with honey or another sweetener (like maple syrup or brown sugar).

PIONEER TIP!

Experts advise against giving raw (unpasteurized) honey to children younger than a year old, because of the risk of botulism. If you're making syrup to give to a baby, you can replace honey with commercial maple syrup or brown sugar.

Tinctures

Tinctures are liquid herbal extracts made by combining the herbs with a solvent. Traditional tinctures are made with a beverage alcohol, but you can also use vinegar or vegetable glycerin (available at many health food stores) instead. Tinctures are typically more potent than infusions, decoctions, or syrups.

+ Start with bulk herbs (fresh is best) and chop them finely. Put them into a clean glass jar and add enough alcohol—80- or 100-proof vodka, gin, or brandy—to cover them with about 2 or 3 inches of fluid. Cover with a tight-fitting lid, place the jar in a warm, dark spot, and leave it there for four to six weeks—the longer, the better.
+ Once a day, shake the jar to keep the herbs from settling at the bottom.
+ When the time is up, strain the herbs and discard them. Transfer the tincture to a small glass bottle (ideally one with a dropper, which makes it easier to get the right dose). Stored properly, it will keep for two years or longer. Be sure to keep tinctures out of the reach of children.

Infused Oils

Herbal oils can be used alone or as a base for creams or ointments. There are two ways to make infused oils: using the sun or using the stove. You can use many types of vegetable oil as your base—coconut (*Cocos nucifera*) and almond (*Prunus dulcis*) are popular choices—and add an equal amount of cocoa (*Theobroma cacao*)

butter to thicken the mixture, if you like (this works best with the stovetop method).

MAKING SOLAR-INFUSED OILS

Place a handful of dried herbs into a clean, clear glass jar and fill the jar with oil (you'll use about 2 ounces, or 8 tablespoons, of herbs per pint of oil). Cover tightly and place in a warm sunny spot. Leave it there for two weeks. When the time is up, pour the mixture through a piece of cheesecloth or muslin, making sure to wring the cloth tightly and catch every last drop of oil.

PIONEER TIP!

When making infused oils, you'll get the best results with dried herbs. Plant material that contains too much moisture can cause the oil to get moldy. (Your oil can also grow mold if it's made or stored in a jar with an ill-fitting lid, which can allow moisture to get in.)

Discard the herbs and replace them with a new batch, then let the oil and herbs steep for another two weeks. Transfer to clean glass bottles. Stored correctly, infused oils will last several months.

MAKING OILS ON THE STOVE

If you don't have a lot of sunshine (or a month to wait), you can make your oil on the stove using a double boiler. Put the herbs and oil into the top section, fill the bottom with water, and bring it to a low boil. Let the oil simmer gently for 30 to 60 minutes, checking frequently to make sure the oil isn't overheating (it will start to smoke if that's the case). The lower and longer you let it simmer, the better your oil will be.

Herbal Ointments

Ointments, also known as salves, are thick, oil-based preparations used to treat superficial wounds (like scrapes, burns, and insect bites) and soothe aching muscles and joints. Here's how to make them:

1. Start with an infused oil (see "Infused Oils") that's been strained. Put the oil into a small pan and add grated beeswax—¼ cup per cup of infused oil. Heat on low, until the beeswax is completely melted, then remove from the heat.

2. Test a small amount for consistency by putting it into the freezer for a minute or two to cool it. If it seems too hard (you can't spread it easily), heat it again and add more oil. If it's too oily, reheat and add more beeswax.

3. When you've got the consistency you want, transfer the ointment to clean glass jars. Stored properly, ointments will last several months.

Compresses

Compresses are small bundles of material that have been soaked in an infusion or decoction and applied to the skin. Linen, gauze, or cotton are often used for compresses. Make sure the infusion or decoction is hot when you soak the material. You should apply the compress to the affected area and change it when it has cooled down.

Poultice

When you make a poultice, you wrap the herbs themselves in a piece of gauze and soak it in the infusion or decoction, then apply it to the skin. You can also use cider vinegar in place of the usual water when you create an infusion or decoction for poultice use. You should apply it to the affected area and change it when it cools down.

HERBAL FIRST AID FOR FRONTIER EMERGENCIES

WHEN THE ORIGINAL PIONEERS had an accident or an injury, they couldn't grab a bottle of Advil or call a cab to drive them to the doctor. Instead, they had access to plants and compounds that allowed them to recover and heal. Today we know that, in contrast to the pharmaceuticals in an average medicine cabinet, herbal first-aid remedies are generally free of side effects and in many cases perform as well or even better than the commercial drugs. Using the herbal healing techniques you have just learned, you will be able to deal with many emergency medical situations you may come across.

Burns and Sunburns

A burn is an injury to the skin that can be caused by several things, including heat, chemicals, sun exposure, and electricity. Most burns are minor—you've accidentally touched a hot stove or spent too much time in the sun—and can be treated at home.

Doctors classify burns according to the amount of damage they've caused. A first-degree burn affects just the top layer of skin (the epidermis) and is by far the most common type. A first-degree burn will be red and painful and will blanch (turn white) when you press on it. It may swell a bit and might peel within a day or two, and will probably heal within a week.

Second-degree burns affect more layers of skin. The skin will blister and be red and swollen, and will take a few weeks to heal. (These burns are more prone to infection, so you should probably see your health care provider.) Third-degree burns, the most severe, affect all layers of the skin and possibly other tissues as well, and take months to heal. These burns always require medical attention.

Sunburn is a type of radiation burn caused by UV, or ultraviolet, light. You can get one from a tanning bed or booth as well as from the real thing. Most often, sunburns are minor (first-degree burns) that make you uncomfortable for a day or so. Occasionally, you can get a second-degree burn from sun exposure, meaning blistering, more pain, and a longer recovery time.

Conventional remedies for minor burns include topical anesthetics/analgesics and oral pain relievers such as NSAIDs. Burns that might get infected are treated with topical antiseptics and antibiotics, which can inhibit healing and cause skin reactions.

┌──────────────────────────────────┐

PIONEER TIP!

Your risk for sunburn depends on the time of day and year (sunburns are more likely on summer days, between 10 a.m. and 2 p.m.), your latitude and altitude (being closer to the equator and farther from sea level means more radiation), and what you're doing (skiing and swimming are done around water and snow, which reflect burning rays).

└──────────────────────────────────┘

Here are some herbal remedies for minor burns or sunburns (for more serious second- and third-degree burns, see your healthcare provider):

+ Aloe (*Aloe vera*): The gel from this cactus-like plant is legendary as a burn remedy. Research shows it improves circulation in superficial blood vessels, inhibits inflammation, and promotes tissue repair.

+ Calendula (*Calendula officinalis*): Calendula, a.k.a. marigold, has both astringent and anti-inflammatory properties and is another classic burn remedy. Studies show it also has antiedemic, analgesic, and wound-healing properties.

+ Lavender (*Lavandula angustifolia*): The essential oil of lavender is a gentle anesthetic and anti-inflammatory with real skin-healing powers. Research shows it can relieve swelling and pain in minor burns.

+ Saint John's wort (*Hypericum perforatum*): Saint John's wort is used topically to treat burns and other superficial skin injuries. It possesses antimicrobial, antioxidant, and anti-inflammatory constituents, and research shows it can modulate the immune response to burn injury in order to speed healing. (Ironically, taking Saint John's wort orally can increase your susceptibility to sunburn, so be sure to use sunblock.)

+ Witch hazel (*Hamamelis virginiana*): Witch hazel is a cooling, soothing remedy for burns (and all types of cuts, scrapes, and other skin injuries). Research shows it can reduce skin inflammation in sunburned people. It also works as a styptic (it stops bleeding).

Burn Ointment

This is a classic remedy that combines skin-soothing, inflammation-fighting and germ-killing herbs. Keep this ointment around the house for cooking mishaps.

INGREDIENTS

1 part calendula (*Calendula officinalis*) flowers
1 part comfrey (*Symphytum officinale*) leaves
1 part comfrey (*Symphytum officinale*) root
1 part Saint John's wort (*Hypericum perforatum*) flowers
1 part olive (*Olea europaea*) oil
Beeswax, grated

1. Put the calendula flowers, comfrey leaves and root, and Saint John's wort flowers into the top section of a double boiler along with the olive oil, fill the bottom with water, and bring it to a low boil.

2. Let the oil simmer gently for 30 to 60 minutes, checking frequently to make sure the oil isn't overheating (it will start to smoke if that's the case).

3. Strain the oil and put it into a small pan and add grated beeswax—¼ cup per cup of infused oil. Heat on low, until the beeswax is completely melted, then remove from the heat.

4. Test a small amount for consistency by putting it into the freezer for a minute or two to cool it. If it seems too hard (you can't spread it easily), heat it again and add more oil. If it's too oily, reheat and add more beeswax.

5. When you've got the consistency you want, transfer the ointment to clean glass jars. Stored properly, ointments will last several months.

Bumps and Bruises

When your body suffers an impact, it can leave a contusion or hematoma (also known as a plain old bruise), which involves localized discoloration, swelling, and inflammation. If you take a fall or bump into something hard enough, the tiny blood vessels just under the skin will rupture, and your skin will develop the telltale black-and-blue color as blood leaks into the surrounding tissues and gets trapped there.

In most cases, bruises are not a big deal and will clear up within a couple of weeks. However, if you experience severe pain and swelling, see a health care provider, as this may be a sign of a more serious injury.

Several herbs have been used traditionally, both internally and topically, to treat bruises:

+ Arnica (*Arnica montana*): Arnica is the classic European herb for bruises and muscle aches and is used as a conventional herbal treatment (for topical application only) as well as a homeopathic remedy, which is extremely dilute (homeopathic preparations are the only safe way to use arnica internally). Studies show it has anti-inflammatory and anticlotting effects, meaning it can reduce swelling and speed the body's efforts to clear away trapped blood.

+ Comfrey (*Symphytum officinale*): Comfrey is a time-honored topical treatment for bruises (especially the deeper ones that affect muscle fibers). Modern research shows it can improve the pain and tenderness of contusions and muscle injuries.

+ Turmeric (*Curcuma longa*): Turmeric relieves inflammation—and the pain and swelling that goes with it—thanks to its chemical constituent curcumin. It's used externally to treat bruises and other skin and muscle injuries.

Scrapes and Cuts

You can injure your skin anywhere: wielding a knife in the kitchen, shuffling papers in the office, or playing with your kids in the park. You also can develop blisters—fluid-filled pouches of skin created by friction—when hiking on vacation or just wearing a new pair of shoes around your neighborhood.

There are many herbs with painkilling and antibacterial functions that can help you heal minor scrapes and cuts.

+ Barberry (*Berberis vulgaris*): Barberry contains the chemical berberine, which has strong antimicrobial and painkilling action. Berberine is also found in goldenseal (*Hydrastis canadensis*).
+ Eucalyptus (*Eucalyptus globulus*): Eucalyptus oil contains antimicrobial, analgesic, anesthetic, and antiseptic constituents, so it can relieve pain and prevent infection.
+ Gotu kola (*Centella asiatica*): A natural anti-inflammatory and antibacterial agent, gotu kola is used throughout India and much of Asia to treat wounds and skin infections. Modern research shows it stimulates new cell growth and the production of collagen, the major protein in skin and connective tissue, which speeds healing and minimizes scarring.
+ Horsetail (*Equisetum arvense*): Horsetail is an analgesic, astringent, antiseptic, and styptic (it stops bleeding) and has been used for centuries by Native Americans to treat superficial skin injuries. In the lab, it's shown antimicrobial action against Streptococcus and other types of bacteria and fungi that can infect wounds.

+ Marshmallow (*Althaea officinalis*): Marshmallow contains antibacterial and anti-inflammatory constituents. It soothes irritated and damaged skin and forms a protective layer to seal out germs and help the skin repair itself.
+ Yarrow (*Achillea millefolium*): Topical applications of yarrow can stop bleeding, reduce inflammation, and prevent infection—like an herbal Band-Aid.

Sprains and Strains

If you sprain something (the most common site for a sprain is the ankle), you might hear a popping sound, but you'll definitely experience almost immediate swelling and pain. If you've strained a muscle or tendon (what many people call a "pulled muscle"), you'll feel immediate pain, and, over the next few hours, increasing stiffness and possible swelling. Both types of injury occur when the tissue is pulled past its normal range of motion and is either stretched or torn in the process.

Here are some herbal remedies:

+ Arnica (*Arnica montana*): Arnica is a classic remedy for soft-tissue (muscle) injuries. It's used topically (as an ointment or cream) and orally (as a homeopathic remedy) and possesses both anti-inflammatory and analgesic effects. Research shows it can reduce pain and inflammation in patients following surgical reconstruction of knee ligaments.

+ Comfrey (*Symphytum officinale*): This herb is used topically to treat injuries to muscles, tendons, and ligaments. Recent research shows that a topical comfrey treatment reduced pain and swelling and restored mobility to sprained ankles better than the prescription NSAID diclofenac.

+ Pineapple (*Ananas comosus*): Pineapples contain the enzyme bromelain, which works as an anti-inflammatory. Research shows it can reduce swelling, bruising, pain, and healing time following injury or trauma.

Itching and Scratching

Plenty of things you encounter both at home and away can cause irritation and itching: bites and stings from insects as well as an inadvertent brush against a toxic plant.

Poison ivy, oak, and sumac contain oils that can cause an itchy, red rash, often involving blisters (you can even have a reaction if you touch something—an article of clothing, even your dog's fur—that's touched the plant, or if you inhale smoke from a fire that contains it).

Several species of bugs—including bees, wasps, and hornets—can sting you, leaving behind venom and sometimes a stinger, plus a welt that's itchy or painful or both. Biting insects, such as ticks, spiders, fleas, and mosquitoes, like to take away something (usually a bit of blood), and leave a bit of saliva that creates a reaction (usually itching and inflammation) in return.

Treatment Options
Herbal alternatives include these:

+ Echinacea (*Echinacea purpurea*): Used topically, echinacea is a mild anesthetic and antiseptic that fights infection and speeds healing. In the lab, it's been shown to reduce inflammation and swelling better than a topical NSAID.

+ Eucalyptus (*Eucalyptus globulus*): Eucalyptus oil works as a topical antiseptic and painkiller; it can relieve pain and itching, speed healing, and prevent infection.

+ Sangre de Grado (*Croton lechleri*): This South American tree is known for its anti-inflammatory and wound-healing prowess. Research shows it can relieve the pain and itching caused by all sorts of insects—including fire ants, wasps, and bees—and poisonous plants. It's also good for treating cuts and scrapes.

+ Tea tree (*Melaleuca alternifolia*): Tea tree oil reduces histamine-induced (allergic) inflammation of the skin and can decrease the welt left from insect bites and stings. It also has antibacterial properties to help prevent infection.

+ Witch hazel (*Hamamelis virginiana*): A powerful astringent, witch hazel can dry up "weeping" rashes and create a virtual bandage over the area by sealing cell membranes and reducing the permeability of surrounding blood vessels. Research shows that it performs better than hydrogen peroxide in helping skin heal (it's also a strong antimicrobial and antioxidant).

Insect Repellents

Several popular culinary herbs and spices contain chemicals with serious bug-repellent powers. Recent studies have shown that extracts of cinnamon (*Cinnamomum verum, C. aromaticum*), clove (*Syzygium aromaticum*), fennel (*Foeniculum vulgare*), and ginger (*Zingiber officinale*) can keep mosquitoes, ticks, and other insects away.

Other herbal alternatives include these:

+ Camphor (*Cinnamomum camphora*): Camphor (the herb) contains camphor (the chemical), which is a natural insect repellent. It's also an effective pain and itch reliever (approved by the FDA), so you can use it to treat bites you've already got.

+ Lemon eucalyptus (*Eucalyptus citriodora, Corymbia citriodora*): The oil from this Australian native is registered with the Food and Drug Administration and was recently approved as an insect repellent by the U.S. Centers for Disease Control.

+ Neem (*Azadirachta indica*): Topical neem preparations have been shown to repel several different species of mosquitoes.

CURING COMMON AILMENTS THROUGH FOOD AND HERBS

- -

Nᴏᴛ ᴀʟʟ ʜᴇᴀʟᴛʜ ᴘʀᴏʙʟᴇᴍꜱ are emergencies. Most, like a terrible cold or a sore throat, insinuate themselves in your immune system and slowly become unbearable. Pioneers faced these issues as well, and they had their own ways of curing their bodies and their minds. In this section, you will learn which ingredients you can use to soothe your back after a long commute or help you sleep after a long day. There are even recipes to cheer you up when you're sad and relax you when you're stressed. The healing power of food and herbs has been well documented throughout history. As a Modern-Day Pioneer, you have the ability to take this valuable knowledge and use it to guide your eating while reaping the benefits of improved health and wellness.

Cold and Flu

Unfortunately, everyone is familiar with colds and the flu. The sniffling, coughing, and aching muscles are symptoms you have likely experienced more than a few times. However, you can prevent becoming victim to the next circulating bug by boosting your immune system with healthy foods.

Most people treat colds and flu with over-the-counter pain relievers, decongestants, antihistamines, and cough medicines. These drugs can cause a long list of side effects, including irregular heartbeat, drowsiness, and stomach pain. Fortunately, there are natural remedies that you, the Modern-Day Pioneer, can use to get healthy without harming your body with chemicals.

Beta-carotene plays a role in the function of skin and mucus membranes that line the nose and lungs. This is your body's first defense against invading germs that could cause a cold or the flu. Beta-carotene increases the presence of T cells, which attack invaders that can cause you to get sick.

Healing with Food

Orange vegetables and dark leafy greens supply you with a bounty of immunity-boosting beta-carotene. Carrots, pumpkin, sweet potatoes, spinach, collard greens, and kale top the list.

Once a cold or the flu has set in, consider incorporating some hot peppers into your diet if your appetite can tolerate it. The capsaicin in chiles can clear your stuffed-up nose by thinning mucous, and cayenne peppers are an excellent source of vitamin A, which is the same vitamin formed from beta-carotene.

Believe it or not, chicken soup stays on the list for foods to eat when you have a cold or the flu. Researchers have found that the soup actually does have an anti-inflammatory effect, which means that it can ease common symptoms such as a sore throat. Get even more benefit by adding plenty of fresh garlic. Garlic's sulfur-containing compounds are antibacterial and antiviral, which fights off infecting viruses and could reduce sickness.

Healing with Herbs

The following herbal remedies will help you with cold and flu symptoms:

+ Andrographis (*Andrographis paniculata*): Andrographis is used in Ayurvedic and Chinese medicine to treat upper respiratory tract infections (it's an antibac-terial and antioxidant). Studies show that it can relieve the symptoms of sore throats and helps to prevent colds.

+ Astragalus (*Astragalus membranaceus*): Astragalus is used in traditional Chinese medicine as a tonic for the immune system. Studies show that it's an antiviral, antibacterial, and immunomodulator that helps prevent infections.

+ Echinacea (*Echinacea purpurea*): Echinacea is a powerful antiviral and immune system stimulant, and has been shown in several studies to reduce the severity and duration of cold and flu symptoms.

+ Elderberry (*Sambucus nigra*): Elderberry has both antiviral and immune-boosting effects, making it a great remedy for colds and flu. Research shows it can fight several viruses at once—and improve your symptoms in just a few days.

+ Ginger (*Zingiber officinale*): Ginger inhibits the bacteria and viruses responsible for upper respiratory infections and also relieves sore throats and the aches of the flu.

+ Isatis (*Isatis tinctoria*): Constituents of this Chinese herb have antiviral, antibacterial, antifungal, analgesic, and antipyretic (fever-reducing) activity.

Cinnamon-Echinacea Cold Syrup

This is perfect for treating colds and flu—especially in kids.

INGREDIENTS

1 part cinnamon (*Cinnamomum verum, C. aromaticum*) bark
1 part dried echinacea (*Echinacea purpurea*) root
½ part fresh ginger (*Zingiber officinalis*) root, grated or chopped

1. Add 2 ounces (about 8 tablespoons) of the herb mixture to a quart of cold water. Bring to a boil, then simmer until the liquid is reduced by half (leave the lid slightly ajar).

2. Strain the herbs from the liquid and discard, then pour the liquid back into the pot.

3. Add 1 cup of honey (or another sweetener) and heat the mixture through.

4. Remove from heat, let cool, and transfer to glass bottles. Store in the refrigerator.

Depression

The term "depressed" is used loosely to refer to feeling down or sad. However, the depressive disorder known as "depression" is a much more serious condition that lasts for extended periods of time, not just a day or two every now and then. It results in feelings of sadness and anxiety and can cause a loss of appetite and a loss of interest in doing things the sufferer once enjoyed. Inability to sleep, as well as excessive sleep, is a symptom, in addition to lack of concentration.

The cause of depression is not known, but its presence is associated with substances called neurotransmitters. Neurotransmitters are chemical messengers in the brain, and those most often linked to depression include serotonin, dopamine, norepinephrine, and y-aminobutyric acid. A deficiency or imbalance in these chemicals may lead to depression. Some nutrients from the foods you eat promote production and action of these neurotransmitters; therefore, nutrient deficiencies can affect proper function and risk for depression.

A variety of chemicals in the brain (for example, serotonin, dopamine, and norepinephrine) influence your mood. Some amino acids consumed through protein in foods are precursors for the brain chemicals, meaning that they are converted to the chemicals once digested or absorbed. Tryptophan and tyrosine are two such amino acids.

Research shows that individuals suffering from depression often have low levels of folate, and this vitamin can help medications for depression work more effectively. Omega-3 fatty acids have been found to have antidepressant effects and can ease the symptoms of depression.

Carbohydrates, especially whole-grain sources, can improve the mood. The spike in insulin that occurs after eating carbohydrates delivers sugar to the cells for energy production, which sends tryptophan to the brain. This influences those neurotransmitters that can improve mood.

Healing with Food

Meat, fish, poultry, eggs, and milk are complete proteins, meaning that they supply all nine essential amino acids, some of which are important for mental health and improved mood. If you are a vegetarian, currently there are two plant sources considered to be complete proteins: soybeans and quinoa.

To increase your folate intake, try Great Northern beans, spinach, asparagus, pinto beans, lentils, and oranges. Wild salmon, flaxseed, and walnuts are almost always recommended for increasing omega-3 fatty acid intake, but don't overlook shrimp, scallops, albacore tuna, and lake trout. These foods also provide amino acids through the protein they supply.

If you're feeling down, a great recipe is the White Bean Tuna Salad, which combines the folate from beans with the protein and omega-3 fatty acids of tuna and walnuts. As a Modern-Day Pioneer, you can use the parsley you've grown yourself.

Healing with Food

Pumpkin seeds, Swiss chard, peanuts, and peanut butter all contain magnesium. Cremini mushrooms, spinach, and eggs supply riboflavin. Choose spinach, almonds, and almond butter and you will get both magnesium and riboflavin.

Pumpkin seeds and nuts make great toppings for a leafy green salad that also includes plenty of spinach. Toast your delicious homemade bread and top it with peanut butter or almond butter for a headache-beating treat. Try sautéing Swiss chard in olive oil with salt and pepper, and add it to scrambled eggs.

PIONEER TIP!

Tyramine is an amino acid that has been found to cause migraines in some people. It can be found in fermented and aged foods, including aged cheese, processed meats, and soy sauce. If you are trying to identify foods that trigger your headaches, pay attention to your tyramine intake and experiment with reducing the foods you eat that contain it.

Healing with Herbs

Many traditional herbal formulas have shown the ability to handle even the toughest of headaches:

+ Butterbur (*Petasites hybridus*): Extracts from this shrub have analgesic, anti-inflammatory, and antiseizure actions. In several recent studies, they produced a marked decrease in severity and frequency of migraines.

- Cayenne (*Capsicum annuum, C. frutescens*): Applied topically, cayenne preparations have been shown to relieve and even prevent the devastating pain of cluster headaches.
- Feverfew (*Tanacetum parthenium*): This is perhaps the best-known herbal headache remedy. It has been shown in several studies to reduce the frequency of migraine attacks—and limit their symptoms when they do occur.
- Lavender (*Lavandula angustifolia*): The essential oil of this flowering plant has been used effectively to treat several types of headache pain. The same is true of peppermint oil (*Mentha x piperita*).
- Willow (*Salix alba*): The salicin from the bark of this tree is a potent analgesic. Its headache-fighting properties are well proven in both laboratory and clinical studies.

Headache Relief Tincture

Keep this relaxing, pain-fighting combination on hand for whenever headaches strike.

INGREDIENTS

1 part California poppy (*Eschscholzia californica*) seeds
1 part feverfew (*Tanacetum parthenium*) leaves and flowers
1 part lavender (*Lavandula angustifolia*) flowers

1. Crush the California poppy seeds and finely chop the feverfew and lavender.

2. Put them into a clean glass jar and add enough alcohol—80- or 100-proof vodka, gin, or brandy—to cover them with about 2 or 3 inches of fluid.

3. Cover with a tight-fitting lid, place the jar in a warm, dark spot, and leave it there for four to six weeks—the longer, the better.

4. Once a day, shake the jar to keep the herbs from settling at the bottom.

5. When the time is up, strain the herbs and discard them. Transfer the tincture to a small glass bottle (ideally one with a dropper, which makes it easier to get the right dose). Stored properly, it will keep for two years or longer. Be sure to keep tinctures out of the reach of children.

Insomnia

According to the Mayo Clinic, insomnia is one of the most common medical complaints. Fortunately, there are many foods that can have calming effects to improve your ability to sleep well and wake feeling rested.

A recent nationwide survey found that one in five Americans takes a prescription or over-the-counter sleep aid at least once a week—and 63 percent of them experience side effects.

PIONEER TIP!

Insomnia can be triggered by several medications, including cold and allergy medications (antihistamines and decongestants), hypertension and heart disease drugs, birth control pills, thyroid medicines, and asthma medications. Caffeine is an obvious cause for insomnia, but it's found in many places beyond your coffee cup, including some over-the-counter pain relievers.

Insomnia can be caused by a variety of factors. Stress and anxiety may trigger it, or it may result from a separate medical condition or current medication. Caffeine and alcohol can cause insomnia, as can eating late at night.

According to the National Sleep Foundation, the amino acid tryptophan can cause sleepiness. Through a series of chemical reactions, tryptophan raises levels of serotonin, which helps regulate sleep patterns, in the brain. Carbohydrates can help make you sleepy because they make the tryptophan more available to the brain for use.

Healing with Food

Tryptophan is found in foods that contain protein. Shrimp, scallops, cod, chicken, and turkey are ideal protein sources. When choosing your carbohydrate source, consider oats, buckwheat, bulgur, barley, and brown rice, or try bananas and baked potatoes. Sunflower seeds and sesame seeds also contain tryptophan.

Other food remedies for insomnia include lettuce, honey, and foods containing vitamin B. Lettuce contains lectucarium, which induces sleep. Vitamin B has been proved to enhance relaxation, which can lead to better sleep; you can find vitamin B in cereals and nuts. Honey, a common home remedy for sleep, can be stirred into a cup of hot water before bedtime.

Many foods can disrupt sleep and are linked to insomnia. If you suffer from insomnia, eat foods that can improve sleep, but also eliminate high-fat and spicy foods, caffeine, and alcohol. These foods can keep you from falling asleep, or cause you to wake up before you are fully rested.

For a better night's sleep, eat a snack about four hours before bedtime that combines carbohydrates and protein. The best choices are proteins with the highest amount of tryptophan, combined with some of the carbohydrate sources that also contain the amino acid. Try a snack of turkey and bulgur.

Healing with Herbs

Here are some useful herbal remedies if you're just not getting the sleep you need after a long day of pioneering:

+ Chamomile (*Matricaria recutita*): Chamomile flowers have been used to make bedtime teas for centuries; they contain mildly sedating compounds, as well as chemicals that reduce anxiety.
+ Kava (*Piper methysticum*): Research shows that this herb can be as effective as the drug Valium in creating the changes in brain waves that help you fall—and stay—asleep.
+ Lavender (*Lavandula angustifolia*): Lavender oil is used topically as a sedative and antianxiety agent.

Research shows it can promote relaxation and induce sleep in people of all ages. In one study, people who used lavender in aromatherapy (they inhaled it or applied it to their skin) before going to bed reported feeling more refreshed in the morning.

+ Lemon balm (*Melissa officinalis*): Lemon balm is a mild sedative and stress reliever. Research shows it can quell anxiety and promote sleep.
+ Passionflower (*Passiflora incarnata*): Passionflower is a mild sedative and sleep aid.
+ Valerian (*Valeriana officinalis*): Valerian is a mild sedative and tranquilizer. Studies show that its chemical compounds can have a direct affect on gamma-aminobutyric acid (GABA), a brain chemical that controls arousal and sleep. Taking valerian can shorten the time it takes you to fall asleep (sleep latency) and improve your sleep quality.

Anti-insomnia Tea

Try this herbal tea when suffering from sleepless nights.

INGREDIENTS

2 parts chamomile (*Matricaria recutita*) flowers
2 parts passionflower (*Passiflora incarnata*) leaves and flowers
2 parts lemon balm (*Melissa officinalis*) leaves
1 part valerian (*Valeriana officinalis*) root
½ part rose (*Rosa canina, R.* spp.) hips
¼ part lavender (*Lavandula angustifolia*) flowers

1. Put all the ingredients into a strainer and place the strainer above a cup.

2. Fill the cup with boiling water. Use about 1 teaspoon of dried herbs per cup of water.

3. Cover the cup: The medicinal value of many herbs is contained in the essential oils, so you'll want to keep the steam from escaping.

4. Steep for 15 minutes or longer. The longer you let it steep, the stronger your tea will be.

5. Drink in the evening, at least an hour or two before bed (you don't want to wake up because you need to use the bathroom). If you want something stronger, you can make this formula into a tincture; take ¼ teaspoon of the tincture at bedtime.

Muscle Cramps

As you move, you contract and relax your muscles. When a muscle involuntarily contracts, it is called a spasm. When the spasm lasts a long time and the muscle can't relax, it becomes a cramp. A muscle cramp can last anywhere from a few minutes to an entire day.

Most often, cramps are caused by a nerve malfunction, and many occur after physical activity or during the night. Dehydration and reduced mineral intake are two dietary causes of this malfunction that can result in a cramp.

Other causes of cramps include:

+ Heavy exercising (or exercising too long)
+ Electrolyte imbalances
+ Muscle fatigue
+ Lack of calcium or potassium

Adequate intake of the electrolytes potassium, sodium, magnesium, and calcium can reduce the risk of cramps due to the role these minerals play in hydration and muscle action. Maintaining a healthy balance of these minerals in the body reduces the risk of muscle cramps.

Healing with Food

Some of the best sources for potassium include potatoes with the skin still on, prunes, and raisins. Lima beans and bananas are good sources as well. If you eat spinach and almonds, you will be getting a little bit of all three nutrients—potassium, magnesium, and calcium.

A spinach salad topped with raisins and almonds provides valuable potassium as well as other nutrients to reduce muscle cramps. If you aren't a fan of prunes because of the texture, try tossing one in your next smoothie just to add sweetness. Lima beans, also a good source of potassium, are a great addition to vegetable soups.

Spinach Salad with Almond Butter Dressing

This salad pairs nutritious spinach with an Asian-inspired dressing. The almonds sprinkled on top add a nice crunch and extra magnesium.

INGREDIENTS + SERVES 4

4 cups spinach, chopped

1 cup bok choy, chopped

1 medium carrot, shredded

¼ cup chopped almonds

¼ cup almond butter

1 tablespoon fresh lime juice

2 tablespoons soy sauce

¼ teaspoon garlic powder

1 teaspoon muscovado sugar

¼ teaspoon crushed red pepper

Olive oil, if needed

2 tablespoons fresh cilantro, chopped

1. Toss the vegetables in a large bowl. Sprinkle the almonds on top.

2. In a small bowl, whisk together the almond butter, lime juice, soy sauce, garlic powder, sugar, and red pepper. If the dressing is too thick, add a teaspoon of olive oil until it reaches desired consistency. Stir in the cilantro.

3. Pour the dressing over the salad and toss to coat evenly. Divide among 4 bowls and serve.

PER SERVING: Calories: 157 | Fat: 12g | Sodium: 499mg | Carbohydrates: 9g | Fiber: 3g | Protein: 5g

HOW A PIONEER STAYS STRONG: Prairie Remedies for Injury and Illness

Healing with Herbs

To fight the pain of most muscle injuries, try these herbal remedies:

+ Arnica (*Arnica montana*): Arnica is a classic remedy for all kinds of aches, including the sports-induced kind. Studies have confirmed its use as a remedy for soft-tissue (i.e., muscle) injuries.
+ Cayenne (*Capsicum annuum, C. frutescens*): These peppers contain a chemical called capsaicin, which can be applied topically to produce a warming sensation and reduce pain (it's the key ingredient in many over-the-counter muscle rubs).
+ Comfrey (*Symphytum officinale*): This herb is used topically to treat all kinds of sports injuries, including injuries to muscles, tendons, and ligaments.
+ Eucalyptus (*Eucalyptus globulus*): The oil from this Australian plant is used topically as an analgesic and anesthetic.
+ Peppermint (*Mentha x piperita*): Peppermint contains menthol, a natural anesthetic and painkiller. Menthol also produces a soothing, cooling sensation.
+ Pineapple (*Ananas comosus*): Pineapple's active constituent, bromelain, can be taken internally to treat a variety of sports injuries and trauma. Studies have shown that it can reduce inflammation, swelling, and bruising.
+ Saint John's wort (*Hypericum perforatum*): This herb produces an oil that's used topically to treat muscle and joint injuries (it's got analgesic, antiedemic, and anesthetic constituents). It also works as an anti-inflammatory and antispasmodic.
+ Yarrow (*Achillea millefolium*): Yarrow relieves pain and swelling and is a classic remedy for swelling, bruising, and muscle soreness.

Stress and Anxiety

Stress is a natural part of life. That's not necessarily a bad thing. Quite often, it's psychological stress that gets you out of bed in the morning or to the gym in the evening. It's what makes you perform well at the office or in the classroom and do basically everything that you need to survive. Unfortunately, too much stress—problems that go on too long or demand too many of your resources—can wreak havoc on your health. Chronic, unresolved stress has been linked to a host of diseases, including cardiovascular disease and cancer. It's also been tied to many mental disorders, such as depression.

According to the National Institutes of Health, low levels of vitamin B_{12} can contribute to feelings of stress and anxiety. Other vitamins play a role in the production and function of neurotransmitters. Some neurotransmitters affect mood, relaxation, and emotions. These include vitamins C, B_6, B_1, B_2, and folate. In addition, the amino acid tryptophan influences the production of serotonin in the brain, which has a calming effect. Low levels of magnesium are also linked to increased and chronic anxiety.

Healing with Food

Papayas, red bell peppers, basil, and arugula are rich in the nutrients that influence the presence and function of neurotransmitters. Poultry, such as chicken or turkey breast, and milk contain both tryptophan and vitamin B_{12}. Bananas also contain tryptophan. Pumpkin seeds, spinach and Swiss chard, and some beans, including black beans and navy beans, contain magnesium.

You can ease stress and anxiety with a simple sandwich that includes chicken or turkey. Bell pepper strips and bananas are ideal for on-the-go snacking, or use your own vegetables and basil for the following de-stressing recipe.

Fresh Red Bell Pepper Dip with Basil

This dip blends sweet red bell pepper, aromatic basil, and tangy yogurt. It is ideal as a dip for vegetables or as a spread for your favorite sandwich.

INGREDIENTS + MAKES ½ CUP

1 red bell pepper, chopped
1 clove garlic
½ cup fresh basil leaves
½ cup plain Greek yogurt

1 tablespoon lemon juice
½ teaspoon salt
¼ teaspoon black pepper

1. Combine the bell pepper, garlic clove, and basil in a small food processor. Pulse until ingredients are almost puréed.

2. Add the yogurt, lemon juice, salt, and pepper. Blend until all of the ingredients come together into a smooth dip. Add more salt and pepper to taste. Refrigerate 30 minutes before serving.

PER 1 TABLESPOON: Calories: 15 | Fat: 1g | Sodium: 153mg | Carbohydrates: 2g | Fiber: 0g | Protein: 1g

Healing with Herbs

Try these other anxiety-busting herbs:

+ Ashwagandha (*Withania somnifera*): Ashwagandha is an Ayurvedic remedy for stress-related anxiety and insomnia. Studies show it inhibits the release of stress hormones and calms the central nervous system.
+ Asian ginseng (*Panax ginseng*): Asian ginseng is one of the best-researched herbs around, and it has been used for centuries to help people manage stress. Recent research has shown it can protect the brain from the damage caused by chronic stress.
+ Ginkgo (*Ginkgo biloba*): Ginkgo is famous for its brain-boosting powers. In the lab, it's shown an ability to offset many effects of stress, such as memory deficits and depression.

+ Lavender (*Lavandula angustifolia*): The essential oil of this fragrant plant has proven antianxiety properties when applied topically or inhaled. In laboratory tests, it performed as well as the drug Valium.
+ Lemon balm (*Melissa officinalis*): This herb relieves stress and induces relaxation. Research shows it can improve your mood, increase your alertness (and mental processing speeds), and produce a general feeling of well-being.
+ Saint John's wort (*Hypericum perforatum*): This herb has been shown to alleviate the cognitive effects of stress, such as lapses in working memory, as well as the decreased physical performance and feelings of anxiety that stress can also produce.
+ Schisandra (*Schisandra chinensis*): This herb balances your nervous and endocrine (hormone) systems and is particularly good at helping you manage psychological stress. Research shows it can increase your mental performance and adjust the levels of the stress hormone cortisol in your system.

Calming Massage Oil

Make this oil with soothing lavender to calm your nerves after a long day on the prairie (or at the office). This infusion contains three tried-and-true herbal relaxants, plus three moisturizing plant oils.

INGREDIENTS

1 part coconut (*Cocos nucifera*) oil
1 part almond (*Prunus dulcis*) oil
1 part cocoa (*Theobroma cacao*) butter
1 part chamomile (*Matricaria recutita*) flowers
1 part lavender (*Lavandula angustifolia*) leaves
1 part lemon balm (*Melissa officinalis*) leaves and flowers

1. Put all the ingredients into the top section of a double boiler, fill the bottom with water, and bring it to a low boil.

2. Let the oil simmer gently for 30 to 60 minutes, checking frequently to make sure the oil isn't overheating (it will start to smoke if that's the case).

3. Allow the oil to cool before use.

CHAPTER 7

HOW A PIONEER CLEANS UP:
An Introduction to Soapmaking

"Better keep yourself clean and bright; you are the window through which you must see the world."

— GEORGE BERNARD SHAW —

THE PRAIRIE WAS A DUSTY PLACE, prone to strong winds that tossed earth around like ocean waves during a high tide. When pioneers came home after a day on the frontier, they would be covered head to toe in grime. Dirt got under their fingernails and inside their ears. They'd find it underneath their clothes no matter how many layers they wore.

So once they were in their house for the night, they'd scour themselves with a bucket of water and a bar of handmade soap.

Made with a caustic solution leached from wood ashes and animal fat, the pioneer soap was often rough and harsh, and it was used to clean everything from overalls to babies. But don't worry, as a Modern-Day Pioneer, your handmade lye soaps bear little resemblance to what a frontier mother may have used to wash out a little boy's mouth as punishment. In this chapter you'll learn the safe way to make gentle soaps using lye and a variety of oils. You'll learn how to create bars that smell sweetly of lavender, exfoliate with oatmeal, and moisturize with shea butter.

SAFETY GEAR

I N A N Y N E W C R A F T I N G E N D E A V O R, taking the time to obtain the proper equipment will make everything else go smoothly. But this is especially important in soapmaking, where you are working with heat and caustic chemicals. The original pioneers were daring, but never careless—you should be the same.

If you fear that you cannot sufficiently control your surroundings to keep and use soapmaking materials safely, do not make soap at home. However, soap is made without accident every day by thousands of Modern-Day Pioneers. By following instructions and using safety gear, you'll be able to relax and enjoy the soapmaking process.

Eye Protection

Make sure that the eye protection you use is resistant to impact, caustics, and heat. If you wear glasses, get goggles that are large enough to wear over them. The danger to your eyes comes from the potential of lye particles, lye solution, raw soap, hot oils, and other liquids splashing you in the face. As long as you work mindfully, you will experience very few—if any—splashing events. However, you do not want to be caught unprotected in the event that one should occur.

Gloves

Regular rubber kitchen gloves provide appropriate protection for your hands and lower arms. Make sure the gloves you buy have textured fingers so that you can keep a firm grip on your equipment. Some soapmakers prefer heavy-duty gloves. Just be sure you can use your fingers freely.

When you are finished with your soapmaking project for the day, clean your gloves well with soap and water. If you clean them and dry them, they'll last quite some time. Turn them inside out to dry and store them only after they're completely dry.

Be sure to protect your arms above the gloves with a long-sleeved shirt. An oversized button-up shirt with sleeves you can roll up is ideal.

Painter's Paper Dust Mask or Filter Mask

Caustic steam will rise when you combine the lye and water. Usually it is enough just to stand back and not breathe the steam, but if you are concerned about sensitivity, take the extra precaution of wearing a painter's paper dust mask or filter mask over your mouth and nose.

Vinegar

Vinegar has traditionally been used as a neutralizer for lye and raw soap spills, but you should not pour vinegar onto an alkaline spill on skin. It would be a good idea to let your doctor know you are making soap, and ask about the best way to handle skin contact with caustics. If you come in contact with lye or raw soap batter, gently wipe the spill from your skin, then flush the area with water. This is when you would douse the area with vinegar if desired. Then flush again with water and finally wash with soap and water. Don't wait to finish stirring your batch before rinsing and neutralizing a smear of raw soap from your skin. Do it as soon as it gets on you.

SOAPMAKING EQUIPMENT

WITH CAREFUL RESEARCH and shopping, you can outfit yourself for soapmaking for far less money than you might think. Use recommended equipment at first, then create your own system variations as you gain experience.

Scale

The best way to measure ingredients for making soap is by weight. Therefore, you will need a good scale. Digital postal scales, available at office supply stores, are the choice for many soapers. They usually run on 9-volt batteries, have the tare feature, weigh in ¼-ounce increments, and have a maximum of ten pounds. This set of specifications is sufficient for most home soapmakers.

Thermometer

You will need an instant-read thermometer. There are many instances in soapmaking where accurate measure of temperature is essential. You may want to get two, in case you need to measure the temperatures of two containers at the same time.

Pots and Pans

When buying your soapmaking pots and pans, stainless steel is the way to go. You can find stainless steel pots and pans at extremely reasonable prices at restaurant supply, warehouse, discount, and thrift stores. You absolutely must not use nonstick, aluminum, cast iron, or tin. These materials are called reactive because they will react with the soaps, ruining both soap and pan. Do not even try "just to see." They will react badly, even violently and toxically, with the lye used in the soapmaking process.

Double Boiler

Double boilers are also used in many kinds of soapmaking. The basic 2-quart, 2-part stainless steel double boiler is perfect for the soap-casting recipes in this book. You can improvise a double boiler using a saucepan and a stainless steel mixing bowl that rests securely but not tightly on the pan. (Always be sure when using any kind of double boiler not to let it boil dry.)

Utensils

Stainless Steel Utensils

Stainless steel stirring spoons, slotted spoons, potato mashers, and ladles are all very useful. You probably already have these in your kitchen, and it is safe to use them for your first few batches. As long as you clean them thoroughly, there is no danger in using them afterward, because the metal does not readily absorb or react with the soap. If you find yourself making a great deal of soap, however, it may be easier to invest in stainless steel tools just for soaping.

PIONEER TIP!

Some stainless steel tools are held together with reactive metal screws, bolts, or brads. You probably won't be able to tell what type of metal the fasteners are, so choose utensils that are all one piece or have "all stainless construction" printed on the package. If you're in doubt, pass it by.

Silicone Utensils

Silicone rubber scrapers, or what many people call "spatulas," are useful tools. Choose a one-piece model so you will never lose the scraper part in a batch of soap.

Measuring Equipment

The small-batch cold-process recipes in this book call for two 4-cup measures: one for mixing the lye solution, and the other for mixing the oils and stirring the soap. The measures are also used in some liquid, melt-and-pour, and hand-milling techniques. They are, of course, always useful for measuring water. It is tempting to use the attractive, thinner heatproof glass, but just stick to the heavy-duty variety as the thin glass will shatter.

Sets of stainless steel measuring cups and spoons are used in nearly all techniques. It's best to steer clear of plastic measuring cups and spoons. While they can be good for some things, they may be corroded by essential oils and fragrance oils or marred by heat.

Soap Molds

Your first batches of soap will very probably be poured into "found" molds. Shoeboxes lined with plastic bags, baby-wipe containers, inexpensive plastic storage containers, and more have all been pressed into service as soap molds. You can use tubes from paper towels or toilet paper rolls. Empty plastic wrap and aluminum foil boxes make small, lidded molds. Beginning soapmakers do not need the latest advance in soap-mold technology. Your mold needs and desires will grow as you gain experience.

If you're using something plastic for a mold, such as a baby-wipe container, be sure to test it for heat resistance. Because of the high temperatures involved in soap-making, you need plastics that will not collapse when exposed to hot soap. The easiest way to check a mold for heat safety is to place it in the sink and fill it with boiling water. If it melts, it is obviously not going to be useful. If it warps and distorts, it is not a good choice either.

You may need some additional supplies to make it easier to get your soap out of their molds. Soapmakers struggle with unmolding all the time. A simple way to ensure ease of release is to line the bottom and sides of the mold. You could brush vegetable oil lightly on the inside of the mold. Then cut plastic sheeting, freezer paper, overhead projector transparencies, or other similar materials to size and press onto the oiled surface. Smooth out bumps and creases in the liner to ensure smooth surfaces on your soap. If all has gone as it should, all you'll have to do is turn the mold over and the beautiful soap will just plop out onto the table. Remove the liner and clean it up for reuse.

Cutting Tools

The simplest soap cutter is a stainless steel table knife. Most soapers prefer nonserrated-edge knives since they make a clean cut. However, soapmakers have adapted all kinds of tools into soap cutters. Dough scrapers borrowed from baking and putty knives and drywall tape spreaders borrowed from home improvement work very well.

TECHNIQUES AND INGREDIENTS FOR YOUR FIRST BATCH OF SOAP

In this book, you will learn how to make soap using the "cold-process." Cold-process soapmaking is the basic form of handmade, from-scratch soapmaking. It is called "cold" process because there is no cooking involved. Beyond heating the oils enough to liquefy them, there is no heat applied during the creation of the soap. You will make luscious, gorgeous, gentle, bubbly soap with a fine texture with this process. The cold-process soapmaking technique is relatively simple and gets easier with practice. In short, a blend of oils is mixed with a simple solution of lye and water, stirred until thickened, then poured into a mold.

The transformation of oils into soap, called saponification, can only happen through the interaction of a lye solution with oils. Used carelessly, lye can cause severe burns and serious injury. It is impossible to overemphasize the necessity of smart safety practices when handling lye, lye solutions, raw, and "young" soap. This chapter describes how to make lye soap safely at home.

Using Lye

All soap is made with a caustic called lye. For the recipes in *The Modern-Day Pioneer* you will use a lye made of sodium hydroxide (chemical formula NaOH), which is used to make solid soap.

Sodium hydroxide is easily available in 18-ounce plastic cans at grocery, hardware, and restaurant supply stores. It is generally stocked alongside the drain cleaners. Do not buy anything other than pure sodium hydroxide. There are other drain cleaners available, but they include substances that are not at all suitable for soapmaking. You may also purchase sodium hydroxide from soapmaking suppliers.

Store your sodium hydroxide in a safe, dry place. The space under the kitchen sink is not a good idea, especially if you have kids. Many home soapers have a "lye safe" just for lye storage. Lye safes can range from a box in the garage clearly marked "Lye! Do Not Touch!" to a metal cabinet with locking doors.

The Modern-Day Pioneer can make a practical and easy-to-create lye safe from a plastic storage box with a tightly fitting lid. Label it clearly and store it where you think it will be safest in your home. Storing your lye safe on a high shelf isn't necessarily recommended, since you can easily drop it, especially if you keep over a few pounds at home. Keeping it on the floor of a closet can work, as can the floor of the garage.

In your lye safe, keep the plastic cans of lye in plastic bags. Label three bags: one for unopened cans, one for partially used cans, and one for empties. Take care how you dispose of empty containers. Neutralize the lye dust by rinsing the containers with a vinegar-and-water solution. If you have a hazardous material drop-off day in your community, take your empty lye cans to the collection point.

In simplest terms, you combine lye, oils, and a liquid to make soap. The liquid may be water, milk, herbal infusions, or any liquid with a relatively neutral pH. Each liquid requires specific soapmaking techniques.

The purpose of liquid in lye soapmaking is to get the lye and the oils together. In solution with water, lye molecules are more easily able to reach the molecules of oil. When they come into contact, the lye and oil molecules all rearrange themselves and become soap and glycerin. If you were to simply add lye to oil, without the liquid, the transformation process would be different and you'd end up with a big, caustic mess.

The amount of lye used in a recipe depends on how much of each oil you use. Each oil has a saponification value. This is the amount of lye it takes to turn one ounce of oil into soap. Soap recipes are calculated to make sure they have the proper balance of oils, water, and lye.

Combining Lye with Water

An important step in soapmaking is combining lye with water. This creates an extremely violent, volatile chemical reaction. It is essential that you add the lye to the water rather than the water to the lye. It releases a great deal of energy in the form of heat immediately upon contact. If you pour cold water on top of lye, you could end up with a volcano-like eruption that would be extremely dangerous. When you add water to lye, the chemical reaction causes the water and lye solution to heat almost immediately to nearly boiling. If water is poured onto the lye, it forms a crust over the top of the lye, which seals in the reaction below. The reaction of the lye and water proceeds normally but in a confined space, causing a buildup of heat energy that eventually bursts open like a bomb, showering the area with dangerously caustic material.

But even when you correctly add lye to water, do so with care. When you add the lye to the liquid, the solution will heat up very fast and will steam. Do not breathe the steam. Usually it is enough just to stand back and not breathe the steam, but if you are concerned about sensitivity to lye steam, wear a painter's paper dust mask or filter mask over your mouth and nose.

When you add water to the caustic, the chemical reaction causes the water and lye solution to heat almost immediately to nearly boiling. This can be alarming, and potentially dangerous, but if you pay attention and use your head, you'll be perfectly safe.

Lye Solution Temperature

The lye-and-water solution will heat up to about 180°F. You need to let the solution cool before combining it with the pre-pared oils. Soapmaking temperatures can range from room temperature (as long as the room is warm enough to keep the oils liquid) to as high as 120°F.

You can take the steaming lye solution outside to let it cool. Just be sure it is in a safe place where no one can get to it and it won't get knocked over. It is also a good idea to cover the container so no leaves or other debris fall into it. The more surface area your lye container has, the faster it will cool. It's better to have an oversized pitcher than one that will be so deeply full that it will take ages to cool. Leaving the lid off the pitcher will help with cooling. You need to be patient and monitor how long it takes so you can plan for the future.

There are some soapmakers who insist that the temperatures of the lye solution and the oil combination must be exactly the same. There are some soapmakers who never even check the temperature. You should start learning your soapmaking techniques by following the temperature guides given in the recipe you are using. After a lot of experience with variations in temperatures, and how those variations affect the process and the product, you can then make your own decisions about how to manage temperature.

Saponification

Saponification is an essential term of soapmaking vocabulary. It means "to turn into soap." The reaction between the lye solution and the oils is called saponification. Saponification starts as soon as the lye solution and oils come into contact. The liquid, such as water or milk, for example, facilitates the reaction by making sure all the various molecules get together.

The saponification process continues until all the lye and the oils have reacted. In cold-process soapmaking, this can take a few weeks or more. As the soap ages, the reaction slows down considerably, and eventually no unreacted alkali remains. "Young" soap will still have some alkalinity, and this level decreases as the soap ages.

Alkalinity, and acidity as well, is measured on the pH scale. This scale is divided into a range of pH measures from 0 to 14. Substances with high pH factors, such as lye, are "alkalis" or "bases," while those with low pH factors, like vinegar, are "acids." Neutrals are found in the middle, around pH 7. Your soap should have a pH between 6 and 10.

A soap is said to be "fully saponified" when there is exactly enough oil and lye to fully react. Since you usually want a little extra oil in your soap, for gentleness and moisturizing benefit, most soaps are formulated with slightly more oil than will completely saponify.

Superfatting

This is also called "lye discount." You may create a gentler soap by calculating a lye discount into your recipe. A lye discount is a reduction from the total amount of lye needed to saponify the oils to a lesser amount. Another way to create a gentler soap is to superfat, by adding extra oils at the end of the stir, before you pour. Overly lye-discounted or superfatted soap is softer and prone to rapid spoilage. However, lye-heavy soap is a worse problem, as it makes harsh, caustic, and unusable soap.

The lye soap recipes you'll find in this chapter are created with a 5- to 7-percent lye discount, and most of them contain one or more superfatting agents. If you want to add more superfatting agents, keep it to 1 tablespoon per pound of oils, or you'll get soap that is soft and spoils more quickly. You may prefer to add the superfatting agent at the beginning and calculate it into the oils when you make your own formulas.

Trace

The term *trace* refers to the presence of traces of the soap mixture on the surface of the mass when some is taken up on your stirrer and dribbled back in. If the dribble makes no mark, your soap has not traced. When it leaves a little lump on the surface that sinks in quickly, that means it's beginning to trace.

A trace state is described from "light" to "heavy." A soap is said to have reached "full" trace when it is at the state desired to do what you need it to do next. When a soap mixture "traces," it has reached a certain level of saponification. You will add color, scent, and other materials at varying levels of trace. As you gain experience, you'll be able to recognize the signs of trace with no problem at all.

FIGURE 7-1: OILS AND LYE JUST COMBINED (NOTE TRANSPARENCY)

Because you'll making 1-pound batches, your initial combination will probably look more like this:

FIGURE 7-2: OILS AND LYE JUST COMBINED IN SMALL CONTAINER

When the oils and lye solution are first mixed, the solution will be transparent, and as you stir, it will become less so. Opacity and a slight graininess let you know that your soap is tracing. There is also a subtle "soap smell" that comes at the same time. It isn't possible to describe it, but you'll come to recognize and be reassured by it.

If you've made gravy or pancake batter, you've experienced the changing texture that many soapers compare to trace. A light trace may be like a thin pancake batter, a medium trace like a medium-thick gravy. If your soap gets gloppy, you've got a heavily traced batch, and you need to get it into its mold as soon as possible.

FIGURE 7-3: SHOWING A MEDIUM TRACE

Trace issues will cease to be issues as you make more and more soap. You must stir your soap to trace before pouring. If your soap hasn't traced, it will likely separate and remain unsaponified in layers of oils and lye solution.

Adding Scent to Your Soap

When you pick up a bar of soap, the first thing you probably do is hold it to your nose and sniff. The packaging, color, and other visuals may attract you, but it's likely the scent that captures or repels you. Some people choose unscented products all or some of the time. Two of the easiest ways to scent your soap is to add essential oils or fragrance oils. When you create blends using both essential oils and fragrance oils, you need to be sure you use the proper measurements for each. Fragrance oil usage is usually about one-third the rate of essential oils. Not all fragrance oils are the same, so be sure you get the manufacturer's or distributor's rate of use for each oil you use.

Fragrance Oils

There are many sources of fragrance oils. For the purpose of soapmaking, a fragrance must be "soap safe." A soap-safe fragrance oil is formulated to react well with the various soapmaking processes. A fragrance that isn't soap safe for lye soapmaking can cause a soap batch to seize— become clumpy and hard as soon as it is added. It can also make soap separate, curdle, discolor, or streak. The scents may fade or mutate, making them unsuitable for soapmaking. Fragrance oils that are designed for use in cold-process soap hold up beautifully through the soapmaking process. It is important that you use "soap safe" fragrance oils. These oils have been tested and selected by suppliers.

Essential Oils

In the study of soapmaking, one of the most interesting topics is essential oils. Unlike fragrance oils, which are mainly synthetic, essential oils are the natural oils from plants. Like fragrance oils, essential oils contribute fragrance to your soap formulas, but they may also have the benefit of aromatherapy, offering health benefits. In order to enjoy the delights of essential oils, you must add a relatively large amount to the cold-process soap batter. The general usage rate is approximately ½ ounce of essential oils per 1 pound of base oils. This varies when using absolutes, concretes, and resins.

Both fragrance oils and essential oils are stirred into the soap batter after it has traced, before pouring it into your mold.

Unmolding

In cold-process soapmaking, you need a recipe that creates a hard, releasable soap.

The soap goes through a "gel" phase during its insulation time. The heat generated by the soap mass inside the towel-wrapped, insulated mold will be enough for the soap to get through that phase.

Curing

Curing refers to the period after cutting during which the soap becomes milder and harder, milder as saponification finishes and harder as water evaporates. You can extend the life of your soap through careful formulation and storage. Over time, exposure to heat and humidity can degrade the quality of your soaps. Soap that sits in water or is allowed to be in the stream of the shower will melt away rapidly, so dry it between uses.

After cutting and while curing, soap needs to be kept at a relatively constant temperature and have air circulation. Depending on the amount of soap you make, you can dry your soap on a paper-covered cookie sheet or a small shelf, or create an entire curing and drying rack system. However you choose to cure it, be sure to turn it every few days during the first couple of weeks so that it will cure evenly.

Lye Safety During Curing

Lye soap is made at home all the time in complete safety. But your safety depends on the use of common sense. If you plan well, everything will go smoothly. The more soap you make, the more you will tailor your safety practices to your situation. Safety essentials are goggles and rubber gloves.

As mentioned earlier, lye is extremely caustic. When you first add the lye to the liquid, the resulting solution is also extremely caustic. After this lye solution is mixed with the soapmaking oils, however, the soap begins to neutralize and becomes safe to touch after it has cured. Always wear goggles and rubber gloves when handling lye, lye solutions, raw soap, and fresh soap. If you are in doubt about how neutralized your soap is, err on the side of wearing goggles and gloves even when they're not needed.

Testing for Neutrality

You can test for neutrality of soap in a number of ways. Using phenolphthalein or litmus papers is the most popular. Phenolphthalein is very reliable, inexpensive, and easy to use. You simply place a couple of drops of the solution on the soap you are testing. If the solution turns pink, it is alkaline. If it stays clear, it is neutral.

You can purchase litmus kits online and at your garden center. Follow the directions on the kit. Often it involves a color comparison chart on the box. You can also purchase an electronic pH meter. Soap is "safe" when it registers between 6 and 10 on the pH scale.

Caustic Messes

While your soap is curing, test it every so often for neutrality. If your soap is more than two weeks old and is still highly caustic, something went wrong in the measurements. The soap should not be used. Find out from your city or county what the proper disposal method is for caustic materials.

Keep a caustic mess contained until you can dispose of it properly. Line a heavy cardboard box with two heavy plastic garbage bags, one inside the other. Fill the box with clay kitty litter deep enough to absorb the mass. Wearing goggles and gloves, pour or scrape the caustic mass into the bags. Add an equal measure of vinegar. If the mass is soupy, add more litter. Label the box and store it in a safe place until you dispose of it.

Evaporation During Curing

Part of the curing process involves the evaporation of extra water from the bars. Ideally, there should be just enough liquid in the batch to ensure success of the reaction of lye with oils. A 4-ounce bar will lose approximately ¼ to ½ ounce of water this way. The bar will shrink a little from its original dimension, but it will stay essentially the same.

Soap Ash

It is very common to find a thin layer of white powder on the top of your batch of soap. This is called "ash," and it is harmless. It is essentially the minerals from the water that have collected on the surface.

Using purified water is the main way to limit the formation of ash. But even soap made with distilled water will sometimes have a layer of ash. It can be because of the composition of the lye or the way the ingredients work together; sometimes there is no identifiable reason.

Placing plastic wrap on the surface of your poured soap is one way to eliminate the ash layer. Try to let the wrap cling to the surface on its own, rather than pressing, as you can add lumps and bumps to the surface if you push down too far. Peel it away when you are ready to unmold.

You can also remove the ash layer by hand. When you cut your bars, you can use a cheese planer to cut away the ash. Some soapers set up their cutters to take off the layer during the cutting process. Or you can just leave it. It isn't harmful, and it is an indication that the soap was made by hand. It is ultimately an aesthetic choice.

PIONEER TIP!

If your soap has a crust of lye crystals, that is not ash. It is still caustic and you must handle it wearing goggles and gloves. You may have added too much lye or stirred improperly, or the lye crystals may be the result of any number of other factors. The soap is probably lye-heavy and will never cure properly.

Cleaning Up

One of the many wonderful things about soapmaking is that in many instances, it is a self-cleaning endeavor. After all, it's soap!

Make sure you don't rinse large blobs of gooey soap, either finished or unsaponified, down your drains. They will clog up your drains almost immediately and take a lot of effort to clean out. Your best bet is to use smart cleanup techniques.

Since the soap is caustic all the way through the process and for a few weeks after, always wear goggles and gloves while handling it. Keep track of all the utensils and equipment that you've used with the lye.

After you're finished with a lye-touched tool, place it in the sink. If you add water, be sure not to hit it with a hard stream that will splatter. Keep adding the utensils as you finish, pouring vinegar on them as you go.

After you've scraped the last of the beautiful soap batter into the mold, wipe the inside of the pan and any other tools you've used. You can use paper towels, but you'll go through a lot of them. A better idea is to get towels out of the rag bag and tear them into paper towel–sized soap cleanup towels.

You can use your soap cleanup towels over and over, saving money and resources. Place the towels in a plastic bag for a day or two, then add them to the wash. The soap will have saponified enough for laundry use and will contribute to the cleansing.

> ### PIONEER TIP!
>
> It is a good idea to clean up as you go. With lye soaps, use the kitchen sink to corral the lye-touched objects as you finish with them. Rinse the lye pouring pitcher with water and a splash of vinegar, then fill it partway with water and more vinegar so you can place the other things in a neutralizing bath.

BASIC RECIPE

AS A BURGEONING SOAPMAKING and Modern-Day Pioneer, you will find yourself always looking for ways to make better soap. The "rules" of soapmaking are different for each soapmaker. As you gain experience with materials, processes, and procedures, you will find ways to customize the basics to suit your own style (always keeping safety in mind). However, all journeys begin with the first step. Your first soapmaking experience should follow a simple, no-frills recipe.

For your first cold-process batch, here is an excellent 1-pound recipe. It will produce an unscented, uncolored soap. You should become familiar with this process before moving on to the scented, fancier soap recipes that follow. You will notice that the total weight comes to 24 ounces. It is called a 1-pound recipe because you are using 1 pound of oil.

For this batch, use two 4-cup glass measuring cups to make the lye solution, heat the oils, and blend the soap. Note that even when you're using measuring cups for mixing, you must always weigh your ingredients. You'll use the first for the lye solution, and the second for the oil mixture.

Remember to keep careful records of each batch of soap you make. This will help you keep track of what recipes you've used and where you are in your schedule for each batch. Later, when you explore variations on the basic recipes, taking thorough notes will help you keep track of what is working and what is not.

PIONEER TIP!

Remember: In soapmaking, all of the liquids are weighed on a scale, not measured in a liquid measure.

Basic Cold-Process Soap, 1-Pound Recipe

INGREDIENTS

Lye Solution
6 ounces water
2.25 ounces lye
Base Oils
10 ounces olive oil
6 ounces coconut oil
Superfat
1 tablespoon castor oil

1. Put on all protective gear, including goggles, gloves, and long sleeves.

2. Place the water in a heatproof glass 4-cup measure. Sprinkle the lye slowly and carefully into the water. Stir until dissolved. Set the lye solution aside to cool.

3. Combine the olive oil, coconut oil, and castor oil in a second heatproof glass 4-cup measure. Melt in microwave or over boiling water. Coconut oil has a low melting point, so it will melt quickly from an opaque white solid to a clear liquid. As each setup is different, be sure to watch your microwave or double boiler closely, and make note of how long it takes. (Do not overheat, as oils take longer to cool than the lye solution does.) Set the oils aside to cool.

4. When both mixtures are at 110°F, pour the lye solution in a thin stream into the oils. Stir constantly until the mixture traces, about 10 to 20 minutes. If using an immersion blender, it will take about a minute. With an immersion blender, take care not to whip air into the mixture.

5. Note that this is where you will add the essential or fragrance oils for the more advanced recipes. Blend thoroughly.

6. Once the soap batter traces and you have mixed in the essential oils (if necessary), pour it into the mold, taking care to scrape all the traced soap out of the cup.

7. Cover the mold with plastic wrap, then wrap the mold in a towel for warmth and let it sit for two days.

8. Wearing your goggles and gloves, try unmolding the soap by pulling out the sides and turning the mold upside down on a brown paper bag or paper towel on the work surface. Push on the bottom of the mold. If the soap does not release readily, place the mold in the freezer for one hour. Try again to remove it. It should release easily this time.

9. Using a stainless steel knife, cut the soap log into bars. Place them on a brown paper bag to dry. Turn them daily to make sure they dry evenly.

10. In four weeks, your soap will be mild and quite firm and ready to use.

11. Store soap in a ventilated container.

This is your first batch of cold-processed lye soap! Congratulations! When you take it to the tub or shower, observe the smell, texture, lather, and rinsability. Although every bath with your own soap is a learning experience, be sure to take time for taking simple delight in what you've created.

SOAP VARIATIONS

Once you've mastered the basics of the cold-process method of soap-making, you are ready to experiment and expand your repertoire. Using the following recipes, you'll be able to make two all-time soap favorites: oatmeal and lavender. These soap recipes use fragrance oils or essential oils and have basic additives. Use the suggested amounts of additives as a guide to making your own simple recipes.

Oatmeal Soap, 1-Pound Recipe

INGREDIENTS

Lye Solution
6 ounces water
2 ounces lye
Base Oils
1 pound olive oil
Superfat
1 tablespoon castor oil
Additive
1 tablespoon finely ground oatmeal

Scent Material
1 teaspoon combination of oatmeal, oatmeal milk, and honey fragrance oil

1. Finely grind the oatmeal to release the skin-soothing properties for which oatmeal is so famous. If you want the look of the whole rolled-oat grain, use it sparingly since it can have sharp edges. Many soapers use baby oatmeal because it has a softer feel.

2. You can make "oat milk" by making an infusion of oatmeal and hot water. Add honey fragrance oil to the mixture.

3. Follow the directions for the procedure for the previous Basic Cold-Process Soap, 1-Pound Recipe using the Oatmeal Soap ingredients.

4. Once the soap batter traces, mix in the 1 tablespoon of finely ground oatmeal and 1 teaspoon of your infusion of oatmeal, oatmeal milk, and honey fragrance oil.

5. Finish the soapmaking process according to the Basic Cold-Process Soap, 1-Pound Recipe.

Lavender Soap, 1-Pound Recipe

Lavender essential oil has a clear to light green color and an herbal, sweetly floral smell.

INGREDIENTS

Lye Solution
6 ounces water
2 ounces lye
Base Oils
1 pound olive oil
Superfat
1 tablespoon castor oil
Scent Material
1 tablespoon lavender essential oil

1. Follow the directions for the procedure for the previous Basic Cold-Process Soap, 1-Pound Recipe using the Lavender Soap ingredients.

2. Once the soap batter traces, mix in the 1 tablespoon of lavender essential oil.

3. Finish the soapmaking process according to the Basic Cold-Process Soap, 1-Pound Recipe.

Shea Butter Combo, 1-Pound Recipe

INGREDIENTS

Lye Solution
6 ounces water
2.4 ounces lye
Oil Blend
2 ounces shea butter
4 ounces almond oil
5 ounces olive oil
5 ounces coconut oil
Superfat
1 tablespoon castor oil

Follow the directions for the procedure for the previous Basic Cold-Process Soap, 1-Pound Recipe using the Shea Butter Combo ingredients.

CHAPTER 8

HOW A PIONEER LIGHTS THE WAY:
An Introduction to Candlemaking

"Man loves company—even if it is only that of a small burning candle."

— GEORG C. LICHTENBERG —

Without cities, streetlights, or car headlights, frontier nights were dark. There was nothing to light the way but the moon. All year, the pioneers squirreled away the tallow they needed. And each fall they would set to work making candles, enough to last through the entire dark winter season. That way, on a moonless or cloudy night, the pioneers could see a candle flickering in their window, and know that they were close to home.

Today, we still associate the warmth of candlelight with peace and comfort. Even with the invention of the light bulb, we still crave the coziness of votives and tealights. Perhaps that is because a candle produces fire as well as light, and fire is essential to human life. After all, a light bulb is merely a fire trying to burn in a vacuum. But a candle offers the real thing: fire you can see, heat you can feel, aromas to smell. In this chapter, you will learn how to roll and pour your own candles, becoming a part of this splendid tradition.

TYPES OF CANDLES

BEFORE YOU DELVE into candlemaking, it will be useful to have a background in the different types of candles available. The kind of candle you'll want to make will differ depending on your need. The kind of candle you'd want to craft as the centerpiece for a dinner party is very different from the candles you may keep on hand in case of a blackout.

+ **Container**—A container candle is set in the shape of the mold in which it is made by pouring.
+ **Pillar**—A popular candle shape, the pillar is a thick candle (usually 3 to 4 inches in diameter). If the pillar is 3 inches in diameter and 6 inches tall, it is called a "three by six," and so on. Most pillars are cylindrical, but they can be made in any shape—oval, hexagonal, square, etc. Commercial pillar candles come in standard sizes, but you can make a pillar candle any size or shape you choose.

+ **Tapers**—As the name implies, these are tapered candles that most of us think of first when we think "candle." The most common candle shape—often found on the dinner table during festivities—tapers are expressly made to fit into a candleholder of some sort, whether for a single candle or for multiple candles.
+ **Tealight**—Tealights are similar to votives, but they are much smaller, flat cylinders usually only ½ inch high and 1½ inches in diameter.
+ **Votive**—The term *votive* comes from the Latin for "to vow"; votive candles were originally used in church to light in front of an icon or a sculpture of a saint while asking for intercession. In recent years, this type of candle has become very popular to be lit at home as well, especially as scented candles of different colors. Votives are usually cylinders 2 to 3 inches high, ordinarily 1½ inches in diameter.

WAX

WHEN ONE THINKS OF making candles, the first thing that comes to mind is wax. Although in times past candles were made of tallow (animal fat), those days are long gone. As a Modern-Day Pioneer, you will likely rely on wax or wax with additives for your home candlemaking. Wax, put simply, is what your candle burns for fuel. As the wick burns, the candle wax melts and is "wicked" into the flame to feed its fire. Most candles these days are made of beeswax or paraffin, or a combination of the two.

Beeswax

Beeswax is the most elegant of the waxes available for candlemaking. Just as silkworms are famous for making fine silk, bees make excellent wax. The bees are essential to life's natural processes, for they pollinate plants, including those that provide us with food.

Beeswax, because it is permeated with honey during its preharvest life, naturally has a wonderful, sweet fragrance. Its odor will vary depending on what the bees are feeding on—which might be wildflowers, clover, avocados, or various herbs. Unrefined beeswax in the natural state has a golden yellow to brownish or reddish-brown color. It also contains plant parts and bits of the bees themselves.

Harvesting and purifying pure beeswax is a time-consuming, difficult process, so it is not surprising that beeswax is far more expensive than paraffin. However, one of its advantages is that it is long-lasting. Beeswax is also very lovely when it burns: It creates a warm, golden glow that nothing else can match, and the sweet honeyed smell permeates the house and people's hair and garments. However, for budgetary purposes, beeswax can be combined with paraffin to make candles that will be long-lasting yet less expensive.

Sheets of beeswax were originally invented by beekeepers. These were, and still are, used (in their natural color only) to line the beehives. This wax liner gives the bees a firm foundation on which to build the honeycomb. Thus, the beekeepers call beeswax sheets "brood foundation." Beeswax candles can be made from foundation sheets. If you have taken to heart the beekeeping advice in Chapter 1, "How a Pioneer Tends," you might obtain beeswax that way.

Paraffin

Since pure beeswax is a rare commodity and so expensive, most beeswax candles you'll find today are mixed with paraffin, a byproduct of the refining process that turns crude oil into motor oil.

Paraffin waxes used for candlemaking are classified by their melting points: low, medium, and high. In general, most homemade candles need to be melted to 125°F to 150°F.

Never buy grocery-store paraffin to use in candlemaking—it is not the same as paraffin wax used to make candles. It has a lower melting point and does not harden sufficiently to make a candle stand up straight.

Some paraffin wax comes with stearin already mixed in, usually 10 percent. Alternatively, you can buy stearin separately and mix it into the paraffin to suit your needs. Stearin, or stearic acid, is added to paraffin to make it harder and to increase opacity.

Although it is possible to make candles from paraffin wax alone, there are definite advantages to adding stearin to paraffin. Here's why:

+ Stearin makes candles easier to remove from their molds because they contract more during the cooling process when stearin has been added to the wax.
+ Candles made with stearin have a longer burn time.
+ Paraffin is translucent and can be dull-looking. Adding stearin makes the candle opaque and much whiter, giving a nicer appearance.

If you are using stearin, check the label on the package. The supplier's information will make clear exactly how to use it and in what proportion.

You can buy paraffin wax in pellets or powered form, which is easier to measure or weigh, and easier to handle. However, bulk is cheaper. Bulk paraffin is normally sold by suppliers and craft shops in 11-pound slabs; the next standard size up is a 55-pound case. The best way to break up the 11-pound slabs is to put one into a heavy-duty disposable trash bag and drop it from shoulder height to the floor.

Recycled Wax

You can save money and help protect the environment by recycling old wax, including cheese coverings, crayons, and sealing wax. Save all your candle ends, as well as any scraps left over from making candles, and store them either in zippered plastic bags (away from heat) or in an airtight tin such as the type in which Christmas cookies are sold. Also, chip, scrape, or melt the dregs of votive cups and save them as well. And, of course, any failed homemade candles with which you weren't satisfied can be reused to make new, successful candles. You can remelt everything (keeping colors separate, if necessary). Strain melted candle ends through a fine sieve or cheesecloth to remove burned bits. Use a hammer to break up large chunks of recycled wax into smaller pieces for remelting. Be sure to save all of the wax that gets spilled during your candlemaking efforts—a putty knife kept handy is a good tool for scraping up spills.

Keep in mind when using colorful wax that some shades lend themselves to reuse more easily than others. Pink can be turned to rose or red, lavender or purple. On the other hand, five pounds of blazingly bright magenta isn't what you'd call versatile. Of course, if your leftover wax is white, you are home free.

You can separate your candle scraps by color if you like, or throw the whole bunch in together—if you are in the mood to experiment, melting different candle colors together can be the way to go. A yellow cheese coating mixed with a green deodorant candle might give you a nice lime color.

PIONEER TIP!

Red seems to be the most powerful—and it can be overpowering—of dyes. Recycled blends of used colors of wax (candle ends, leftovers) that have red in them will ordinarily turn out with a reddish cast, even if red is not the largest proportion of color in your mixture.

WICKS

If the first component of a candle is wax, it follows that the next is the wick. Indeed, the wick is the heart of the candle, not only in that it lies at the center but also in that it is what determines if a candle will burn, and how well it will do so. Today's wick is a braided or cored bunch of threads, usually made of cotton but sometimes of linen or other fabric. The material is then subjected to a process known as "mordanting," where it is pickled in a chemical solution that is intended to make it fire-retardant.

Candlemaking suppliers sell packaged wicks to those who choose to make their own candles. These prepackaged wicks are ordinarily classified by the diameter of the candle with which they should be used:

+ 0–1" = extra small
+ 1–2" = small
+ 2–3" = large
+ 4" or greater = extra large

There are two basic kinds of modern wicks, cored and braided. Cored wicks are woven around a central core made up of paper, cotton, zinc, or lead. This helps them to stand upright.

Braided wicks come in a flat type and a square-braided type, in a full range of sizes. The flat-braided type is just like a braid of hair: a three-strand braid made of many tiny threads. Flat-braided wicks are sized according to the number of these small threads, called "plies," in each wick.

Square-braided wicks look like square columns with rounded corners. They are available in various sizes and are classified according to different numbering systems.

Wick Priming

Prior to use, all wicks need to be primed. This is a process that saturates the wick with wax in advance of its being placed in the candle mold, or dipped. Priming is done to eliminate air that may have become trapped in the plies of the braid.

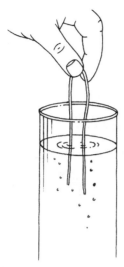

FIGURE 8-1: PRIMING THE WICK

2. Dip the length of wick into the wax. Air bubbles will form as the air escapes. Continue to hold the wick in the wax until you don't see any more air bubbles (this usually takes about five minutes).

3. Once the wax no longer bubbles, remove the wick from the pot of wax and stretch it out. Allow it to cool thoroughly.

4. When completely dry, the wick should be stiff. At this point, it is ready to use.

Usually, when you pour the wax over the wick, or dip the wick, the air is forced out naturally. However, this can't be relied on, and so it's best to prime the wick before use. This is especially important for the poured container candles you'll learn to make later on in this chapter.

To prime a wick, follow these steps:

1. Heat some wax to 160°F (using your thermometer to check the temperature).

Always trim the wick to within ½" of the wax surface before lighting the candle. For larger candles, especially pillars, allow the candle to burn at least two hours before extinguishing to distribute the liquid wax evenly. Don't burn large diameter candles for longer than three hours at a time. Otherwise you risk destabilizing the candle.

CANDLEMAKING EQUIPMENT

I N ADDITION TO WAX AND WICKS, making candles at home requires some basic equipment, most of which is neither expensive nor complicated. As a Modern-Day Pioneer, your kitchen and household probably already contains most of the bare essentials.

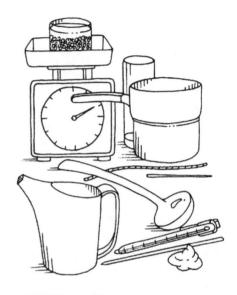

FIGURE 8-2: CANDLEMAKING EQUIPMENT

PIONEER TIP!

If you choose to use any of your cooking implements and/or pots for making candles at home, dedicate any and all candlemaking equipment to that end only. Not only will you avoid confusion, but you will also keep your food safe from contamination from wax, additives, dyes, and the like.

Thermometer

As in so many other Modern-Day Pioneer activities, your thermometer is vital. You can buy a special wax thermometer or use a candy or other cooking thermometer that covers a scale from 0°F to 300°F. It should have a clip so that you can immerse it deep enough into your pot of melting wax to get an accurate reading.

Make sure your thermometer is accurate. You must always know the precise degree to which your wax has been heated. Check your thermometer regularly and discontinue use if it is no longer accurate.

Double Boilers

Obviously, a system for melting wax is the primary consideration in candlemaking. For the novice candlemaker, the best melting method is the double boiler. Double boilers are extremely easy to improvise. You need only an outer pot to hold water and an inner pot in which to melt the wax. The outer pot must be large enough to hold an amount of water sufficient to rise two-thirds of the way up the inner pot. For the poured candles in this book, you can use a shallow round pot, big enough to melt as much wax as you will need. You can put one saucepan over another, or rest a fireproof bowl on a saucepan, but your wax may melt unevenly. Ideally, the inner pot will have a handle (a metal pitcher is excellent). A large can, such as the kind fruit juice is sold in, will work if you are willing to ladle out the wax. You can pour from such a can if you use mitts to protect your hands from the heat and are very careful.

If you improvise your double boiler, you will need a support for the inner pot, such as a metal trivet (the kind used on the dinner table to protect it from a hot dish). A support can be improvised as well, for instance by using three short cans (tuna fish or cat food cans will do). Cut out both ends and wire them together to make a three-pointed support. Or, cut out one end only and fill them with water so they don't float.

PIONEER TIP!

Never put your wax-melting container directly on the heat source. And keep a careful watch on the water level in your outer pot. *Never* let it boil dry. Add water frequently while melting wax.

You can also buy ready-made double boilers of many sizes. Cast aluminum and stainless steel double boilers for cooking are readily available wherever cookware is sold.

Whichever kind of double boiler you use, you will need to replenish the water in the bottom pot frequently in order to keep your boiling water at the correct level. Your working surface must be level and have ready access to a water supply. You also need a heat source that is not an open flame. Your electric stove will work fine; a steady hot plate will suffice as well. Clean your melting vessel with paper towels after each use.

Miscellaneous Equipment

There is more to candlemaking than melted wax and wicks. Depending on what kind of candle you make and which method you use, there are many supplies that will be necessary. These ancillary but necessary items are listed more or less in the order of importance, though all will eventually prove useful as you continue to expand your efforts. This list is not necessarily all-inclusive—you may think of other tools or implements that will be useful. Like the original pioneers, you must be innovative and resourceful.

Cake Pans and Cookie Sheets

Cake pans and cookie sheets are multipurpose. You can line them with nonstick pan spray or vegetable oil and pour unused melted wax to cool. They are also useful as pads for containers of hot wax.

Scale

A scale is an important piece of equipment as well, one you can't do without. Chances are you already have a kitchen scale that will do. It should have a range of 0 to 10 pounds, in ounces. You can use a gram scale. If you do, however, you will need to convert between grams and ounces and pounds. A scale is necessary for weighing not only wax but also additives such as stearic acid.

Pyrex Measuring Cups

These come in 1-cup, 2-cup, 4-cup, and 6-cup sizes, and are heat resistant. You can use the cups to determine the volume of wax by displacement. Put wax in one cup in a block or chunks; then put water in the second cup and note the amount it takes to fully submerge the wax in the first cup. Subtract the volume of water added from the level of water needed to cover the wax. The result is the volume of wax you have just measured. Since Pyrex measuring cups can be heated, you can also use such a measuring cup (or any heatproof calibrated vessel, such as a flask used in chemistry) as a wax melting insert when melting small amounts of wax in an improvised double boiler.

Oven Mitts and Potholders

Oven mitts or potholders are essential when it comes to protecting your hands when you handle a pot of hot wax.

Metal Ruler or Straightedge

An artist's T-square is good, as are the heavy metal rulers they use. It's even a good idea to have both—for cutting and for calibrating lengths of vessels, candles, and wicks. These tools are available at art supply shops, which often also sell craft materials. You can use the straightedge to cut sheet wax for the rolled candles you'll learn about later in this chapter.

Cutting Surface

A cutting surface can be a laminated kitchen counter that can't be cut-marked or a wooden or plastic cutting board such as those used for chopping food. You can even use a piece of heavy cardboard.

Cutting Tools

For cutting tools, X-Acto knifes work well. The blades are extremely sharp and run cleanly along a straight edge. Your cutting tool is for cutting sheets of wax for rolled and stacked candles and for trimming the seams of finished molded candles. Scissors are also useful, especially for cutting wicks.

Stirrers

If you are adding stearin to paraffin wax, you'll need to mix it in as it's melting. Practically any old thing will do for stirring the melted wax, but old long-handled wooden spoons are ideal. If you don't have any, chances are you can pick up some cheaply at a garage or yard sale, or at a flea market. Another handy stirrer can be had for free at your paint store. Paint stirrers are flat paddles given away with the purchase of paint, and paint store salespeople are usually happy to give you a few extra because they are imprinted with advertising for the brand of paint and/or the store. So when you have an occasion to buy paint, ask for extra stirrers and stash them away.

Ladle

You might also need a ladle—choose one impervious to heat, with a deep bowl and a comfortably angled handle to avoid spilling.

Greaseproof Paper and Paper Towels

This includes waxed paper, parchment, brown craft paper (or brown paper bags flattened out), and foil. Keep a good supply on hand to cover work surfaces. And don't forget about paper towels—they are essential for cleanups, to use as oil wipes, to mop up water spills, and many other chores.

Dowels

When making the container candles later in this chapter, you'll need a straight rod of some kind to tie the wick to while you pour wax around it. Your dowel can be a chopstick or a piece of cardboard, anything that will support the weight of the wick.

Wick Sustainers

These are little metal disks that are used to anchor the wick in container candles, votives, and tealights. Wick sustainers are available wherever candlemaking supplies are sold. To use, you push the wick through a small hole in the sustainer and pinch the metal together so that it sits flat on the container base.

Paint Scraper

A paint scraper is excellent for easily scraping spilled wax off a hard surface, such as a counter. You might also use a putty knife.

Weights

Small weights with a center hole are required to weigh down wicks. Washers, curtain weights, and nuts will all do.

SAFETY TIPS FOR CANDLEMAKING

BEFORE YOU BEGIN TO WORK with wax, it must be heated to its particular melting point. Take care not to overheat your wax. The "burning point" of wax is that temperature at which the properties of the particular wax have been stretched beyond the safety mark. For example, paraffin should not usually be heated hotter than 200°F. Never leave melting wax on the heat source unattended—it is as volatile as cooking oil and can catch fire if overheated. Always keep a large pot lid handy to smother a fire, should one start. Also keep damp cloths handy for the same purpose.

Waxes are highly flammable (that's why candles burn!) and can catch fire. The temperature at which they will combust is the "flash point." This is approximately 440°F, depending on the type of wax you use. *Never* heat wax to the flash point. Watch your thermometer carefully.

If your wax does catch fire, stay calm and do the following:

+ Turn off heat immediately. Do not move the pan.
+ Smother flames with a metal lid or damp towel.
+ Never use water to put out a wax fire.

It is also smart to have an ABC-type fire extinguisher on hand, as well as baking soda (dumped into a fire it will smother the flames immediately).

PIONEER TIP!

Always remember that the wax you are pouring is hot, and that it can burn you if spilled on your skin. Don't pour when you are feeling jittery or are distracted. Teach yourself to pour in a smooth steady stream by practicing with water, using the vessel in which you plan to melt the wax.

CLEANUP TIPS FOR CANDLEMAKING

ALWAYS COVER YOUR WORK SURFACE with disposable paper. Don't use old newspapers to cover working surfaces as the newsprint may transfer to the under-surface if wax spills on it. Use brown wrapping paper or tin foil (use foil on your stove) to facilitate cleanup. Or, if you can devote an entire countertop to your candle-making, get a laminated one with a smooth surface from which you can easily scrape up cooled wax.

After each candlemaking session, be sure to clean up your workspace—especially if it's in your kitchen. Then you won't have to clean up before you start another candle-making session. Gather all your tools and materials—knives, scrapers, wicks, colorants, scent bottles, etc.—wipe or scrape any waxy residue, and store them in the place you regularly keep them. Always keep rags and paper towels handy. Use them to wipe any waxy surfaces while they are still warm. After you have cleaned up all waxy containers and surfaces, dispose of the paper towels or rags. Do *not* inciner-ate them.

Don't ever pour liquid wax down your drain. It will solidify and cause severe blockage—not to mention a huge plumb-ing bill. Also, don't pour your hot double boiler water down your drain. It may have wax in it unbeknownst to you. Dispose of the water outside. Or, let it cool until the wax hardens and then remove the wax before pouring the water down the drain.

Pour leftover melted wax into muffin tins or other small cups. Once it's cooled you can then pop out the hardened wax and store it in plastic bags for future use. Don't throw away your leftovers, even the small scraps, including candle ends or the bottoms of container candles. Wax costs money. Recycling saves money and work.

HANDMADE ROLLED CANDLES

ROLLED CANDLES are made from sheets of wax, and as the name implies, the wax is rolled around a wick, much as you would roll a sheet of dough around a filling to make jelly rolls. This is the simplest method of making candles. It's easiest for the beginner—and a good introduction into the world of candlemaking.

Wax sheets specially made for rolling are available at craft shops and from candlemaking suppliers and they come in dozens of lovely colors (although later in this chapter you will learn how to make your own).

There are two types of commercially prepared wax sheets for making rolled candles. The majority are made of pure beeswax, which, although more expensive, are longer burning than paraffin or paraffin with stearic acid. The second type of sheet wax is a mixture of beeswax and paraffin, which is less expensive than pure beeswax. Also available, though in shorter supply, are sheets of paraffin without beeswax. These are the least expensive of all, but have the disadvantage of a much shorter burn time.

Most wax sheets for rolled candles are formed in a honeycomb pattern. This type of sheet is embossed with a hexagonal indentation—it looks like the wax from a honeycomb. The most common size is 8" × 16", but you can cut the sheets to suit your specific purpose. The honeycomb-patterned sheets are rolled out under an embossing wheel. You can purchase these in the natural beeswax colors (pale honey to dark brown), or you can purchase them in various colors that have been dyed after the wax was bleached.

Another type of wax for making rolled candles is smooth and flat. These are useful when you don't want a textured candle. The pure-white smooth sheets make an elegant-looking candle that gives a stylish appearance.

Keeping Your Sheets Warm

Sheets of beeswax bought preformed in a honeycomb pattern are ready for use. However, they need to be warm enough to be pliable before you start to roll. A blow-dryer is a handy tool to keep on hand for warming sheets of wax. Beeswax is the easiest to work with because of its natural flexibility.

Paraffin or beeswax/paraffin blend wax sheets are used in the same manner, but paraffin tends to be brittle. Therefore, a blend or straight paraffin will be a bit more difficult to handle, requiring extra attention in order to keep the sheets warm enough to be pliable. If your wax sheets have become cold and aren't pliable enough to roll, you can do several things:

+ Using your blow-dryer, waft warm air over the sheets of wax.
+ Iron them with a warm iron between sheets of paper.
+ Quickly dip the sheets into hot water.

Making Your Own Wax Sheets

Although using purchased wax sheets is the easiest way to make rolled candles, if you are adventuresome—and if you have some leftover wax you want to make use of—you can make your own wax sheets.

You'll need:

+ A piece of plywood the size of the sheet you want.
+ A large, deep pot for melting the wax.
+ A deep steamer of the type used for asparagus or corn will work, as will a deep stockpot.

To prepare the plywood, soak it in water for 1 hour or more (to prevent it from absorbing the hot wax). Dip the plywood into the melted wax, using tongs or pliers to hold it firmly. Allow the wax-covered plywood to cool for about a minute. Dip the wax-covered board into the wax again, and again allow it to cool. Repeat this process five or more times depending on the thickness of the wax sheet you want. Scrape the wax at the edges of the board, then peel off the sheet.

Homemade wax sheets lend themselves to various uses. Although purchased sheets come in various colors, you can tint your own wax sheets any color you like, or make multicolored layers for an interesting effect.

What's nice about homemade sheet wax is that you don't have to warm it up before using it. It will be warm when you remove it from the board. While it is still warm, you can form it into different shapes as you roll it.

Should the wax cool too much, just drop it into hot water (100°F to 110°F) for a minute or two to soften it again. Keep a pot of warm water at hand for this purpose.

Preparing the Wick

Pick your wicks based on what you plan for the diameter of your finished rolled candles. There is no need to prime (pre-wax) the entire wick to make a rolled candle. However, the tip of the wick needs to be primed prior to being lighted. To do this, simply pull a small corner piece of wax from the edge of the sheet and press it around the end of the wick.

Rolling Your Candle

You can make rolled candles any diameter you like. You can make tall slender rolled candles with two or three sheets. Medium- and large-size rolled candles can be made simply by adding more sheets until you reach the size you prefer. Rolled candles lend themselves to various shapes, the most common and easiest being a simple cylinder. To make this type of rolled candle, you lay out the sheet (preferably on a warm surface) and lay on it a wick cut to the proper size. Begin rolling at the short (8-inch) end of the sheet and keep rolling until you reach the end.

What You Will Need

+ Sheets of wax made for rolling (either store-bought or homemade)
+ Wick (or wicks if you plan to make several). Use a flat-braided wick for beeswax, a square-braided wick for paraffin.
+ A blow-dryer or warming tray
+ A sharp knife or razor blade
+ A straightedge or ruler
+ Scissors (for cutting wick)
+ A hard cutting surface

Steps for Making Rolled Candles

1. Make sure your cutting surface is properly prepared. It should be covered with a piece of heavy cardboard or a mat.

2. Decide what size rolled candle you want to make. Cut a wick (or wicks) 2 inches longer than the size of the finished candle. Set aside.

3. Warm your wax sheets until they are pliable enough to roll easily. Use a blow-dryer (set on low) or put them on a heating pad or warming tray. Be sure to watch your wax sheets carefully while they are warming. Depending on the warmth of your room, they can easily melt on a heat source. If you accidentally overheat and get a melt, just save the wax to make poured candles.

4. Lay the sheet of wax flat on a smooth surface, such as a countertop or a table. Then bend a ⅛" fold at the end of the short side to make a place for the wick. Press the wick gently into the edge of the wax before beginning to roll. Make sure the wick is firmly embedded in the wax.

5. Next, roll up the wax tightly, making sure that the wick is closely held in the wax at each turn. Keep rolling with a firm and even pressure. This is to avoid letting air bubbles form between the layers. Take care to roll in a straight line to keep the ends flat (for cylindrical candles).

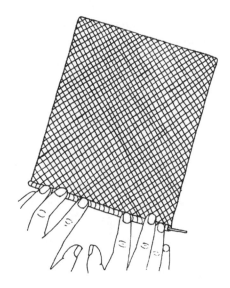

FIGURE 8-3: ROLLING A BEESWAX CANDLE

6. When you have rolled the entire sheet, press the final end into the candle so that it adheres to the last layer of wax.

7. Once you have finished rolling your candle, cut the wick to ½" in length and neatly trim the bottom end with your knife or razor to get a flat surface on which the candle can rest.

If your candles seem uneven or the layers aren't quite close enough, roll the finished candle on your countertop back and forth (like fashioning a roll of cookie dough) until the candle has a round shape and the layers all hold together. Do this with a gentle but firm hand.

Making a Rolled Taper

You can carve a taper shape into your rolled candle. To do this, use a sharp knife to trim the wax into a cone shape, then smooth the edges with a heated butter knife. Trim the wick to ½".

Making a Diagonal Rolled Candle

To make a diagonal rolled candle, cut your sheet of wax in half to make two triangles, using your straightedge or ruler and a razor blade or other sharp implement such as an X-Acto knife. Cut the wick to fit the longer edge (the 8" edge) and roll the wax sheet toward the pointed end. Take care to keep the long, straight edge even in order to end up with a flat bottom. This method will give you a spiral-shaped candle that is very attractive.

Making a Square-Shaped Rolled Candle

Using seven sheets of beeswax (9" × 12" each) and a primed wick 10" long, plus 2 ounces of melted beeswax, you can make a square candle from the textured sheets of beeswax. These are quite easy to make, with little mess as you need melt only a small amount of wax.

1. Lay the primed wick across one beeswax sheet as described above. Roll up the entire sheet around the wick.

2. Place another sheet of beeswax next to the edge of the end of the first sheet and again roll tightly. Keep the edges even as you roll so that they remain the same length.

3. Using your metal ruler, press the sheets against a third sheet of beeswax at a 90-degree angle, pressing the roll into a square shape as you turn it over each time.

4. Continue adding the remaining sheets, using the ruler at each turn to make the sides square. After you have the edges shaped, lightly score each remaining sheet against the ruler to help you fold (not roll) the wax around the inner core of squared wax sheets.

5. Press the end of the final sheet firmly into place as you bend it around the candle. This step will ensure that the finished candle does not unroll as it burns.

6. Holding the finished candle upside down over a cookie sheet lined with paper to catch the drips, use a small spoon to pour some of the melted beeswax into the cracks between the layers of wax sheets. Smooth some melted wax evenly over the bottom to seal the candle together and give a flat surface.

POURED CONTAINER CANDLES

POURING IS THE MOST VERSATILE WAY to make candles, with a long history dating back far beyond the original pioneers. The first rudimentary lamps were made by pouring oil and wax into containers. Most of these used some sort of liquid fuel, such as oil or animal fat, that would harden at room temperature, especially in cold climates. In this section you will learn to make candles that are poured into the containers in which they will be burned.

Choosing a Container

Container depth is important. Generally speaking, due to the need of the wick for adequate oxygen to burn the candle properly, it's a good idea to select containers no more than 5 or 6 inches tall. Shorter ones—even very small ones—are ideal as they burn well and can be made in quantity and set around different areas of your rooms to give a candlelit feeling to the entire space. For example, baby food jars or other votive-candle-size containers can be utilized this way.

Not only jams and jellies, but all sorts of foods come in glass jars suitable for mak-

ing container candles. These often come in interesting shapes. The possibilities are almost endless. Once you become aware of them, you'll notice jars of food that will make excellent and attractive containers, so save them up and you'll have plenty of interesting-looking and original candle containers on hand!

Always pick containers that are either the same diameter at the top and at the bottom, or are wide-mouthed at the top. Do not use anything with a narrow neck.

Glass and metal are the best materials for containers. Ceramic will also work, but it is opaque and will not give a glow as the candle burns down. Never use wood, milk cartons, or any other flammable materials for containers. Glass is a good choice, but make sure it is heavy enough not to crack under the burning candle's heat. All sorts of glass containers will work fine. For example, glasses made of heavy recycled glass (usually pale green: they are made from old Coke bottles) are perfect. Goblets or glasses of heavy glass, often hobnailed (that is, they have bumps on the surface), are very useful and can be refilled indefinitely. Another good choice is the square-shaped heavy glass contain-ers that contain a jelled room deodorizer that evaporates as it is exposed to air. When empty and washed, these types of jars make perfect container candles.

PIONEER TIP!

Before you remove the labels from food jars to use for making container candles, make a note of how many ounces the jar holds. You can put the lid on the empty jar with a label marked with the jar's volume. This saves you measuring time.

Here are some more interesting ideas for unique container candles:

+ Metal ice cube trays—though new ones may be hard to find in this era when plastic rules—make splendid container candles. Using an ice cube tray has a double advantage. It's easy to pour and you get the effect of a multi-wick candle. When lighted, the tray of little cubes gives a brilliant light.
+ You can also make neat miniature con-tainer candles in a minimuffin tin. Line the cups with foil liners before pouring in the wax. When the wax has hard-ened, lift out each minicandle. For a dinner party, you can set one of these little miniature candles at each per-son's place, perhaps placed on a saucer.
+ Slice oranges in half and juice them. Then, carefully pull out the membrane and pulp until you are down to the shell of the orange peel. Fill with wax. When the wax is cool but not solid, insert a cored wick. These ingenious candles are wonderful for outdoor parties.

What You Will Need

+ Wax—Usually plain paraffin with a melting point of 130°F. Remember that the kind of wax you use will influence whether or not you should add stearin:

  127 mp wax is sold specifically for use in container candles. It has a soft consistency and low melting point, and holds scent in until the candle is burned, without additives.

  128 mp wax is also specially blended for use in containers (and votives), but it may require additives.

  130 mp requires additives.

+ Stearic acid—Optional but will give a longer burn time

- Wick—Medium-sized, one for each container; cored wicks are preferable, but not essential. The wick should be 1" longer than the height of the container you are using
- Wick sustainers—One for each container
- Double boiler
- Thermometer
- Ladle and/or vessel for pouring— Preferably with a handle
- Small sticks—A dowel, chopsticks, or even a slim garden stake will work for suspending the wick over the container
- Weights—You need to weight the wick in the container if you are using a noncored variety; small washers or nuts will work fine
- Utensil for poking holes in the wax— This can be a skewer, a chopstick, a pencil, or a small stick
- The containers you have chosen

Basic Steps to Making a Container Candle

Assemble all of your tools and materials in the order in which you will be using them before you begin your candlemaking operation. You don't want to have the wax melted and then start looking for a container or other needed tool.

1. Measure the wax. To ascertain how much wax is needed to fill your container (or containers, if you are making multiples) fill the container with water and pour the water into a measuring cup to determine the container's volume. Then dry the container thoroughly.

2. Begin melting wax in your double boiler.

3. After the wax has reached the proper melting point (usually 150°F to 160°F), prime your wick as directed earlier in the chapter.

PIONEER TIP!

Keep a close eye on your thermometer. Make sure that the wax is not overheating while you prepare the wick and container for pouring.

---

4. Attach a wick sustainer to the primed wick. Put the wick sustainer on one end, which will be the bottom. If you

are using an uncored wick, you will need to tie your small weight to the wick, to ensure that it stays anchored while pouring the wax.

5. Lay the dowel or chopstick across the top of your container. Tie the top end of the wick to it so that the wick hangs steadily in the container.

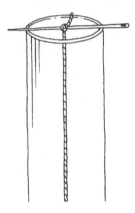

FIGURE 8-4: THE DOWEL AND THE WICK

6. Warm the container before pouring wax into it. You can do this step one of several ways: place it in a warming oven (150°F) for a few minutes; put it in the sink and run hot water into it; or set a pan of water on the stove on low heat and put the container (or containers) in the water to warm them before use. Make sure that the container is dried thoroughly before use.

PIONEER TIP!

If you are using glass containers, warm them slowly (the hot water method is safest). If metal, don't let them get so hot that they burn your fingers. Always use a hot pad to handle a heated container.

7. If you are adding stearin to pure paraffin, add it to the wax now and stir well.

8. Begin pouring slowly, to one side of the dowel holding the wick. Make sure you keep the wick centered in the container, using the bottom tab or weight to do so. You may need to hold it in place for a few moments to allow it to set. This "tack pour," of about ½ inch of wax in the bottom of the container, is an important step, for a wick that is off-center will cause the candle to burn lopsidedly. Allow the ½ inch of wax at the bottom to cool sufficiently enough to stabilize the centered wick.

9. Once the tack pour has cooled, continue pouring the wax until it is about ½" from the top.

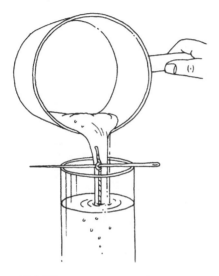

FIGURE 8-5: POURING THE WAX

10. Wait a few minutes for the wax to begin to congeal. Then, with your skewer, poke a few holes into the cooling wax. Pour a bit more wax into these holes. This second pour (the "repour" or "cap pour") is to fill in spaces caused by air bubbles that formed in the first pour.

11. Repeat the repouring process until the wax cools.

12. Wax shrinks as it cools, and the candle will develop a depression in the center. Pour some more melted wax into this center when the candle is firm to the touch in order to make a flat surface.

13. When the candle has cooled completely (this takes from eight to twenty-four hours, depending on the candle's diameter), trim the wick to ⅓" above the candle's surface.

CHAPTER 9

HOW A PIONEER KEEPS WARM:
An Introduction to Quilting

"The abilities of man must fall short on one side or the other, like too scanty a blanket when you are abed. If you pull it upon your shoulders, your feet are left bare; if you thrust it down to your feet, your shoulders are uncovered."

— THOMAS PAINE —

QUILTING WAS AN ESSENTIAL PART OF FRONTIER LIFE. Without it, a family would freeze in their beds during the winter nights. More than just a necessity, quilting also provided the original pioneers with a restful activity and a sense of community. Generations of women would join together for quilting bees. So often their days were full of difficult and backbreaking work; every waking moment was teeming with tasks to ensure their household's survival. A quilting bee was a much anticipated respite, an excuse to socialize and enjoy the company of neighbors and family. Gossip was shared faster than quilt patterns as the women sat around a quilt frame helping each other with their quilts. Because fabric scraps were exchanged, everyone had bits of each other's cloth in her quilt, symbolizing their shared lives.

For the Modern-Day Pioneer, quilting is a wonderful way to get back to a simpler time, while creating a beautiful and useful keepsake.

THE QUILT

LTHOUGH THERE ARE EXCEPTIONS, the basic quilt consists of three layers. The first is the backing, or bottom layer, which is generally made of a plain fabric and is sometimes called a lining. The term backing is less confusing because no other part of a quilt or quilted project is likely to be referred to as such, while lining might refer to other things.

The middle layer is the batting. This gives the quilt its insulation properties. The thickness of the batting combined with the style of stitching determines how heavy or puffy the quilt will be. This middle layer is sometimes called the filling or padding, but these terms bring to mind more old-fashioned products than the commercial quilt batting used in modern quilts.

The final layer is the cover. This is the decorated layer often called a quilt top or, more rarely, the face. Since *top* might refer to the headboard end of the finished quilt and *face* can be confused with *facing*, the term *cover* is somewhat preferable and is what will be used in this chapter.

Types of Quilts

There are two primary types of quilts: the pieced and the appliquéd. Pieced refers to a quilt cover made up of many, sometimes hundreds, of small pieces of cloth stitched together. These pieces might go together to create one large pattern such as a star on the cover. More often, the pieces are arranged in repeating geometric patterns. Sometimes these patterns are alternately turned to one side or another or dark and light colors are used to create diamond or stripe effects on the overall cover.

Appliquéd quilts are made of cutout shapes stitched onto a contrasting background. If the design consists of one large picture, it is said to have an allover pattern. Often the appliquéd picture is repeated, much like the pieced pattern, and sewn onto blocks, which are then sewn together.

A comforter, or comfortable as it was called some hundred years ago by the original pioneers, is a tied quilt, which means instead of rows of stitching joining the layers together, threads are caught through the layers at even intervals and tied in knots. It's a quilt that isn't quilted. A plain quilt, on the other hand, is exceedingly quilted. The cover is made from one solid-colored piece, often white, and this is where it gets its name. It is then quilted all over in the most intricate of patterns, often very detailed garlands of flowers, feathered wreaths, or figures of animals, people, houses, or ships.

Construction of a Quilt

Pattern refers to the guide you will follow to make your quilt but also to the design itself. The pattern (guide) will show you how to cut the pieces that will make up a particular pattern (design). Sometimes a template, a cardboard or plastic cutout, is used to cut the pieces. Sewing these pieces together along a seam line is called piecing. Sewing one piece on top of another is called appliquéing.

If the pattern repeats across the cover of the quilt, each of these repeats is called a block. Sometimes the blocks are sewn directly together, but sometimes they are separated by a strip of fabric called a panel. When the blocks and panels are sewn together, it is referred to as setting the quilt. When the layers of the quilt are put together, it is called assembling the quilt.

Often there are strips of cloth sewn around the outside edges of the set blocks. These are called borders. The size of the borders can be easily changed, which is handy if the pattern you are using isn't going to make your quilt quite the size you want. Borders can be plain, designed to frame a fancy quilt, or they can be very intricately pieced, appliquéd, or stitched.

Sometimes they are intended to be the part of the quilt that hangs over the edge of the bed and therefore are present only on the sides and bottom of the quilt. The top, the headboard end, is finished with the top row of blocks or with a narrow border. The process of finishing the raw edges around the quilt is called binding. The material used for this purpose is called binding as well.

Stitching that is used to hold pieces or layers together temporarily until more thorough stitching can be completed is called basting. The tiny decorative stitching that holds the layers together and gives the quilt its distinctive beauty is the quilting stitch.

TOOLS AND SUPPLIES

QUILTING SHOPS AND CATALOGS offer many marvelous gadgets for the quilter that can simplify part of the process or make cutting or sewing more accurate. Yet the Modern-Day Pioneer can begin quilting with very little expense. After all, the original pioneers did without these modern "necessities." Consider getting more advanced equipment as your hobby expands, but you can start with the essentials.

Pins and Needles

Needles and pins are the most basic of quilting tools, and everyone, even a non-sewer, will most likely have a few somewhere in the home. Needles come in numbered sizes. The larger the number, the smaller the diameter of the needle. To quilt, you will need two distinct kinds of needles, each for a separate type of sewing: sharps and betweens.

+ **Sharps:** Sharps are the most common type of needle. They are called sharps because they begin tapering right below the eye, becoming narrower all the way to the sharp point. You will be using sharps for basting, piecing, and any other hand sewing that you do besides the quilting itself. Sizes 7 and 8 are your best choices for this work.

+ **Betweens:** The needles you should use for quilting are called betweens. The most common theory is that they get their name because they are somewhere between the sharp and the darning needle in characteristics. They do not taper like the sharps but come to a sudden point very close to the end.

Size 7 or 8 is recommended. The finer the needle, the smaller the holes left in the fabric and the easier it will glide through the layers. Some experienced quilters even prefer size 9 needles.

+ **Pins:** Extrafine pins are best for quilting because they leave smaller holes in your fabric. Pins with ball heads, as opposed to the standard flathead pins, are desirable because they are less likely to catch the threads as you sew. The colored glass–headed pins are better still because they are easy to find in your work, unless, of course, you accidentally match a pin to a piece of fabric.

Thread

The thread is what holds your quilt together. If a thread breaks in your finished quilt, you'll have a hole that is difficult to mend effectively. Part of a seam's strength comes from the stitch you use, but the rest comes from the thread itself. This is why it is important to consider the type of thread you will use for your quilts.

+ **All-Purpose Thread:** The basic all-purpose thread is what you will use for piecing, appliqué, and all other stitching with the exception of the quilting itself.

As a general rule, try to use a color of thread that matches the fabric you are sewing. If an exact match isn't possible, a shade lighter is less noticeable than a shade darker. When piecing—that is, stitching two pieces of fabric together—the thread will be hidden within the seam and will not show from the outside unless it is vastly different from the fabric. If you are working with many different colors of fabric, there is no need to switch threads with each pair of pieces. A light shade, similar to the lightest fabric or an appropriate hue of gray or tan, should blend with all of them.

The color of your thread becomes especially important with appliqué because the thread will be visible. Try to match the fabric exactly and switch colors with each piece unless you want the stitching to accent the pieces.

+ **Basting Thread:** Basting should be done with a contrasting color for ease in finding the threads that need to be removed. Avoid very dark colors as they may leave behind tiny specks of the cotton coating that are difficult to brush away.
+ **Quilting Thread:** You will need a stronger thread especially made for quilting. Besides being more durable, the stiffer thread is less prone to tangling. Quilting thread is sold in most sewing departments and comes in many colors as well as the standard white. Whether your quilting stitches blend or contrast with the fabric is a matter of choice.

You will also find special thread made for machine quilting. If you decide you will be doing a great deal of machine quilting, you might want to give this a try. Otherwise, what little machine quilting you'll be doing can be done with all-purpose thread.

Sewing Scissors

While everyone has scissors in their homes, getting the appropriate scissors for quilting might be worth the investment. Trying to cut fabric with dull scissors will not only frustrate you, but will also make your pieces fray and will interfere with the accuracy of your cutting. It could easily affect the appearance of the finished quilt.

+ **Fabric Shears:** Any good-quality shears will do fine. Buy a new pair, if possible, and mark them in some way as your fabric shears. Never use them for anything else.
+ **Thread Scissors:** A handy addition to your sewing basket, but not a necessity, is a pair of small scissors for clipping threads. You will find them so much easier than general-use scissors to handle for the quick snip either at the sewing machine or at the quilt frame.
+ **Rotary Cutter:** One of the new gadgets that can be worth the investment is the rotary cutter. A rotary cutter has a circular blade that works much like a pizza cutter. It is always used with a cutting mat and often with a clear ruler.

Rulers

You will need at the very least a 6" ruler with ¹⁄₁₆" markings and something longer for measuring the larger pieces. A yardstick works well for this purpose. There are acrylic rulers that are extremely handy for cutting quilting pieces. They come in a variety of sizes. A 6" by 6" square one and another 18" long are recommended if you are able to invest in them.

Thimbles

Thimbles are intended to protect the finger that pushes the thread through the fabric from becoming sore or even punctured by the eye end of the needle. Thimbles are generally worn on the middle finger.

Sometimes a second thimble is worn on the hand under the quilt. This hand helps push the needle back up through the quilt and might need the protection of a thimble as well. The standard metal thimble is the most readily available and probably the best choice for a beginner. Once you have settled on the type of thimble to start with, check it for a correct fit. It should not squeeze the fingertip but should not fall off easily either.

Pattern Materials

In order to translate a picture of a pattern into something you can use to cut and sew your quilt, you will need a few basic supplies. Pencils, paper, cardboard, and rulers are probably already available to you. Patterns can be made with no more specialized equipment than these. However, there are a few things that will make the process easier.

+ **Graph Paper:** Most patterns are pictured on a grid. The chore of translating that to the size you want for your quilt is much easier with commercial graph paper. Marking a grid yourself can be tedious, and if you are not accurate, your pattern won't be, either.

If you are designing your own quilt, graph paper can be helpful. Shading light and dark squares to try different variations of a geometric design can save you time later.

+ **Template Material:** The quilting projects in *The Modern-Day Pioneer* do not require templates, because the fabric pieces are all squares or rectangles. But for more complex patterns, most quilters either make templates out of cardboard or use commercial plastic templates. Keep in mind that if you are cutting several pieces from the same pattern, the cardboard will begin to wear down and your last pieces will be slightly smaller than the first. The plastic template is also clear, so when you lay it on your fabric to mark it, you can see exactly what your cut piece will look like. Cardboard, however, won't melt if you use your template as a pressing guide to turn under seam allowances, as plastic will. It may shrink slightly, but it won't be enough to matter unless you are making a great many identical pieces. The solution is to make several cardboard templates of each size.

Marking Tools

At several points in the process of making your quilt, you will need to mark lines or designs on your fabric. You will not want any of these marks to show on the finished quilt, yet they need to remain long enough for you to use them effectively.

Unlike dressmaking, where you pin your pattern to the fabric and then cut around it, when you cut your quilt pieces, you will be drawing around your pattern, then cutting them out. A hard lead pencil is often used for this purpose. A soft lead pencil will smear and make your thread dirty. It is recommended that you use an art gum eraser or an eraser made especially for fabric to get rid of any lines that show after stitching rather than counting on them to come out in the wash.

There are special quilt pencils that may be a little safer. They also come in different colors to ensure that one will show up on any type of fabric. Many quilters love architects' silver pencils because the mark shows up on nearly everything. Just don't iron over the marks, as this will set them onto the fabric.

Tailor's chalk can also be used, but it doesn't make a very fine line, and it often rubs off before you are ready. It is handy, however, for quick-fix marking while you are quilting if a line isn't showing up sufficiently or if you've decided to add an extra line. Keep it sharp with an emery board.

Once all the pieces of your quilt are cut and sewn together, you will need to mark out a quilting design. This is your guide to the quilting itself. The simplest method is to use commercial stencils. They are available in quilt shops and catalogs. Draw the design onto your quilt cover through the slits in the stencil with your quilting pencils or a regular hard lead pencil. Another method is to use dressmakers' tracing paper as if it were carbon and draw over the design. Tracing paper comes in a variety of colors to show up on different colors of fabric. It should wash out of any fabric you would be using in quilts. If you are tracing the same design several times, be sure to make more than one copy as continual tracing will eventually wear through the paper.

Before these supplies were available, tailor's chalk was rubbed over a paper pattern that had been pricked at intervals with a pin. The chalk would be brushed off when the quilt was done. Unfortunately, with all the handling and rolling of the quilt as it is stitched, the chalk might brush off too soon.

Hoops or Frames

You will need to be able to hold your quilt in place while you stitch the layers together. While it is possible to quilt a small project without any kind of hoop or frame, your stitches will be more even and the result smoother if you use something. Since it takes both hands to do the quilting, something that holds the quilt for you is helpful for even the smallest project, but it is a necessity for a large one.

+ **Hoops:** Embroidery hoops come in many sizes, and the heavier ones can accommodate the layers of a quilt. A small project might be worked on one of these. There are sturdier quilting hoops the size of embroidery hoops that have an interlocking feature. This keeps the thickness of your quilt layers from causing the outside hoop to pop off.
+ **Frames:** The standard quilt frame is designed to accommodate any size quilt. The whole width of the quilt is available to the quilter at once and the ends that are finished or waiting to be worked are rolled out of the way.

Modern quilting frames can be tipped for more comfortable sewing or set level for group quilting. Their biggest disadvantage is they take up about as much room as a piano, (though they are easier to move) and not every home can accommodate one.

Sewing Machines

While not absolutely necessary, the modern sewing machine can be a very useful tool for quilting. Piecing is not only faster and straighter when done on a machine, but it is also stronger. If you have a sewing machine, make sure it is clean and in good working order before attempting to quilt with it. Replace the needle with a new one to avoid skipped stitches. A feeder foot or walking foot would be a good investment to ensure all three layers move along under the needle at the same rate. In the next chapter, "How a Pioneer Mends," you'll learn more about what to look for in a sewing machine.

QUILTING FABRICS

THE FABRIC will be a major factor in the appearance and durability of your finished quilt. The wrong fabric can cause frustration during construction and even disappointment when the sewing is done. Knowing what to look for and what to avoid at the fabric store can make all the difference.

Fabric Terms

Don't be confused by the terms you hear tossed about in the fabric store. Here are a few of the most common ones to help you start speaking the language.

Yard goods refers to fabrics sold by the yard or fraction of a yard. The tightly woven finished sides of a length of fabric are called the selvage. The threads that run from selvage to selvage are called the cross-wise threads, with the lengthwise threads running, of course, the length of the fabric. Bias refers to an imaginary line in the fabric on the diagonal with these threads.

The seemingly miles of fabric wrapped around a cardboard core and displayed in the store is called a bolt. Fabric can be anywhere from 36" to 60" wide (measured selvage to selvage), but most cotton fabrics suitable for quilting are between 42" and 45".

A fat quarter, a quilter's favorite, is a half-yard of fabric, cut in half lengthwise. In other words, it is a piece approximately 18" by 22". A normal (skinny) quarter would be 9" by around 44". Fabric stores cut them and fold them into attractive little squares for quilters because they are a handy size.

Broadcloth refers to a plain-weave fabric with a semiglossy finish. Most quilting fabric is broadcloth or broadcloth weight.

Cottons and Blends

Cotton has been the preferred fabric for quilt making for around 300 years. It is colorfast, washable, easy to work with, and durable. Its only close rivals are today's cotton-polyester blends. An old-fashioned quilt pattern done all in cotton resembles an antique quilt because of the traditional fabric. Cotton is soft to the touch and the preferred material for baby quilts. Pure cotton creases easily. This can mean a great deal when you are turning under a raw edge on a small piece for appliqué.

On the other hand, cotton-polyester quilts will keep that brand-new look longer. It's the polyester that gives the blended fabrics their permanent press quality, making them look smooth and crisp. The colors will be a bit brighter and slower to fade than those in 100 percent cotton. Some quilters say 30 percent polyester should be the maximum, but 60/40 cotton-polyester blends are common and often used.

Mixing Blends with Pure Cotton

A quilt should probably be made from only one type of fabric: all cotton or all blends that have as close to the same percentage of cotton as possible. This is especially true if the quilt is made up of large pieces. However, it won't be disastrous to do a little mixing. The smaller the pieces in the quilt, the less the differences in the fabrics will show.

Fabric bought in remnant bins, at garage sales, and even scraps left over from your own sewing may keep their exact content a secret. A clue will be how wrinkled they are after being washed. The more they wrinkle, the higher the cotton content. If you must know if two or more fabrics are of similar content, carefully burn small equal-size pieces in heat-proof dishes and compare the ash. Polyester will melt, rather than burn, and leave tiny beads behind.

Solids and Prints

Now that you know what types of fabrics to look for, you are ready to make your selections. As far as color choices go, there are two basic types of quilts: the scrap quilts that use up lots of leftover fabric and the quilts in which all the fabric pieces coordinate with one another.

For scrap quilts, the more variety in color and texture the better. In fact, in charm quilts, no two pieces should be from the same fabric. All you have to consider is the placement of the pieces, trying not to put pieces of similar color or similar size prints next to each other.

For the color-coordinated quilt, your tastes will be your best guide, but consider a few suggestions. Before you go shopping, cut a window in a piece of cardboard the size and shape of the primary pieces of your quilt. As you look at fabrics, test how the print appears in the window. You don't want a fabric where the motif is too large for the piece or one where the pictures are so far apart it would be possible to cut a piece and miss the picture entirely.

Fabric for Backing

The fabric for the quilt backing is as important as the cover. Most of the same rules apply, because it will be quilted along with the cover and will ultimately receive the same care.

Unbleached muslin is a traditional quilt backing. It is often sold in widths up to 108". Special quilt backing, sometimes called sheeting, is sold in some fabric stores. It can be as wide as 112" and can eliminate the necessity of piecing the back to fit even a king-sized bed.

Types of Batting

The last component of your quilt is the batting. Commercial batting is generally polyester, but you might find cotton batting available in some specialty stores. Quilt batting is folded and rolled very tightly to fit into the plastic bag it comes in. A day or so before you are ready to assemble your quilt, it should be unrolled and laid flat. Smooth the wrinkles gently with your hand. A light misting with water will help the worst of the wrinkles disappear.

Preparing New Fabric

Once you have chosen the fabric to use in your quilt, the hard part is over, but you aren't quite ready for quilting. New fabric needs some preparation before it is ready to be cut for your quilt. A little extra work now can save considerable grief later.

> ### PIONEER TIP!
>
> Because all new fabric is going to fray in the wash, a load made up entirely of new fabric pieces can become a tangled mess. Therefore it's better to toss a length or two in with a regular load of wash. Clipping the selvage corners will also help minimize tangling but will put more loose threads in your washer. Untangle the pieces and cut away the loose threads before you put the pieces in the dryer.

Preshrinking Your Fabric

Cotton shrinks more than cotton-polyester blends do, and some cottons shrink more than others. You want the fabrics you've chosen for your quilt to do all their shrinking before they are pieced together. To do this, simply launder them the way you would the quilt. The gentle cycle and cold water is probably fine for most quilts, but a baby quilt might need a hot water wash at some point in its life. If your fabric can't handle that, it's better to find out now.

Straightening Your Fabric

Most fabric is not exactly straight with the grain when you buy it, meaning that the lengthwise threads are not exactly perpendicular to the crosswise threads. If you do not correct this, your quilt will not be straight, either.

To see if your fabric is straight with the grain, pull a thread near one raw edge until it breaks and cut along the line you've created. Repeat this until you've cut from one selvaged edge to the other. Fold this newly cut edge in half and hold the fabric up to see if the selvages hang in a straight line. If they do not, your fabric should be straightened.

Fabric is straightened by pulling on the bias to force the lengthwise and crosswise threads into alignment. Stretch the entire surface of the fabric, not just across the center. And remember, unless the fabric is the same length as the width, corner to corner is not the true bias. Stretch several places along the bias and test again.

THE MODERN-DAY PIONEER'S WALL HANGING: GETTING STARTED WITH A SIMPLE PROJECT

THE QUILTING STITCH, while time consuming, is not particularly difficult. It does take some practice, however. If you practice on a small wall hanging, you'll have fun and something worth keeping when you're done. This simple wall hanging uses picture print fabric so there is no piecing or appliqué to do. An inexpensive embroidery hoop serves as the frame and hides the raw edges at the same time.

Supplies You Will Need

Picture Print Fabric

You will need a piece of printed fabric with a picture at least 3" or 4" across. An equal radius of neutral color surrounding the picture would be ideal. Fabrics printed to look like patchwork quilts, sometimes called cheater's quilting, often have large picture "blocks" that work well for this project.

Embroidery and Quilting Hoops

You will need an inexpensive embroidery hoop to use as a permanent frame for your miniquilt. Embroidery hoops can easily be found in sizes anywhere from 3" to 14" in diameter. Choose one of appropriate size to frame the picture you've chosen. The best way to do this is to have your fabric with you when you pick out the hoop.

You will also need a good-quality quilting hoop for the actual stitching. For lap quilting—that is, quilting without a freestanding frame or hoop—a hoop of about 8" in diameter is a convenient size. If your picture is to be smaller than that, you may be able to do your quilting in the same hoop you will use for framing later. Or you can enlarge the project by basting strips of fabric along each side. These extensions will fit into the quilt frame and hold the work in place.

Don't be confused into thinking lap quilting means quilting with no hoop at all. It is possible to quilt this way, but without stretching the quilt out flat in a hoop, your stitches will be too tight and your finished quilt will be puckery.

└─────────────────────────────┘

Ruffle

If it seems appropriate to your picture, you may want to put a ruffle around your wall hanging. A length of commercial ruffle a couple of inches longer than the circumference of the hoop or frame will be sufficient. Ruffles are available in many colors, sizes, and styles. Again, it is best to have your fabric with you when you shop for the trim. Be sure the ruffle is stiff enough that it will stand out around the hoop.

Other Supplies

The other supplies that you'll need for this project are:

+ Quilt batting
+ Backing fabric
+ Quilting thread
+ Basting thread
+ Needles and pins
+ A thimble
+ Liquid or hot glue

Assembling Your Quilt

Now that you have all of your materials, it's time to put together your miniquilt.

Cut

Cut the printed fabric in a square 2" or 3" larger than the hoop frame you have chosen. This is now the cover of your miniature quilt.

Place your cover right side up on the quilt batting and smooth both layers out with your hands. Cut the batting slightly larger than the cover. Place both of these layers on the wrong side of the backing fabric and cut around it as well, making it the same size as the batting. If these layers were cut exactly the same size as the cover, they would have to be placed exactly on top of one another to ensure that there is batting and backing behind all the edges of the cover.

Baste

Pin baste the layers together, checking the back to be sure it is as smooth as the front. A pin every 2" or 3" will be enough.

With a contrasting thread, baste the layers together. Knot the thread and begin in the center with a running stitch. To do a running stitch, weave the needle in and out of the fabric several times before you pull it all the way through. These stitches can be ½" long or longer and don't have to be pretty. You'll be removing them as you quilt. Stitch to one corner and cut the thread. Repeat for the other corners, always beginning in the center.

If your hanging is more than 6" or 7" across, you could run stitches from near the center to the sides and to the top and bottom as well. The purpose of basting is to hold the layers securely so nothing shifts when you quilt.

The Quilting Stitch

The ideal quilting stitches are straight, even stitches through the layers of the quilt that look the same on the back as the front. Expert quilters take as many as ten or twelve stitches per inch. Beginners should be happy with eight.

For this project, you will begin by quilting along the outline of your picture. Follow these steps and practice making stitches that are as tiny and even as possible. A few lines of stitching inside the pic-ture can be very effective. However, don't try to outline every detail. Think in terms of foreground and background and outline a few key areas.

Bury the Knot

Thread an 18" length of quilting thread onto a between needle. Tie a simple knot in the thread close to one end. Along the stitching line and about 1" away from where you want to begin stitching, insert the needle through the top layer of the fabric only and out at the point where you will begin stitching.

Pull the needle through and gently tug the knot through the cover so it will be hidden in the batting. Sometimes scratching it with your thumbnail will encourage it through the cloth. If you are having trouble, you might use the tip of the needle to lift the fabric near the knot and pull it over the knot as you tug on the thread.

Be sure to enter the thread on the line where you will be stitching. This prevents the shadow of the knot or any tail behind the knot from showing as it might if you bury the knot outside the stitching line. This is especially important if you are using colored thread.

Downward Stitch

With the index finger of your non-dominant hand under your work at the point where you will begin stitching, balance the frame against your body. Insert the tip of the needle about ¹⁄₁₆" from the exit point of the thread. Use your index finger to stop the needle as soon as it emerges from the quilt.

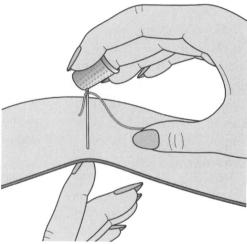

FIGURE 9-1: A CUTAWAY VIEW OF THE QUILT DURING THE FIRST DOWNWARD STITCH

Upward Stitch

Gently place your thimble-protected middle finger on the eye end of the needle, and rock the needle to the side until it is nearly lying on the surface of the quilt. Push up with your finger under the quilt. At the same time, push down on the top of the quilt with your thumb, just ahead of the needle. This makes it possible for the needle to get into a position nearly perpendicular to the part of the quilt it is going to enter.

The index finger under the quilt pushes the needle through the layers and the thumb stops it as it emerges. The thumb is the key to tiny stitches on top and the index finger is the key to tiny stitches on the bottom.

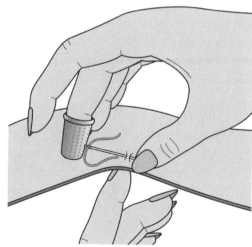

FIGURE 9-2: A CUTAWAY VIEW OF THE QUILT DURING THE FIRST UPWARD STITCH

When the tip of the needle comes through the fabric and is stopped by the thumb, relax your thumb and rock the needle upward again, forcing the tip back through the layers. Your hand should look like Figure 9-1 again except there will be a stitch on the needle.

Running Stitch

At first you might want to push the needle on through the cloth after only one or two stitches. Practice making tiny stitches initially, then see how many stitches you can get on a needle before you have to pull it through. There is a limit to how many stitches will work before you need to use pliers to get the needle through all the layers, but four or five stitches on the needle will help ensure your stitching is straight.

Tying Off

When the thread is getting short enough to cause difficulty, it is time to tie it off and begin with another length of thread. While the thread is still on the needle, tie a knot in the thread about ¼" to ½" from the surface of the quilt. If you poke the end of the needle in the loop as you tighten the knot, you can guide the knot to end where you want it to.

Run the needle into the top layer of fabric at the point it had emerged and out again about 1" away. Be sure you do this along a stitching line. Pull until the knot has gone through the fabric and is in the batting layer. Tug the thread a little and clip it near the cloth. The knot and tail will be buried inside the quilt.

Echo Stitching

Once you have gone all the way around the picture on your quilt, try echo stitching to get in some more practice. Echo stitches are rows of stitches running parallel to a design, mimicking its curves and angles. Think of the ripples on the surface of a pond.

To judge where to run the row of echo stitches, use a ruler and hard lead pencil to mark a few spots ¼" from the finished row. A dot every 1" or so should be enough to guide you around the picture again. Continue the echo rows until you have filled the entire area that will be visible when the picture is centered in the hoop.

Finishing Touches

First, be sure to remove any remaining basting stitches. Erase any pencil marks that are visible. If your work seems smudged by your pencil marks or prolonged handling, you may want to wash it.

Your quilt will seem surprisingly puckered after being quilted and washed. Be certain all the pencil marks are gone and then iron it. Ironing a finished quilt isn't usually recommended because it flattens the batting. However, this project will look better on your wall if it is ironed. Stretch it out as you go so you don't iron puckers or creases in the unquilted areas.

Framing the Quilt

Center your miniature quilt over the inside hoop of the embroidery hoop frame. Loosen the outside hoop and center the adjustable screw at the top of the picture. You will be hanging the finished quilt from this screw.

Push the outside hoop down over the inside hoop, adjusting the quilt to see that it stays centered. Tighten the screw a little at a time, pulling the ends of the quilt tight as you go.

When the quilt is centered and before the screw is completely tight, ease the outside hoop off a fraction. Run a few drops of glue between the exposed inner hoop and the quilt and along the line between the back of the outside hoop and the quilt. Slide the hoop back in place and tighten thoroughly, making any necessary last-minute adjustments. Allow the glue to dry. Next, trim off the excess fabric flush with the back of the hoop frame.

Adding the Ruffle

Trim the raw edge at one end of the ruffle. Press and stitch under a narrow hem. Use the ruffle to measure around the hoop frame to find where to put the second hem. Starting with the hemmed edge at the center top, lay it out carefully around the hoop. You will be gluing the base of the ruffle against the raw edge of the quilt and the back of the hoop. Ideally, the gathering stitches of the ruffle should just be hidden behind the hoop frame.

Find the point where the ends of the ruffle will meet, allow for the hem, and trim and hem the second end. Glue the ruffle in place. If you are using liquid glue, you might need to push an occasional pin through the ruffle into the edge of the quilt to hold the ruffle in place until the glue dries. Inserting the pins at a sharp angle is going to be most effective. Let the glue dry; then hang your first quilt on the wall to enjoy.

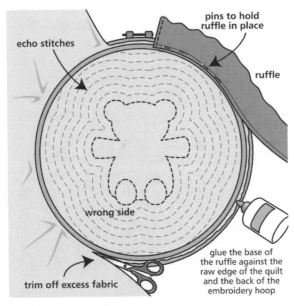

FIGURE 9-3: THE BACK VIEW OF THE MINIQUILT
DURING THE FINISHING STEPS

NINE-PATCH BABY QUILT

ONCE YOU'VE GOTTEN THE HANG of the miniquilt, try this more advanced project. Don't have a baby? This would make a wonderful gift or an excellent lap robe or throw. Note that the directions for this quilt are for machine piecing. However, if you do not have a machine, you can, of course, stitch the pieces by hand.

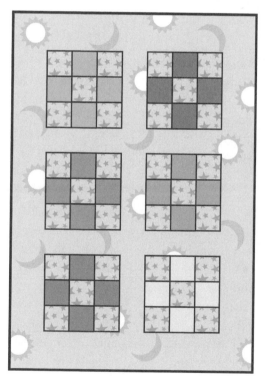

FIGURE 9-4:
THE LAYOUT OF A NINE-PATCH BABY QUILT

Fabric Requirements

Nine-Patch refers to a pattern of nine squares, generally of only two colors, which alternate in three rows of three. The nine-square blocks are framed with panels of a coordinating fabric to keep the blocks from blending into one huge checkerboard. This 36" by 52" quilt calls for six blocks made of nine 4" (finished size) patches, separated and framed by 4" panels.

Amounts of Fabrics

The yardages that follow assume the fabric you are buying is about 42" wide. If the width of the fabric is significantly different, adjust the yardages accordingly. And remember, it's better to have too much than too little. You can start your stash of scraps for future projects.

You will need:

+ 1 yard of a primary print for panel and border pieces
+ ⅔ yard of a secondary print
+ ⅙ yard each of six solid-color fabrics that coordinate with the prints
+ 1⅔ yards for backing
+ Piece of batting at least 38" by 54"
+ 10 yards of yarn or crochet cotton for ties
+ A sharp tapestry needle or large embroidery needle

You should be able to cut the thirty secondary-color patches from exactly ½ yard of fabric. If you are using the primary print fabric for the backing, 2½ yards should be sufficient for the panels, borders, and the backing. One yard of the secondary fabric should be enough if you want to use it for the backing as well as the thirty patches. Cut the backing piece first and cut the smaller blocks or panels from what is left.

Cut and Arrange the Pieces

Since all the pieces are squares or rectangles, there is no need to make templates. Be sure to iron the fabric first so your measurements will be accurate.

The patches on the finished quilt will be 4" by 4". Allowing ¼" all around for the seams, each patch will need to be cut 4½" square. Measure 4½" from the cut edge of your fabric and pull another thread or cut with a rotary cutter. If you are using a rotary cutter, you can fold the fabric and cut through as many as four layers at once if you are careful about keeping the edges lined up. Remember to cut away the selvage before you cut your strip into 4½" squares.

The Patches

You will need thirty squares of the primary color and four of each of the six solid colors. But here is the fun of the Nine-Patch: If you discover you are short on the print fabric, use it for four patches per block instead of five and cut one more of each of the solid-color fabrics. Or, if you have a lot of scraps of juvenile prints, use a different print for the patches in each block. You could pick a different solid color to go with each print or choose one that goes well with them all.

Panels and Borders

You will need to cut the border and panel pieces 4½" wide. You will need nine pieces 12½" long to fit vertically between and on either side of the blocks, and four pieces 36½" long to run horizontally above, between, and below the rows of blocks.

Cut the fabric into seven strips, each 4½" wide. Four of these strips will be used for the horizontal panels and borders. The other three will become the vertical panels and borders. Trim away the selvages, but there's no need to cut the strips to the exact length. You can save time by doing that as you sew.

Backing and Batting

The finished cover will be slightly less than 36" by 52". Your backing and batting will both need to be cut a couple of inches larger than this. Pull a thread to cut the edge with the grain; fold the cut edge in half, selvage to selvage. Pull on the diagonal until the selvages hang evenly.

Three Patches Equal a Row

Begin with two patches that will be next to each other in a block. With right sides together, line up the edges and stitch ¼" from the raw edge. Being sure to keep track of which patch should be in the middle of the row, stitch a third patch to the first two. Set this row aside and repeat the process with each row of patches. You should have eighteen rows.

If all your blocks are the same, you can sew 4½" strips of fabric together in the order the blocks should be arranged in the top and bottom rows. Cut the connected strips into 4½" units. Do the same with strips arranged for the middle row. This can save considerable time if you are making a full-sized quilt.

Press the seam allowances toward the darker fabric. This ensures that the allowance will not show through the front of the cover.

Matching Seams

Group the pressed three-square units together by block again. With right sides together, line up the edges and seams. To be sure the seams match, pin the strips together exactly on the seam line. The seam allowances should be pressed to stagger rather than overlap, minimizing the bulk. You will not be sewing through more than four layers of cloth when you stitch the strips together. This also makes it easier to line up the seams. Run a pin in and back out along the stitching line of the unit you've placed on top. Check the bottom unit. Does the part of the pin that is visible line up exactly with the stitching? If not, make the necessary adjustments.

When both seams are matched, check the fabric between the pins. Is it lying flat naturally? You need to be able to stitch without gathering or stretching one patch to fit the other. If you can't, you need to redo a seam. Use another unit to help you determine which seam is the culprit. It's easier to make a piece smaller than larger, but don't automatically solve the problem that way. Your finished block might end up a different size than the rest of the blocks and your problems will have increased considerably.

Three Rows Equal a Block

When the seams line up, stitch the units together ¼" from the edge and repeat the process with the third row of patches. Set the new block aside and make the other five blocks the same way.

Press the seams. The direction isn't going to make a great deal of difference because whichever way you choose, you will be pressing darker allowances toward lighter fabric about half the time. An alternative would be to press the seams open, but this is a little more time consuming. If you have a great deal of contrast between the hue of the fabrics in your quilt, it might be worth the extra effort. Otherwise, consistency is probably more important than which direction you choose.

Unless your blocks are all the same, you'll need to decide their placement on the finished quilt. Lay them out on a large surface such as the floor. You can spread your panel/border strips between them to get a better idea of what your quilt will look like. Trade the blocks around until you are satisfied.

Once you've made your decision, stack your blocks in order, bottom row blocks, middle, then top row. Left and right won't make any difference at this point unless you have used one-way fabric. In which case, you'll need to keep careful track of what you are doing.

Set the Quilt

Spread three of the panel strips across your lap. With right sides together, sew a panel strip to one side of the first block. You won't need to pin since there are no seams to match. Simply line up the edges and sew. When you come to the end of the block, cut the thread and trim the strip, using the block as a guide.

Repeat the process with the other end of the block. Sew the second block in the stack to the panel you've just trimmed, and then sew a third panel to the other end of it. You now have a completed row of your quilt.

Set this aside to press and repeat the process with the rest of the blocks. Iron the seams toward the panels and lay them out to recreate your chosen layout.

Return to the sewing machine, if you are using one, and spread the remaining four panel strips across your lap. Sew the strips and the rows of blocks together, trimming the excess from the panel strips at the end of each row. Press the seams toward the panels and your quilt cover is finished.

Easy Assembly Method

This method of assembling a quilt works well with small projects. The idea is to sew the cover and the back together with the right sides of the fabrics facing each other, a little like a pillowcase, then turn it right-side out. This saves the need for any form of binding or hemming of the edges of the quilt.

Backing and Batting

Spread the batting out on the floor or other large surface. Smooth out any wrinkles. Spread the backing piece over it, right-side up and pin them together in a few places. Baste the pieces together loosely and remove the pins. You won't need a great many basting stitches in order to hold these together for the next step.

Assemble

Spread the cover, right-side down, on top of the backing. Carefully smooth out any wrinkles. Place a pin every few inches around the outside edge. The edges of the backing and batting should extend beyond the edge of the cover.

Stitch a ¼" seam around the outside edge of the cover, leaving only 10" to 12" open on one side of the quilt.

You will need to stitch the backing to the batting at the opening. Move the cover out of your way and stitch along what would have been the stitching line, coming as close as possible to where the cover is stitched down without catching the cover in these stitches.

Trim and Turn

Trim the backing to about $\frac{1}{16}$" outside the cover's edge. The finished edge will lie smoother after it's turned if the two fabrics in the seam allowance are of different widths. Trim the batting close to the stitching and clip the four corners almost to the diagonal stitches.

Turn the quilt right-side out through the opening you left. Poke the corners out using a blunt object like the eraser end of a pencil. Never use a sharp object for this as you can easily rip open the seam or poke a hole in the fabric.

Press around the edge of the quilt, being careful to open the seam out as much as possible. Rolling the seam between your fingers helps to open it out. Turn the edges under in the opening and press them flat. Remove the basting stitches from the backing.

The Blind Stitch

You need to close up the opening you left to turn the quilt, but you want it to look as much like the machine stitches as possible. If done correctly, the blind stitch is nearly invisible.

Refer to Figure 9-5 and follow these steps.

1. Knot an appropriate length of the same thread you used to stitch around the quilt.

2. Bury the knot in the seam allowance, bringing the needle out at the end of the machine stitching.

3. Holding the layers between the thumb and forefinger of your nondominant hand, take a tiny stitch exactly on the crease of the cover.

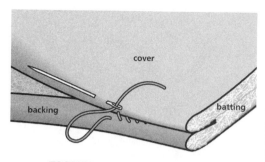

FIGURE 9-5: THE BLIND STITCH

4. Insert the needle in the backing even with where the needle left the cover and take another tiny stitch.

5. Repeat with another tiny stitch in the cover beginning exactly across from the end of the last stitch.

The trick is to do all your forward movement with the thread inside the folds of cloth and not in the space between the layers.

Tie the Quilt

The only thing left to do is secure the layers together. This quilt is going to be tied at the corners of every patch. This puts ties evenly spaced over the entire surface of the quilt at close-enough intervals to hold the batting in place.

Baste

Spread the quilt out on a flat surface again and smooth it out. Begin in the middle and pin the layers together every 6" to 8". Flip the quilt over to be sure the backing is as smooth as the front. Move pins if necessary.

Since this is a relatively small project, pin basting will be sufficient while you tie. However, if you are reluctant to get a few scratches from the pins as you work, baste the layers together, beginning in the center and working outward the same way you basted the miniquilt. Knot your contrasting thread and work a running stitch from the center to each corner, then from the center to each side.

Yarn for Tying

Cotton or acrylic yarn is recommended for tying. Some quilters use wool because it shrinks and frizzes into tight little knots when the quilt is washed, and there is no danger of the ties coming out. There's also no danger of anyone lying on the quilt, because those knots are as hard as buttons. Acrylic and cotton ties will last well enough and, if done correctly, will not come out anyway.

The color you choose for the ties will depend on whether you want the ties to decorate the surface of your quilt or blend to near invisibility. There's no rule that says the ties must all be the same color, either. Consider how your yarn or yarns look with all the different fabrics before you make your decision.

The Tie Stitch

There is no need to cut a length of yarn from the skein. Simply thread the loose end of it onto your sharp tapestry needle or embroidery needle. The smallest needle available that will still allow the yarn to go through the eye will be easiest to draw through the layers of your quilt.

Beginning near the center of your quilt, insert the needle about ⅛" diagonally from the corner of a patch and out again ⅛" on the other side. Draw about 4" of yarn through the quilt. Take a second stitch back through the same holes. Tie the yarn in a double knot and trim to about ¾" or whatever length you desire.

With the thumb and forefinger of your nondominant hand, untwist the yarn slightly. Stick the needle in the yarn just above the knot and run it outward to fray the yarn. This will decrease the chances of the knots coming untied.

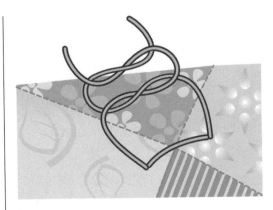

FIGURE 9-6:
DOUBLE STITCH AND DOUBLE KNOT TO TIE

Rethread the needle and repeat across the surface of the quilt, working outward from the center. Sometimes it's easier to catch any skipped sites by checking the back of the quilt. The little loops of yarn should be evenly spaced over the entire surface.

Sometimes ties are tied in bows instead of frayed. This can be very pretty but is not recommended for a baby quilt as tiny fingers can catch in the loops. However, it might work very well on the living room throw.

SIGNING YOUR WORK

Any work of art deserves to carry the artist's signature. Your quilted wall hangings, especially ones that express your special interests or milestones, should be signed. Nearly all quilters put their names on their quilts. Most also include the date—at least the year. Some record the date the quilt was begun as well as the date it was finished. Many quilters include their maiden name to help future genealogists. Many include the quilt's name and sometimes more information about the pattern.

Some quilters put their name and whatever other information they want on a piece of cloth and stitch it to the quilt, while others sign directly on the quilt.

Most quilters put their names on the backs of their quilts. The information is on the quilt forever, but doesn't detract from the appearance of the quilt.

Generally, if a quilter puts her name on the front, she will try to make it less conspicuous. Some will use quilting thread to sew their names in tiny stitches taken only through the cover of the quilt. A few will even work their names into the stitching pattern.

You can sign your quilt with ink or a permanent marker, or sign it in pencil and stitch over the lines. Cursive letters are easier than printed letters because they are joined. A single strand of embroidery thread works best for the stitching. Use a simple backstitch, sometimes called a stem stitch.

If you decide to sign in ink, iron over it to set it. Covering the signature with a cloth dipped in vinegar and water and then wrung out and ironing over that is even better—you don't want the ink to run when the quilt is washed. If you are signing a piece of cloth to appliqué to the quilt, backing it with iron-on interfacing or butcher paper first makes it easier to sign. Remove the paper before you sew it to the quilt.

CHAPTER 10

HOW A PIONEER MENDS:
An Introduction to Sewing

"Man is born broken. He lives by mending."

— EUGENE O'NEILL —

YOU HAVE ALREADY SEEN how hard the original pioneers worked. They grew and harvested their own food and made their own candles and soap. They healed, brewed, and crafted without so many of the conveniences we take for granted today. They were fierce and self-sufficient. This was not a path for the prim and proper.

And that was doubly true for the pioneer's clothing. The frontier was no place for top hats and ball gowns. Simple patterns with durable material were valued above lace and silk. Even so, sleeves were still ripped and dresses were still stained. But the pioneers could not go out and buy replacements—ready-made clothes were nearly unheard of and even fabric could sometimes be hard to come by.

So they learned how to mend their own clothes, from tears and holes to popped buttons and loose hems. They could alter their closet to make items bigger or smaller; they knew just where to put a pocket to cover up a stain. In this chapter, you will learn their secrets.

BEFORE YOU BEGIN

READY-MADE CLOTHES can be bought for relatively little nowadays, leading many people to dismiss the notion of mending or altering in favor of buying something new. But the very practices that make clothes cheap also increase the chances that a brand-new piece will have some little things wrong with it. Knowing how to quickly fix whatever is wrong will mean your money isn't wasted. Understanding how to fix tears, repair ripped seams, or raise a hemline will always be useful.

You can't expect to be able to make your favorite old garment look like new. Plan, instead, to solve problems that keep you from using certain garments, or to extend the life of favorites. In a sense, every major mending or altering project is an experiment. You don't always know what you're going to turn a garment into when you start ripping out seams. There's always a chance it won't go back together the way you hope. However, if the piece of clothing is not wearable as it is, there's little to be lost in giving it a try.

Little except your time, that is.

> ## PIONEER TIP!
>
> If a piece of clothing is beyond repair, check out Chapter 9, "How a Pioneer Keeps Warm," to see if it could be incorporated into a quilt project! If not, cut the fabric into squares to use as dishtowels.

Even the original pioneers had to throw clothes away sometimes. If a garment has a whole list of problems, chances are you won't be able to correct them all. Your time will be wasted if there is still something wrong after hours of work. Ask yourself the following questions:

+ Is the garment wearable as it is?
+ If I can't fix it, can I at least return it to its current condition?
+ What is the *best* I can hope for after mending or altering?
+ How long is it likely to take?
+ What is my time worth relative to the cost of replacing the item of clothing?

Some of these questions will be easier to answer after you've had more experience altering and mending. Sometimes a project is worth tackling for the experience alone. You never know what new construction technique you might discover while you're taking something apart. There are other reasons to give mending and altering a try. You will get some sewing practice and a more intimate knowledge of clothing construction as you notice how store-bought items are put together. It will also make you a better shopper as you become more adept at recognizing flaws and potential problems.

If you've had some practice stitching missed seams on T-shirts and mending a few tears, you'll be ready when the opportunity arises to save a favorite dress or an expensive new jacket from the rag sack.

SUPPLIES

$\mathbf{T}$HE PREVIOUS CHAPTER, "How a Pioneer Keeps Warm," contains details on most of the supplies that a beginning sewer should have on hand. A mender will use the same sewing scissors, basic needles (sharps), pins, basic thread, measuring tape, and rulers that a quilter would find handy. But there are a few supplies particular to mending and altering clothing that a Modern-Day Pioneer should take note of.

Darning Supplies

Darning is a technique perfect for fixing certain kinds of holes and tears. But it requires certain specialty items.

Darning Needles

Darning needles are only slightly thicker than the sharps needles, but they are much longer. The length makes it possible to work a weaving pattern with your thread over a hole being darned.

Darning Thread

Darning thread is thicking and heavier than all-purpose thread.

Darning Gourds and Mushrooms

Darning gourds, shaped like a child's rattle, and darning mushrooms, which are similar but with a broader top, might seem terribly old fashioned, but they are useful for more than just darning socks. Nearly any hand mending will be neater if you use one. You can find them in well-stocked fabric stores, but the ones you find in antique stores will have more character.

The Sewing Machine

Like the original pioneers, you can mend and alter anything by hand. But the sewing machine makes this task much easier. Seams sewn on a machine are stronger and neater. For some Modern-Day Pioneers, using a sewing machine may be the most thorough and time-effective way to mend clothing.

When shopping for a sewing machine, the bare essentials you'll want for construction sewing are straight and zigzag stitching in a variety of lengths and widths. If you're planning on doing a small or moderate amount of sewing, this may be as much as you'll ever need.

HOLES AND TEARS

It's going to be impossible to mend a tear in such a way that it completely disappears. If the tear is in a piece of dress clothing and is located where it will show, it may not be worth the trouble. If the garment is comfortable enough that it can have a second life as at-home work clothes, mend the tear while it's still small. Tears in work clothes can catch on things, making them potentially dangerous as well as annoying.

Holes in garments are treated pretty much like tears except that they are more difficult to hide. Assume the garment is now work clothes and patch or darn it to stop further damage.

Patching Tears in Woven Fabrics

For very small tears, iron-on patches might be the best solution. They are available in a few colors. Choose the one closest to your fabric or slightly lighter, and cut it just slightly larger than the tear. Follow the package directions to apply it to the underside of your garment. They adhere better to some fabrics than others. Cotton takes them very well.

If the fabric can't take the heat needed to iron on the patch, you must try another solution.

Cut a piece of scrap fabric the weight of your garment fabric or lighter and slightly larger than the tear. Weight is going to be more important than color, although a close color match is nice. Back the tear with the fabric, pinning it carefully so the fabric around the tear is lying flat on the patch. With thread that matches the garment, sew along the tear with a wide, close-together zigzag stitch. If the tear closes entirely, one row of stitches might hold it together. More likely it will take two or three overlapping rows. Carefully trim the backing fabric away close to the stitches.

Darning Tears on Woven Fabrics

If the tear is at a barely noticeable place, like under the arm, and you want a more professional-looking mend so you don't have to reduce the garment's use, you can try darning the tear. Placing the area around the tear in an embroidery hoop might make it easier to keep it flat. Using a darning needle and two strands of thread or the heavier darning thread, begin about ½" beyond and above the tear. Do not make a knot. Simply leave a tail and trim it off later.

Choosing the direction that most closely runs perpendicular to the tear, weave the needle in and out of the fabric in line with the grain, taking about eight stitches per inch. Extend the stitches about ½" past the tear. Turn and weave another row of stitches parallel to the last row. Continue this weaving pattern over the area, treating the tear as if it weren't there.

If the tear is on the grain line, which is likely in woven fabrics, you won't need to go in the opposite direction. However, if the tear is diagonal or an L shape, darn in a crosswise direction, weaving in and out over the first set of stitches.

Tears in Knitted Fabrics

A very fine knit like a T-shirt can be mended with a zigzag stitch, in the same way you would mend woven fabrics, as long as you are careful not to stretch it out of shape. The hand-darning method will also work because it won't stretch with the fabric.

Heavier knits—ones on which you can easily see the rows of knit stitches—will need to be mended taking the knit stitches into account. To mend the hole before it becomes larger, find a similar weight yarn if possible and, using a blunt tapestry needle, try a little free-form darning. Be sure to catch any loops that do not have yarn running though them. These will run if they aren't anchored.

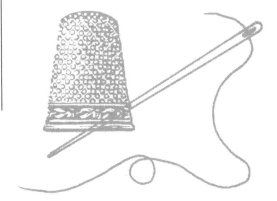

Patching Holes

To mend a hole, begin with a scrap of fabric of similar weight. Cut it slightly larger than the hole. Trim the loose thread away at the edges of the hole. Pin the patch to the underside of the fabric. From the outside, stitch around the edge of the hole. From the inside, stitch around the outside edge of the patch. If you don't like the outline of the hole showing on an outside patch, sew around the empty hole to keep it from fraying and then apply the patch. If you are using a machine, use the zigzag stitch for sewing patches; this better prevents further fraying.

If you have a very small hole, especially in lightweight fabric, the round of stitches at the hole will probably be enough. Trim the patch fabric away close to these stitches.

Darning Holes

Darning a hole works pretty much the same way as darning a tear except you'll always have to go in both the lengthwise and the crosswise directions. Don't try to darn any holes that are larger than a quarter. Also, if a spot on a garment is wearing extremely thin, darn it before it wears through entirely. This is easier than putting your own fabric over the hole.

Darning gourds or mushrooms might help you keep your darning stitches smooth. Center the hole over the smooth top, and gather the fabric around the handle to hold with your nondominant hand while you darn. These darning tools work better for holes than for tears. They tend to pull a tear open rather than help you hold it closed.

PIONEER TIP!

The verb "to darn" is related to the Middle Dutch *dernen*, meaning to stop up a hole in a dyke. This suggests that darning is a task that's better to do while the hole is small and manageable.

BUTTONS AND BUTTONHOLES

A T A TIME BEFORE ZIPPERS AND Velcro, a pioneer's clothes were held together by buttons or pins. Today, the Modern-Day Pioneer can use a solid understanding of buttons and buttonhole construction to fix all kinds of clothing problems. Most of these issues are easily solved, if you simply take the time to do it. Here's what you need to know in order to handle these minor problems with ease.

Buttons

Not being able to sew on a button is the sewing equivalent of not being able to boil water. No one actually believes you when you say it. The only tricks are to match the button if the original is lost, match the thread used to sew the other buttons, and sew it on with approximately the same amount of thread.

First, check the lower seam allowances. Sometimes manufacturers will sew on extra buttons there. Other clothes come with one button in a tiny plastic bag with the label. If you saved it and can find it, you're in luck. If your button was lost and you can't quite match it, see if you can't move a button from the least conspicuous place and put your almost-match in its place. Avoid the problem of matching buttons as often as possible by noticing loose buttons and restitching them before they come off.

If the button has torn the fabric beneath it, mend the hole with an iron-on patch or by darning, then replace the button. If you have darned it, reinforce the area by holding a small square of twill tape behind the mend and sewing the button through it as well as the fabric.

Reducing Buttonholes

Sometimes a button will not stay buttoned, even though there is no particular pressure on it. The fault is probably the buttonhole. Check to see if the buttonhole stitching has started to come out. If it has, replacing it will most likely solve the problem.

Cut any loose threads. Line the exposed raw edges of the buttonhole with tiny buttonhole stitches, using thread that matches the other buttonholes as closely as possible. Also, use the other buttonholes or

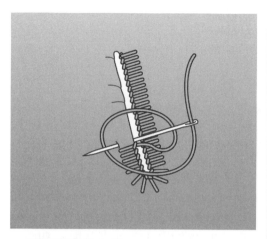

FIGURE 10-8: THE BUTTONHOLE STITCH

the needle holes from the lost stitches to determine the depth of your stitches. Refer to Figure 10-8 and follow the steps below.

1. Hide a small knot on the underside of the garment, or take three stitches on top of each other to anchor your thread.

2. Bring the needle and thread to the outside through the buttonhole to begin.

3. Insert the needle back through the buttonhole and out at the end of the stitching line.

4. Loop the thread around the needle, going behind the eye end and under the point.

5. Pull the needle through, adjusting the thread so the "knot" you've just made is at the raw edge.

6. Repeat steps 3 through 5 very close to the last stitch.

Other Suggestions

If reworking the buttonhole isn't enough to keep the button from slipping out, or if the original stitches are still in place, the buttonhole may have just been made a little too large. Reduce its size by taking a few looping stitches over one end of the buttonhole. Test it as you go so you don't end up making the buttonhole too small.

If you have a sweater, blouse, or dress that tends to separate between the buttons, see if it can't be sewn closed. Try pulling the garment off and on with only the top one or two buttons undone. Determine exactly how many buttons you actually need to use. If the buttonhole band has a row of topstitching, that would be a natural place to stitch. Heavier sweaters will be better if you stitch them loosely by hand using a hemstitch along the edge of the button band. Begin even with or just below the first button, and stitch down until you are even with the last button. Don't stitch clear to the hemline if you want it to appear as if the buttons still work.

MAKING CLOTHES SMALLER: DARTS AND SHAPING

CLOTHING MANUFACTURERS tailor their garments to fit some mysterious standard. A lucky few actually fit this standard. Everyone else buys the nearest fit. Sometimes that doesn't seem to be near enough.

Now that you know how the seams and hems on garments are constructed, you don't need to be afraid to change a near fit to a perfect fit. This is going to work better with new garments, because stitching lines and fold lines may show in even slightly worn clothing. Be sure you aren't working with a fabric that shows pinholes, like silk. Test the hem allowance with a pin before you begin. If your new garment is cotton, there's a chance it'll shrink a little so wash it before you alter it. Otherwise, alter it first. Washing will only set the creases in the seams, darts, and hems.

Put the garment on inside out. Pin the seams and darts until the garment fits. If you are altering the back seam, or if you are dealing with a close-fitting garment, you might enlist a friend's help. Be careful not to make it too small. Sit down and move around in this smaller garment. Take it off carefully so the pins don't either scratch you or fall out.

Shift the pins a little to make sure you are altering each side evenly. Mark along the pins with chalk and stitch the seams and darts. Try the garment on again, right side out this time, then finish the seam allowances.

MAKING CLOTHES LARGER: ADDING PANELS

ENLARGING GARMENTS takes some creative thinking. If the seam allowances don't give you enough fabric, you'll have to find it somewhere else. Rather than making your alterations disappear, try to make them look like original trim and hide them in plain sight. This works best with casual wear, but some dressier clothes might lend themselves to this type of altering, too.

Pants and Skirts

+ Take out the stitching in the side seams. It may be necessary to cut through the waistband. Take out a little of the hemstitches on each side of the side seams. Press the old allowance flat, and trim the edges so they are even.
+ Cut two strips of fabric as near the same weight as the garment. Cut them as wide as the amount you want to add plus seam allowances. Make sure the strips are long enough to hem at the bottom, and turn under for the width of the waistband at the top.
+ Sew these strips into place at the sides of your garment. Redo the hem and turn under, and topstitch at the waist.
+ Cover the side panels with colorful braid or woven ribbon. You may be surprised at what you can find that will go with the color and style of your pants or skirt. Adding a little of the same trim to the edge of the pockets will further encourage the idea that the trim is original. For skirts, you might want to add three off-center stripes to the front rather than at the side seams.

PIONEER TIP!

While these panels work well with jeans, they are really best for shorts, skirts, and children's clothing. Unless you are fixing expensive jeans, the ribbon might turn out to be more expensive than replacing the pants.

Shirts and Blouses

To use panels to widen shirts and blouses, choose a contrasting fabric to create vertical stripes down the front.

+ Open up the shoulder seams.
+ Cut vertical lines straight with the grain from hem to shoulder front and back and on both sides.
+ You can sew your panels in with two seams or by folding under the edges and topstitching as you overlap it with the cut edge of the shirt. This latter alternative is more likely to give the appearance of a stripe of trim. If there are darts in line with where you want to cut, take out the stitches up to a couple of inches from the side seams. Press the darts flat.
+ Make the cuts, and sew in the panels with two seams. Trim the top of the panels to align them with the shoulder seams, and repair these seams. Repair the hem.
+ If you had to take out a dart, try the shirt on inside out and find the lines for the new darts.
+ Make sure both sides look the same, especially where they cross the panels. Consider replacing sleeve bands with your panel fabric or adding a breast pocket.

Sleeves

If a sleeve is too tight, you can put a similar panel along the top of the sleeve. Add a matching panel across the shoulder seams or along the bottom of the shirt.

If the armhole is tight too, open the shoulder seam and widen it with a panel. You can turn it under at the neckline or redo the facing. If there is a collar, you'll need to completely redo the neckline.

Dresses

Dresses without waistlines might be altered with panels the same way as shirts or blouses. If there is a waistline, you might open up the waist seam and sew in separate panels for the bodice and the skirt, but be sure to have them meet.

If the dress is gathered, you might take the skirt off entirely, or at least up to the zipper. Add the panels to the bodice, and regather the skirt onto the larger waistline. If you want the skirt to be fuller, don't remove the skirt except right at the point where you add the panels. Add slightly wider panels to the skirt so it gathers appropriately.

CAMOUFLAGING MENDED AREAS OR STAINS

THERE ARE ANY NUMBER of ways to disguise a mend or cover a stain. You will have to consider each case individually, using your own imagination and sense of style.

Cover-Ups

Depending on the location of the stain or mend, you might be able to cover it with a pocket, trim, or an appliqué (essentially, a decorative patch).

The location has to be just right for a pocket to work. Even if it does work, there's the problem of fabric. Generally it is better to use contrasting fabric than it is to try to make the pocket from a near-match fabric. Use the fabric again around the collar, or match it to a new set of buttons. If it's a short-sleeved dress or shirt, you might stitch a narrow fold of your pocket fabric behind the sleeve band and extend it just ¼" beyond.

Whether a row of ruffle or other trim is going to work will also depend on the location. Perhaps a second row in a more logical place will keep the first from looking odd. Maybe three rows of narrow ribbon sewn on the diagonal across one side of a casual shirt and repeated along the bottom of the other side will work, if the ribbons pick up colors in the shirt.

Children's clothes lend themselves to the use of appliqué for cover-ups. If the exact location seems wrong for a single appliqué, consider how it might look if it is part of a scattering of related appliqués.

Cut It Away

Consider how you might modify a garment to get rid of a stain or serious tear. If it's on a sleeve, can the sleeves be cut off above the problem and either banded or hemmed? If it's near the bottom, can the garment be shortened?

If the problem is in the center front of a sweatshirt or sweater, consider slitting the garment down the center, adding ribbing to cover the cut ends, and turning it into a cardigan.

Sometimes a neckline can be changed to remove the problem. You can use a near-match fabric to face your new neckline. Press it so the stitching is just under, rather than right on, the edge. This is a trick you might use to make something you're tired of look like something new.

APPENDICES

STANDARD U.S./METRIC MEASUREMENT CONVERSIONS

VOLUME CONVERSIONS	
U.S. Volume Measure	**Metric Equivalent**
⅛ teaspoon	0.5 milliliter
¼ teaspoon	1 milliliter
½ teaspoon	2 milliliters
1 teaspoon	5 milliliters
½ tablespoon	7 milliliters
1 tablespoon (3 teaspoons)	15 milliliters
2 tablespoons (1 fluid ounce)	30 milliliters
¼ cup (4 tablespoons)	60 milliliters
⅓ cup	90 milliliters
½ cup (4 fluid ounces)	125 milliliters
⅔ cup	160 milliliters
¾ cup (6 fluid ounces)	180 milliliters
1 cup (16 tablespoons)	250 milliliters
1 pint (2 cups)	500 milliliters
1 quart (4 cups)	1 liter (about)

WEIGHT CONVERSIONS	
U.S. Weight Measure	**Metric Equivalent**
½ ounce	15 grams
1 ounce	30 grams
2 ounces	60 grams
3 ounces	85 grams
¼ pound (4 ounces)	115 grams
½ pound (8 ounces)	225 grams
¾ pound (12 ounces)	340 grams
1 pound (16 ounces)	454 grams

OVEN TEMPERATURE CONVERSIONS

Degrees Fahrenheit	Degrees Celsius
200 degrees F	95 degrees C
250 degrees F	120 degrees C
275 degrees F	135 degrees C
300 degrees F	150 degrees C
325 degrees F	160 degrees C
350 degrees F	180 degrees C
375 degrees F	190 degrees C
400 degrees F	205 degrees C
425 degrees F	220 degrees C
450 degrees F	230 degrees C

BAKING PAN SIZES

American	Metric
8 x 1½ inch round baking pan	20 x 4 cm cake tin
9 x 1½ inch round baking pan	23 x 3.5 cm cake tin
11 x 7 x 1½ inch baking pan	28 x 18 x 4 cm baking tin
13 x 9 x 2 inch baking pan	30 x 20 x 5 cm baking tin
2 quart rectangular baking dish	30 x 20 x 3 cm baking tin
15 x 10 x 2 inch baking pan	30 x 25 x 2 cm baking tin (Swiss roll tin)
9 inch pie plate	22 x 4 or 23 x 4 cm pie plate
7 or 8 inch springform pan	18 or 20 cm springform or loose bottom cake tin
9 x 5 x 3 inch loaf pan	23 x 13 x 7 cm or 2 lb narrow loaf or pâté tin
1½ quart casserole	1.5 liter casserole
2 quart casserole	2 liter casserole

LENGTH CONVERSIONS

U.S. Length Measure	Metric Equivalent
1 inch	2.54 centimeters
1 foot	30.48 centimeters
1 yard	0.9 meter
1 mile	1.6 kilometers

GUIDE TO VEGETABLE YIELDS AND PLANTINGS

VEGETABLE	AVERAGE HARVEST PER 100 FEET	RECOMMENDED PLANTING PER PERSON
Beans, bush	120 pounds	20–30 feet
Beans, dry	10 pounds	100 feet
Beans, pole	150 pounds	20–25 feet
Beets	100 pounds	10–20 feet
Broccoli	75 pounds	10–15 plants
Brussels sprouts	60 pounds	10–15 plants
Cabbage	150 pounds	10–20 plants
Carrots	100 pounds	25–30 plants
Cauliflower	100 pounds	10–15 plants
Celery	75 heads	5–10 plants
Corn	10 dozen ears	50–100 plants
Cucumbers	120 pounds	15–25 feet
Jerusalem artichokes	150 pounds	10–20 feet
Kale	75 pounds	10–20 feet
Leeks	150 leeks	10 feet
Lettuce	50 pounds (80 heads)	10–15 feet
Onions	80 pounds	50–100 feet
Parsley	30 pounds	5–10 feet
Parsnips	100 pounds	10 feet
Peas, shelling	15 pounds	50–100 feet
Peppers	50 pounds	5–10 plants
Potatoes	100 pounds	30–50 feet
Pumpkins	200 pounds	5–10 feet
Radishes	100 bunches	15–25 feet
Rutabagas	150 pounds	10–20 feet
Spinach	30 pounds	30–40 feet
Squash, summer	150 pounds	5–10 feet
Squash, winter	125 pounds	25–30 feet
Tomatoes	100 pounds	10–20 plants

COMMON VEGETABLE WATERING
AND FERTILIZING CHART

VEGETABLE	WHEN TO WATER	WHEN TO FERTILIZE
Beans	Regularly once pods begin to form	After heavy bloom and once pods set
Beets	Only during dry conditions	At time of planting
Broccoli	Only during dry conditions	Three weeks after transplanting
Brussels sprouts	At transplanting and during dry spells	Three weeks after transplanting
Cabbage	Only during dry conditions	Three weeks after transplanting
Carrots	Only during dry conditions	Preferably in the fall for the following spring
Cauliflower	Only during dry conditions	Three weeks after transplanting
Celery	Once a week	At time of planting
Corn	When tassels appear and cobs start to swell	When 8 to 10 inches tall and again when silk first appears
Cucumbers	Frequently, especially when fruits are forming	One week after bloom and again three weeks later
Lettuce	Once a week	Two or three weeks after transplanting
Melons	Once a week	One week after bloom and again three weeks later
Onions	Only during drought conditions	When bulbs begin to swell and again when plants are 1 foot tall
Parsnips	Only during dry conditions	Preferably in the fall for the following spring
Peas	Regularly once the pods begin to form	After heavy bloom and set of pods
Peppers	Once a week	At first bloom and after first fruit set
Potatoes	Regularly	At bloom time or time of second hilling
Pumpkins	Only during dry conditions	Just before vines start to grow, usually when plant is about 1 foot tall
Radishes	Once a week	Preferably in the fall for the following spring
Spinach	Once a week	When plants are one-third grown
Squash, summer	Only during dry conditions	Just before vines start to grow, usually when plant is about 1 foot tall
Squash, winter	Only during dry conditions	Just before vines start to grow, usually when plant is about 1 foot tall
Tomatoes	Deep watering once a week	Two weeks before and after first picking

INDEX

Note: Page numbers in *italics* indicate recipes.

Tinctures, 156–57, 158–59, *177*
Tomatoes
    about: canning, 40, 44, 52
    Fried Green Tomatoes, *88*
    Tomato Ketchup, *45*
Trees, planting, 18–19
Turmeric, 164

Upward stitch, 253–54

Valerian, 179
Vegetables. *See also specific vegetables*
    about: blanching, 61; drying, 67–68; freezing,
        60–61; growing. *See* Container gardening;
        Gardening; pressure canning, 49–51
    Root Vegetables in Beef Broth, 95

Water
    for baking, 104–5, 111
    collecting/using rainwater, 29
    for homebrewing, 133
Water-bath canning, 42–47
Watering/fertilizing chart, 295
Wax (beeswax, paraffin, recycled), 213–15
Whisks, 76
Wicks, 216–17
Willow, 176
Window boxes, 23–24
Witch hazel, 162, 167
Worm composting (and worm bin), 27–28

Yarrow, 165, 183
Yeast, 103–4, 131, 147